Leeds Centre Working Papers in Victorian Studies
Volume 4

Unrespectable Recreations

Edited by
Martin Hewitt

Trinity and All Saints/Leeds Centre for Victorian Studies

Published by the Leeds Centre for Victorian Studies,
Trinity and All Saints, University of Leeds,
Horsforth, Leeds, LS18 5HD

ISBN: 0 9540159 0 8
Printed and bound by the University Print Services, University of Leeds

Contents

'Hacked Until The Blood Ran': Violence and gamesmanship in   9
Victorian middle-class rugby
Tony Collins

Bull-baiting in Industrialising Townships, 1800-1850   19
Emma Griffen

The Cheek of the Young Person: Sexualized Popular   31
Discourse as Subtext in Dickens
Caroline Jackson-Houlston

The Joy of Sex?: Paradoxes of representation in the Age of   46
Photography
Nicholas Jagger

'... one of the most mischievous Acts that ever passed the   59
British legislature'. The 1830 Beerhouse Act and its
consequences
Paul Jennings

Ludicrous Politics: Nautical Melodrama and the Degradation   71
of Law
Matthew Kaiser

Popular Sunday Newspapers, Class, and the Struggle for   81
Respectability in Late Victorian Britain
David Scott Kamper

Circumambulatory; or, The Adventures of Three Gentlemen   95
and a Lady in Search of a British Public
Mary Elizabeth Braddon (circa 1860)
Gabrielle Malcolm

Drugs, Doubling, and Disguise: Sherlock Holmes and 'The   107
Man with the Twisted Lip'
Nancy Anne Marck

Gounod and The Gods: Audience Behaviour in Irish Theatres 117
1840-1900
Nuala McAllister

The Pleasures of War: War and Popular Culture in Age of 129
Victoria
Michael Paris

Dandy rats at play: the Liverpudlian middle classes and horse 143
racing in the nineteenth century
John Pinfold

'The Mysteries of Midnight': Low-Life London 'Penny 160
Dreadfuls' as unrespectable reading from the 1860s
John Springhall

Respectability takes a holiday: disreputable behaviour at the 176
Victorian seaside
John K. Walton

Wanton Women and Malignant Murderesses: the female 194
criminal and the Victorian reader
Chris Willis

Contents

'Hacked Until The Blood Ran': Violence and gamesmanship in Victorian middle-class rugby
Tony Collins   9

Bull-baiting in Industrialising Townships, 1800-1850
Emma Griffen   19

The Cheek of the Young Person: Sexualized Popular Discourse as Subtext in Dickens
Caroline Jackson-Houlston   31

The Joy of Sex?: Paradoxes of representation in the Age of Photography
Nicholas Jagger   46

'... one of the most mischievous Acts that ever passed the British legislature'. The 1830 Beerhouse Act and its consequences
Paul Jennings   59

Ludicrous Politics: Nautical Melodrama and the Degradation of Law
Matthew Kaiser   71

Popular Sunday Newspapers, Class, and the Struggle for Respectability in Late Victorian Britain
David Scott Kamper   81

Circumambulatory; or, The Adventures of Three Gentlemen and a Lady in Search of a British Public
Mary Elizabeth Braddon (circa 1860)
Gabrielle Malcolm   95

Drugs, Doubling, and Disguise: Sherlock Holmes and 'The Man with the Twisted Lip'
Nancy Anne Marck   107

Gounod and The Gods: Audience Behaviour in Irish Theatres   117
1840-1900
Nuala McAllister

The Pleasures of War: War and Popular Culture in Age of   129
Victoria
Michael Paris

Dandy rats at play: the Liverpudlian middle classes and horse   143
racing in the nineteenth century
John Pinfold

'The Mysteries of Midnight': Low-Life London 'Penny   160
Dreadfuls' as unrespectable reading from the 1860s
John Springhall

Respectability takes a holiday: disreputable behaviour at the   176
Victorian seaside
John K. Walton

Wanton Women and Malignant Murderesses: the female   194
criminal and the Victorian reader
Chris Willis

Leeds Working Papers in Victorian Studies

These papers are collected in the first instance for the purpose of discussion at the colloquium on 'Unrespectable Recreations: The Victorians at Play', held under the auspices of the Leeds Centre for Victorian Studies at Trinity and All Saints, University of Leeds, on March 17th 2001. This colloquium is the thirteenth in the series of biannual Victorian Studies colloquia which have been organised by the Centre since 1994. Established in 1994, the activities of the Centre include the colloquium series, a programme of seminars and day schools, M.A. and PhD. programmes in Victorian Studies, and the sponsorship of the *Journal of Victorian Culture*, which is jointly published by Trinity and All Saints and Edinburgh University Press.

Over the course of the colloquia series, a format has evolved in which in order to maximise the time available for discussion, papers to be presented at the colloquia were collected and distributed in advance. For several reasons it seems sensible to make these papers available in a more permanent form. In particular, it makes it easier to distribute them to those who are unable to attend the day itself, but who are interested in participating in the ongoing discussion of the issues covered. It also places in more permanent form papers which may never be developed in this form into published work.

It must be stressed, however, that these papers are presented simply as *working papers*, as *work-in-progress*. Of course the degree to which they are preliminary or tentative varies; some are closer to finished work than others. But all are presented here as conditional statements of their author's ideas and understandings, in the expectation that they will be developed and refined and ultimately published elsewhere, as finished and polished pieces of work. I also hope that the availability of this collection of papers will enable the debate on the topics considered here to be extended beyond the confines of those who attended the colloquium itself. To that end, conventional and (where available) e-mail addresses of the authors are provided; all would welcome contact from anyone interested in discussing their work further.

I am very grateful to the authors whose work appears in this volume, both for their willingness to participate in the colloquium, and for their co-operation in producing this volume, especially in keeping to the potentially very restrictive limit of 5000 words on contributions, and in providing copy in good time. I am especially grateful to Mike Huggins of St Martin's College, Lancaster, who first came to me with the suggestion for this topic, and who has been active in soliciting many of the contributions in the volume, and to the colloquia itself

There is still a tendency to consign the Victorians to that part of history which our contemporary psyche deems 'repressed', and to think of them as puritanical and almost joyless; or to accept that Victorian culture was not entirely a matter of strict religiosity and suspicion of enjoyment, but to file this under 'hypocrisy'. There were of course powerful behavioural codes, and these did often constrain what was accepted as proper within narrow grounds. But there were several of these codes, across classes, within classes, for different days of the week and seasons of the year. And whatever the pressures of labour or advancement, the Victorians, like any others, sought relaxation or escape vigorously and in a multitude of ways, ways which all too often worried at the boundaries of the 'respectable'. As literary and social historians move beyond the easy middle-class sources, or the canonical novels, the contours of Victorian pleasure-seeking become more apparent. Yet we still know surprisingly little of many of the kinds of activities which did not lend themselves to autobiographical reminiscence, associational record, or conventional journalistic description, and it is hoped that the work contained in this volume will encourage further explorations in this area.

I hope the essays will also make it clear that this endeavour cannot be prosecuted effectively from within a narrowly single-discipline position. A rounded understanding of the leisure cultures of Victorian Britain requires approaches and insights from a broad range of disciplines, not just history and literature as conventionally defined, but the histories of theatre, religion, and cultural studies. As in the case of the previous volumes in this series of Working Papers, therefore, I hope these essays reflect the potential of cross-disciplinary fertilisation, and in so doing, help to justify the "Victorian Studies" project.

Martin Hewitt
Leeds Centre for Victorian Studies

'Hacked Until The Blood Ran': Violence and gamesmanship in Victorian middle-class rugby

Tony Collins
Department of History
De Montfort University
The Gateway
Leicester, LE1 9BH
tonycollins@mac.com

How much of a 'gentleman' was the Victorian sporting gentleman?
The question is not simply one arising out of curiosity. The moral tenor of modern sport is still largely derived from the tenets of Victorian middle-class sporting ethics. Discussions about the use of drugs in sport are framed in terms of a debate about what constitutes 'fair play'. Concerns are regularly voiced about the levels of violence in football and rugby. Players' disputes with match officials, whether tennis umpires at Wimbledon or soccer referees at Old Trafford, are used by the press to demonstrate the decline in sportsmanship. And, of course, the tendency to hark back to a golden age when sport was played for its pure enjoyment without concern for financial considerations, is a feature of almost all discourse on sport.

However, the reality of Victorian middle-class sport was somewhat different from its self-image or when viewed through the somewhat rosy spectacles of future generations. Violence was not only widespread but was privately held to be one of sport's most appealing features. The art of twisting the rules to one's advantage – 'gamesmanship' – was commonplace and outright cheating was upheld if done in the right context. Monetary rewards were regularly paid. And far from playing for pure enjoyment, winning was critical to those who played: and if they could not win, many simply stopped playing.

Rugby presents possibly the most illuminating example of this contradiction between words and deeds. Until 1995 the Rugby Football Union (R.F.U.) steadfastly upheld the Victorian principles of amateurism, insisting that as a sport it had a moral quality that set it aside from, if not above, all others. Its determination to keep its amateur ideals pure in the

1890s led to the cleavage in the game which resulted in the vast majority of its clubs in the north of England leaving to create the semi-professional Northern Union in 1895, which later became the Rugby League. The 1970 official centenary history of rugby union claimed, in language possibly more suited to 1870, that it was 'a chivalrous and character-building game'. For its devotees rugby union was, to quote the motto of the Barbarians club, a 'game for gentlemen of all classes but never for a bad sportsman in any class'.[1]

Gentlemen and Payers

Who was the Victorian sporting gentleman? In his *Sport and the British* Richard Holt gives a precise definition:

> Fair play was the watchword of the gentleman amateur. The term 'amateur' has come to mean anyone who does not play for pay, but the original meaning was more subtle. Amateurs were gentlemen of the middle and upper classes who played sports that were often enjoyed by the common people – athletics, rowing or cricket, for example – but who played these and other games in a special way. Fair play meant not only respecting the written rules of the game, but abiding by what was generally understood to be the spirit of the game.

Holt develops this theme further. 'The middle class amateur ... had greater pretensions to be 'civilised'. ... The middle-class sportsman saw himself as someone who could hold his passions in check and for whom the enjoyment of the game was more important than the result'.[2]

That many apparent paragons of Victorian sporting virtue failed to live up to such standards is perhaps not surprising. Over the past two decades, a number of historians have uncovered the extent of 'shamateurism' among gentlemen cricketers who were ostensibly amateurs. The highly profitable amateurism of W.G. Grace in particular has come under scrutiny and the work of historians such as Sandiford, Vamplew and Birley have highlighted the extensive financial arrangements which county cricket clubs entered into in order to support the cricketing ambitions of their gentlemen amateurs. Indeed, many amateur cricketers received more money from their county clubs than the professionals in the same team. Possibly the most egregious example of this state of affairs was highlighted by the strike of some of the professionals in the England side to play Australia in August 1896. The professionals in the side received £10 wages per test match while the amateurs received £25 'expenses' – and the captain, W.G. Grace, picked up £40 per match, double the normal match expenses he was paid by Gloucestershire.[3]

However, cricket had always had a place, albeit strictly subordinate, for professionalism. The fact that money made its way across the divide to many of its gentleman amateurs of the sport was generally viewed with equanimity by the sport. But rugby believed itself to be different. In 1886 it introduced a strict code of amateurism, which not only forbade payments to players but almost every other form of remuneration, including gifts, jobs or payments in kind. Violation of these laws was punished by banishment from the game. Nevertheless, similar 'understandings' about expenses were not unknown in the oval ball game. For example, Andrew Stoddart, England captain at both rugby and cricket, took over as captain of the 1888 rugby tour of Australia and New Zealand for a payment of at least £200. Fellow tourist, the Welsh international and Cambridge rugby blue, W.H. Thomas was paid £90 for the thirty week tour and demanded a further £3 per week when the tour was extended to cash in on its success. Closer to home, Oxford blue and Tadcaster player William Bromet claimed expenses of £6/13 shillings for turning out for the Yorkshire county side in 1895. The biggest outrage for many of Yorkshire's leading clubs, such as Bradford, Halifax, Huddersfield and Leeds, was the fact that the leading southern sides charged them for travelling north to play them. In 1887 Bradford paid Blackheath players £57/15 shillings and those of Richmond £42/10 shillings in match expenses.[4] The antagonism caused by such financial demands was exacerbated by the fact that the southern teams refused to pay expenses to northern teams which travelled south to play. When Bradford declined to pay Blackheath's expenses in 1893, 'The Club', as it proclaimed itself, immediately cancelled the fixture. Nor was this was a practice confined to devotees of the rugby code of football – the Corinthians, a name even today synonymous with amateurism, charged their soccer opponents £150 per match and were well-known for their liberal dispensation of expenses.[5]

Hacking and violence in rugby
Although serious, these examples of breaches in the gentleman's code could be thought to be aberrations, untypical of the game as a whole. Such a defence, which was occasionally advanced by supporters of the R.F.U., would be tenable if it could be demonstrated that such behaviour was indeed anomalous when compared to the conduct of the game as a whole. To what extent therefore did the way that gentlemen played rugby otherwise conform to the ideals of 'fair play'?

As could be expected for a sport which was so closely associated with the public schools, the pattern for its playing styles and ethics was set in those schools where it was the sport of choice. At its heart was a belief that the violence of the sport would help to foster 'manliness'. Thus Harry Garnett, president of the R.F.U. in 1889, was introduced to hacking as a boy at Blackheath Proprietary School: 'Boots were made specially with an extra sole piece at the toe, pointed like a ship's ram, and hardened against the bars of the fire, or with a hot poker'. Hacking was inflicted on opponents 'with the utmost violence'. None of this was surprising to those involved in rugby at the time, not least because Garnett's old school was notorious for its unswerving devotion to hacking. Despite being asked to stop the practice by the school's headmaster in the 1860s, they continued to hack their way through opponents, and at one point forced the adult Richmond club to abandon a match with them in protest against their tactics. Further north, E.H. Dykes, who founded the Leeds Parish Church rugby team in 1874, learnt the importance of hacking and tripping as a pupil at Durham school. '"Hack him over" was the cry when anyone was running with the ball, and it was the commonest thing to see fellows hacked off their feet. A scrummage was mainly an opportunity for hard hacking'. Such was the seriousness with which hacking was taken that Durham boys would prepare for rugby matches by hammering their shins with pokers in order to harden the skin.[6]

It was inevitable that such extreme displays of violence by those ostensibly being educated to become society's leaders would come to public attention. Although the immediate catalyst for the formation of the R.F.U. in January 1871 was the perceived need to combat the growth of the Association code of football, highlighted by the fact that the soccer clubs had arranged an England versus Scotland fixture in November 1870, the underlying context was a public outcry over violent play in games of rugby. A letter from 'A Surgeon' had appeared in *The Times* complaining about the number of injuries he had dealt with following games of football at Rugby School and this had been taken up by the *Lancet* and others to call for the game to be reformed or abolished. The initiative to form a rugby union came from the Richmond club, with the stated intention of countering the adverse publicity which the sport was attracting. Richmond had opposed 'unnecessary' hacking since 1866 – although even they were not opposed to hacking players who were running with the ball or those who were contesting for the ball in a scrum. The aim of the new union was to draw up a common code of rules which would enable clubs to play against each other without having to negotiate compromises over the idiosyncrasies of each others' rules. Hacking was explicitly forbidden under rule 57 of the new union, although it was generally understood that clubs playing each other could make their own arrangements about its enforcement. It is also safe to assume that the R.F.U.'s rule 58, outlawing the use of 'projecting nails, iron plates or gutta percha' on boots, was a direct response to the activities of those players most devoted to hacking.[7]

Despite the formation of the R.F.U. and its public banning of hacking, it was clear that the practice was not merely a predilection of overly-aggressive schoolboys – it continued across the adult game throughout the 1860s and 1870s. Although many of the newly-founded clubs played their own variations of the original Rugby school rules of football, violence was an integral – not to say very appealing – part of the game. Blackheath, despite being one of the founders of the Football Association, continued to play Rugby School rules with full hacking. W.H.H. Hutchinson remembered that Hull's original rules while prohibiting hacking did allow tripping, a feature which was also explicitly outlawed in the R.F.U.'s first set of rules of 1871. The nature of the games that were played can be gauged by Hutchinson's memory of a match against Harrogate, when an opposing player 'got me by the hair of the head and stuck to it for all he was worth'. J.G. Hudson, one of the founders of the Leeds club also looked back fondly at a Leeds versus Manchester match of 1865, which consisted predominantly of 'a good set-to at each other's shins in mid-field'. Herbert Gregg, a founder of the Manchester club, also looked back at the 'many bloody battles I have taken part in against Liverpool, also Preston, Rochdale and many other clubs' during the 1860s and 1870s. The first Yorkshire versus Lancashire match in 1870 was marked by the Lancashire players' keenness to indulge in hacking their opponents.[8]

Harry Garnett continued to be as enthusiastic about hacking as an adult player as he had been as a schoolboy. Throughout his career, he disdained to wear shinguards, believing them to be 'unmanly', and refused to allow his team mates to wear them too, telling a fellow Otley player in the 1870s, 'If you don't take that off, I will see if I cannot hack it off'. Nor was he unique in such an uncompromising stance. When York played a game against York Training College in the mid-1870s, they were aghast to see that their opponents turned out wearing shinguards. York captain Robert Christison protested but, perhaps forewarned against what was about to transpire, the Training College players refused to abandon their protection. Undeterred, York proceeded to hack away at the covered shins of their adversaries. Christison proudly recalled 30 years later that despite the College players' precautions they still looked 'a good deal worse for wear' when they removed their shinguards after the match. As late as 1879 Manchester played Manchester Free Wanderers in a game where both sides agreed to allow hacking.[9]

Even after hacking disappeared from the adult game, the 1880s still saw examples of violent play on the part of teams composed of 'gentlemen'. When Bradford toured Scotland in 1885, their game against Edinburgh Academicals was marred by 'some of the foulest play ever perpetrated' by the Scotsmen, who left four Bradford players seeking hospital treatment following the match. The fact that some of this rough play was on occasion due to middle-class players seeking to assert their dominance over the more working-class northern clubs can be seen by the comments of Blackheath's C.B. Grundy about a game against a Yorkshire team in 1881: 'Their idea evidently was, "There's a team of southern amateurs, let's frighten them by playing rough". And they did play rough! But they never made a greater mistake in their lives. At half-time Blackheath had thirteen men left and the others eleven. The rest had been take in cabs to the nearest hospital'. It is also worth pointing out that the soccer amateurs of Corinthians F.C. were also widely noted for their 'robust' style of play, in which individual dribbling of the ball and shoulder-charging opponents played a prominent part, a style which was viewed by many as being more violent than the style of play based on passing the ball used by the professional sides in the north and the midlands.[10]

'It's not the winning but who is taking part'

But it was not just the violence of playing styles which suggests that the idea that 'it is not the winning, but the taking part that is important' was honoured more in the breach. Until 1885 neutral referees were not obligatory at rugby matches and the common practice was for disputes over the rules to be decided mutually by the captains of the two teams. Although in theory this appeared to be the perfect application of gentlemanly ethics, in practice it was far from it. Looking back on the 1870s, Harry Beardsell of Huddersfield remarked that in his playing days, 'the captains were the referees and if any disputes occurred they squabbled until one or the other gave way'. Indeed, it became an unwritten rule that the time spent arguing over disputed points during the course of a match had to be added on, in a similar way that injury time was added to the length of a match. As York's Robert Christison admitted, such arrangements meant that team captains tended to be drawn from the more argumentative members of a club.

Gamesmanship, best described as using the letter of the law to undermine the spirit of the law, was also rife. The Leeds player, Ben Cariss, allegedly became the first person to deliberately kick the ball deep and out of play to give his side a territorial advantage. Although this tactic has subsequently been a feature of rugby union for the past 120 years, at the time Cariss was frowned upon by many because the traditional aim of the game had been to avoid putting the ball into touch. As late as 1878 controversy ensued when A.N. Hornby, the son of one of Lancashire's major textile manufacturing families, sought to protect Lancashire's slender lead in a Roses match by instructing his team to kick the ball out of play as soon they received it in order to waste time. Perhaps the most notorious example of a departure from the 'spirit of the game' occurred in 1889 during England's game against the touring New Zealand Maori team at Blackheath. Andrew Stoddart had his shorts ripped in a tackle and players of both sides formed a circle around him so that he could protect his decency while changing. However, as the circle was being formed, England's Frank Evershed picked up the ball and scored a try. Despite vigorous protests by the Maori side, referee Rowland Hill, who as secretary of the Rugby Football Union was one of the strongest advocates of the amateur ethos, awarded the try. [11]

As can be seen from these examples, winning was vitally important to the gentlemen of the Victorian middle classes, not least because their victories in sporting contests confirmed their own belief in their superiority over those they saw as the lower social orders or lesser races. Indeed, for many members of the middle-classes, sport without victory lost its meaning. And when they consistently lost, many simply withdrew from the sport. To those who espoused the belief that it was 'the playing of the game for its own sake' which was important, defeat should not have detracted from their enjoyment of, or participation, in rugby – but it did. In 1881, the original Hull club, founded in 1865 by the sons of local shipowners who had been to Rugby school, passed a resolution stating 'that this club cease to exist' after suffering a series of crushing defeats by clubs they viewed as their social inferiors. The following year York, one of the oldest rugby clubs in England, decided to fold and merged with the local York Melbourne club following a string of heavy defeats. In 1883 Yorkshire Wanderers, claimants to be the oldest and most socially-exclusive rugby club in Leeds, voted not to continue their playing efforts after losing every single match of the previous season. [12]

Whilst some withdrew from the sport, the reaction of other middle-class players and administrators was to seek to restrict the involvement of working class players in the game in order to reduce the perceived threat to their control of the game. The introduction in 1886 of strict regulations outlawing any form of payment for play was an attempt to curb the growing on-field dominance of working class players – the great fear was that the introduction of professionalism would result in the complete eclipse of the gentleman player, as had happened in soccer following the legalisation of professionalism in 1884.

These growing fears about working-class participation in rugby were also related to the gradual extinction of hacking. In part, hacking's decline was due to new attitudes to violence in sport. As the keenness of the R.F.U. to officially oppose hacking demonstrated, public opinion was not favourably disposed to the violence engendered by the hacking game. Rugby could not be expected to increase its popularity among broader sections of the population while its players insisted on engaging in such bloody practices. Growing middle-class intolerance of cruel and bloody sports involving animals, which had culminated in the outlawing of sports such as cock-fighting in the middle of the century, was mirrored by concerns about human recreations, most prominently by the 'rational recreation' movement. Although the rational recreationists directed their attention at the working classes, the idea that the middle classes should set an example for others to follow became increasingly important to the administrators of newly popular sports in the 1870s. Such leadership was especially important to the enthusiasts of Muscular Christianity, which became the moral thread running through the philosophy and attitudes of those leading the rugby game.

But it was also no coincidence that the decline of hacking coincided with the entrance of the working classes into the rugby game. Whilst rugby's rulers generally welcomed the new adherents of the game, their participation could not question or threaten the sport's leadership, either on or off the field. Hacking and other associated forms of violence in the game were, like duelling in Europe, activities which were to be confined to those social strata which shared a common moral culture. Thus by the mid-1880s there was a new outcry against the growth of violence in the game, this time initiated by the R.F.U. itself, which was allegedly caused by working-class players who did not understand the rules, or, more ominously, by working-class 'veiled professionals' who were prepared to use violence in order to win at all costs. The irony of such complaints when viewed in the context of rugby's history was unintentionally highlighted by a supporter of the R.F.U. writing to the *Yorkshire Post* in 1886:

> A great many of the Horbury team were artisans and colliers. Now, I don't object to any working man – collier or whatever he may be – as long as he understands the game he is playing, but when in ignorance he puts on his working boots ... I am not surprised at smashed legs. ... It is a disgrace to the prestige of 'Dear Old England' for time-honoured fair play.[13]

A mere ten or fifteen years earlier, many players would have viewed 'smashed legs' as a desirable outcome at the end of a match!

Conclusion

Such comments also revealed the underlying tension in the construction of rugby's gentlemanly ethos. No matter how strongly rugby's rulers emphasised its chivalrous characteristics, they could not (nor, indeed, did they want to) escape the fact that the game's violence was central to its appeal. This was not because its participants were inherently more aggressive than players of other sports but because rugby saw its role in society as being the third aspect of a trinity which encompassing masculinity and national identity. Although this tended to be more implied than expressed towards the end of the Victorian period, the link was made very clear in the earlier decades of the sport. The rugby-supporting F.W. Campbell of Blackheath argued at the founding meeting of the Football Association in 1863 that abolishing hacking would 'do away with all the courage and pluck of the game, and I will be bound to bring over a lot of Frenchmen who could beat you with a week's practice'. At the founding of the Wakefield Trinity club in 1872, one of the curates pointed to the physical virtues of the game 'which were supposed to make one Englishman equal to five Frenchmen' and, although lacking the preceding Francophobia, an 1876 article in the Manchester-based *Athletic News* responded to those who felt that the game was too violent by arguing that 'English youths inherit the traditional pluck and energy of their race' by taking part in it.[14]

The point is not that Victorian middle class rugby players were any more violent or inclined to bend the rules than working class players – rather that there was no appreciable difference in the type of behaviour displayed by members of either class. As A.A. Sutherland, the rugby correspondent of Robert Blatchford's *Clarion* pointed out, there were great similarities between hacking and 'purring', a working class activity common in the North West which involved two men kicking each other's shins until one could no longer continue.[15] The only difference was that while such behaviour was perfectly acceptable when employed within the shared social circles inhabited by the former public school boys who led the game, it was unacceptable to the game's rulers when exhibited by those of less exalted social milieu.

The growth of the ethos of the 'gentleman amateur' in rugby was therefore not the result of a codification of ideals but a response to a suspicious public opinion and to the influx of working class players into rugby in the 1880s. The early traditions of public school and middle-class rugby were in effect 'uninvented' and replaced by an ethical system which aimed at justifying the continued control of the game by its public school educated rulers. The gentleman rugby player may or may not have existed – but whatever his reality, middle-class sporting bodies such as the Rugby Union felt that it was necessary to invent him.

Endnotes

[1] U.A. Titley and A.R. McWhirter, *Centenary History of the Rugby Football Union* (London: R.F.U., 1970), 9. For a social context of the early development of rugby see Tony Collins, *Rugby's Great Split* (London: Frank Cass, 1998) and Eric Dunning and Ken Sheard, *Barbarians, Gentlemen and Players* (New York: New York University Press, 1979).

[2] Richard Holt, Sport and the British (Oxford: Oxford University Press, 1989), 98 and 174

[3] Keith Sandiford, *Cricket and the Victorians* (Aldershot: Scholar Press, 1994). Wray Vamplew, *Play Up and Play The Game* (Cambridge: Cambridge University Press, 1988). Derek Birley, *The Willow Wand* (London: Sportspages, 1989).

[4] Letters of Arthur Shrewsbury to Alfred Shaw, 14 March and 22 June 1888, in the Arthur Shrewsbury archive at Trent Bridge Cricket Ground, Nottingham; *Yorkshire Owl*, 18 November 1895, *The Yorkshireman*, 2 May 1888.

[5] *Yorkshire Post*, 11 March, 4 October and 13 December 1893.

[6] *Yorkshire Evening Post*, 12 January 1901 and 9 February 1901.

[7] For the circumstances of the formation of the R.F.U. and the text of its first rules, see O.L. Owen, *The History of the Rugby Football Union* (London: Playfair, 1955), 59-72.

[8] *Yorkshire Evening Post*, 1 and 8 December 1900.

[9] *Yorkshire Evening Post*, 12 January and 22 February 1901.

[10] *The Yorkshireman*, 7 November 1885; C.B. Grundy quoted in John Lowerson, *Sport and the English Middle Classes* (Manchester: Manchester University Press, 1993), 84. On the Corinthians' 'robust' style of play, see Tony Mason, *Association Football and English Society 1863-1915* (Brighton: Harvester, 1981), 207-209, and Derek Birley, *Land of Sport and Glory* (Manchester: Manchester University Press, 1995), 34.

[11] *Yorkshire Evening Post*, 15 December 1900, and 9 and 22 February 1901.

[12] *Yorkshire Evening Post*, 27 February 1904 and 21 March 1903; *The Yorkshireman*, 29 September 1883.

[13] *Yorkshire Post*, 2 April 1886.

[14] Campbell quoted in Derek Birley, *Sport and the Making of Britain* (Manchester: Manchester University Press, 1993), 259. *Wakefield Express*, 23 November 1872; *Athletic News*, 30 November 1876.

[15] *Clarion*, 7 October 1893.

Bull-baiting in Industrialising Townships, 1800-1850.

Emma Griffen
Sidney Sussex
Cambridge
CB2 3HU
eg213@hermes.cam.ac.uk

The focus of this paper is an area where popular recreations had become more 'unrespectable' than most by the early nineteenth century: Birmingham and the Black Country. I hope to demonstrate that dismissing the sports of this region as 'unrespectable' is unhelpful, and to illustrate some of the ways in which the study of their sports may further our understanding of social relations and local politics in the area. The paper consists of two parts: in the first I describe popular recreation in the Black Country; and in the second I explore some of the implications of the patterns of recreation there described.

The key event in the festive calendar throughout Staffordshire and the Black Country was the annual wakes. In common with wakes and feasts held elsewhere in the country, races, shows and stalls formed the staple of the week's entertainment. Inhabitants of Birmingham remembered 'dancing, drinking, singing, fighting, skittle playing, racing, jumping in sacks, dipping in tubs of water for money', and 'grinning through collars... leaping in sacks... bobbing at treacle rolls [and] climbing up poles for legs of mutton' at the annual wakes.[1] In addition, however, and in contrast to other regions, bull-baitings always formed a part of the week's entertainments; indeed, no west Midland wake was complete without its bull-baiting. They were integral to popular celebrations in this region, sufficiently deeply rooted to lead one local historian to refer to 'the fetishism of the bull-baiting cult' in the region.[2]

The excitement began the day before, when local people could come and inspect the bull that had been provided for their sport – at Handsworth, for example, 'the bull was always got in readiness on the Saturday before the wake, and kept at the Jolly Bacchus stables, to be inspected by the company visiting the house all day on Sunday'.[3] The entertainment began early the following morning, when the organisers of the sport endeavoured to walk the bull to the stake: at the appointed place, large crowds would have already assembled. The waiting and the arrival of the bull together formed part of the entertainment, and both were remembered clearly by one adult who had been taken as a child to the wake at Uttoxeter, on the Staffordshire-Derbyshire border, in 1819:

> It [the bull-baiting] was announced to take place at noon on the Wakes Monday in the Market Place. It was fine September morning about ten o'clock, and when we got there we found a considerable crowd collected, waiting for the sport to begin. These were not the days of railways, but vehicles of all sorts were bringing in their contingents of blackguards from Bromley, Tean, Land End, and the surrounding hamlets. I had never seen such a concourse of people together before ... After waiting about an hour there arose a Babel of yells and shouting, and there was a terrible rush in the direction of the Red Lion ... The poor brute came quietly enough, led by a strong rope, surrounded by a host of roughs more brutal than himself[4]

The organisers of the bull-baits might be 'professionals', who toured the wakes with an experienced game bull, or publicans or other individuals, who had managed to procure a bull; However the bull was obtained, its owner covered his costs by charging the owners of bull-dogs to run at the bull. But the absence of individuals with the means to buy a bull would not be allowed to prevent the traditional sport. A wake without a bull was unthinkable, and when times were hard, wake-goers would club together to pay for the bull by subscription. Similarly, a cap would be passed round to raise the few pence needed by the dogs' owners to enter their dogs in the baiting if necessary. A wake always signified a bull-baiting, and a good opening baiting was a matter of local pride in the Black Country townships; consequently stories about the theft of bulls the night before the wake were long remembered. In the memories of the contributors to the Notes and Queries columns of the *Birmingham Weekly Post* the two events, wakes and bull-baitings, were similarly run together. Though not entirely confined to the wakes, there was a strong connection between wakes and bull-baiting; in Birmingham, one inhabitant remembered, the bulls were sometimes brought into the town after being baited at wakes nearby; 'these were chance baitings, however', he added. 'The regular matches were got up during the holidays or wakes'.[5]

Large crowds were always drawn to the bull-baiting. In 1828 a constable directed to suppress a bull-baiting found 'upwards of a thousand persons assembled' between seven and eight on the Monday morning.[6] The crowds were filled with working people from the neighbourhood: many adults in the late nineteenth century remembered going as children – one even remembered being carried to a bull-bait by his nurse – and numerous reminiscences recalled the presence of women as well as men.[7] The bull-baiting brought the crowd together at the beginning of the week's festivities; the opening bull-bait lay at the core of the week's holiday, and was a central and distinctive feature of popular sports in this region.

The wakes were the most important element of the recreational calendar of the west Midlands. They attracted large numbers of visitors from surrounding districts, and because the neighbouring settlements celebrated wakes at different dates, there were numerous opportunities for reciprocal visiting throughout the period from early July to early December. In Birmingham and the Black Country, the high density of wakes holidays provided a particularly packed festive calendar. An elderly buckle-maker from Birmingham remembered that the various parish and neighbouring wakes, provided the opportunity for working men to enjoy a wake 'nearly every month'.[8] Even in the more isolated industrial settlements in northern Staffordshire most communities could expect to enjoy more than one wakes holiday. Wakes consequently formed a very important source of entertainment in the Black Country. By contrast, there is rather little evidence of Guy Fawkes celebrations in the region outside the largest towns. It may be that street bonfires were neglected by commentators, attracting little comment because they were relatively inoffensive compared with bull-baiting. However the wakes season extended until November, so it may be that the Fifth of November was a less important occasion for celebration.

Shrovetide, however, remained an important popular festival in the Black Country, and like the wakes, was dominated by blood sports and violence. The ancient customs of cockfighting and throwing at cocks at Shrovetide were particularly vigorous, and appear to have been slower to decline here than elsewhere. In parts of Warwickshire throwing at cocks certainly continued well into the first quarter of the nineteenth century, since the magistrates of that county issued orders against the sport in 1814 and 1824.[9] In Birmingham, throwing at cocks developed into a spectator sport in the early nineteenth century; the sport consisted in shooting at the cock with a gun, rather than knocking him down with wooden batons; apparently, however, 'the birds breast acted as a shield, and to kill the cock at one shot was not so easy a matter'.[10] In this form, the sport reportedly continued until the 1860s.

Cockfighting was also popular all over the west Midlands, particularly at Shrove Tuesday, but at other times as well.[11] It was remembered that in the early part of the nineteenth-century cockfighting contests in the Black Country were 'extremely frequent', and that 'very few public-houses in the Black Country towns [were] considered perfect without their cock-pits'.[12] Monday was the established day for cockfighting in Birmingham, particularly during winter. In that town, one writer listed half a dozen public houses that were remembered half a century after the suppression of the sport as 'notable cocking-fighting houses', and added that there had been 'several others, now forgotten'.[13] The sport was no less popular in Staffordshire, which remained a stronghold of the sport until the twentieth century.

The other major popular sport in the west Midlands was pugilism, and it was practised throughout the year. 'Prize-fighting held sway in a large part of the Black Country,' it was recalled, and informal set-tos were extremely common: 'hardly a week passed without matches being arranged either between local youths or men of note' a working man remembered in the late nineteenth century.[14] The collieries had their own championship, and at one colliery, every Monday was largely given over to prize-fighting.[15] Fields to the north-west of the city provided the location for many of these prize-fights, and the wakes provided the occasion for many more – for 'plenty of unprofessional boxing'.[16]

Of course pugilism was by no means confined to this district – it was nationally popular as a spectator sport, and the tendency of men to fall to blows was familiar everywhere. However, the evidence suggests high rates of participation in fighting sports across the Black Country. The Staffordshire newspapers contained numerous reports of fights that had ended in death – some had been organised challenges, and others had begun as personal, often drunken, quarrels. One can assume that these cases represent a very small minority of the fights contested, and that fist-fighting was an extremely common occurrence. Along with bull-baiting, cockfighting, and pugilism, the only other popular sports frequently mentioned with reference to the west Midlands were dog-fighting and badger-baiting.

II

It is clear that blood sports and violence dominated the recreational calendar of the west Midlands in the early nineteenth century. These were of course hardly unknown elsewhere, yet their high profile here was unusual, and the ritualised bull-baiting at the Black Country wakes was particularly distinctive. The campaign to suppress bull-baiting consequently bore down on Birmingham and the Black Country far more heavily than it did elsewhere, and as reforming pressure increased the west Midlands became the site of a long-running battle between the authorities and the bull-baiters.

Official attempts to prevent bull-baiting began in Birmingham in the late eighteenth century, and spread to many Black Country townships during the first two decades of the nineteenth. As bull-baiting was not strictly illegal, these attacks consisted in largely uncoordinated attempts by local officials to prosecute bull-baiters for nuisance when the sport was conducted in public spaces. Following the passage of the Cruelty to Animals Act in 1822, many local authorities turned their attention to bull-baiting on private premises – usually innkeepers' yards – believing that the recent Act had made the sport illegal. A decision at the King's Bench in 1827 ruled that bulls had in fact been intentionally excluded from the Act, and provided protection for bull-baitings held on private land until 1835, when a fresh Act unambiguously outlawed the baiting of all animals with dogs, and rapidly secured what uncoordinated action had failed to achieve.[17] By the end of the 1830s the local newspapers had ceased reporting convictions for bull-baiting during the wakes season, and bull-baiting had been confined to the memories of the region's inhabitants.

How should the popularity of blood sports in this area be explained? In the first place I think it important we should resist a cultural explanation of the place of bull-baiting in the west Midlands – that is, one that seeks to locate these recreations in the culture and values of the early industrial worker. Explanations of this kind date back so far as the early nineteenth century. It was always promised by reformers that the abolition of bull-baiting would encourage an improvement in popular manners and morals; and the first generation of commentators following the suppression of bull-baiting unanimously agreed that the predicted moral improvement had indeed occurred. All agreed that the disappearance of bull-baiting, dog-fighting, cock-fighting, and to a lesser degree prize-fighting, provided a satisfactory testimony to the great improvement in the manners of the working population that had occurred over the nineteenth century. In the view of one: 'In the gradual decline of cockfighting, bear-baiting, bull-baiting, and badger-baiting may be traced the slow but sure progress of civilisation and refinement'.[18]

Nor are cultural explanations confined to nineteenth-century scholars, as similar assumptions concerning the brutality of early-nineteenth-century working-class culture have continued to permeate late twentieth century discussions of the popularity of blood sports in the west Midlands. People with such harsh living conditions could not be expected to share our sensitivities: 'the common people lived rough lives, and enjoyed rough, unrefined pleasures', it is argued.[19] This formula makes it possible for us to understand the culture of violence, without condemning the people we are studying. But blood sports remain, as ever, no more than an indicator of brutality: they are the litmus test of civilisation; once

24

you know that people enjoyed *these* sports, you know all you need to about they kind of people they were.

Though there is no doubt some validity in this common-sense view of how people could tolerate what disgusts us today, I believe that stressing the brutality and degradation common to both the sport and the people obscures as much as it reveals. In particular, this approach has not encouraged a serious analysis of the suppression of the sport: given its association with the basest elements of human nature, the elimination of bull-baiting is seen quite simply as an inevitability. Consequently, historians who have been struck by the taming of the violent excesses of wakes, have nevertheless had very little to say about why the bull-baiting was suppressed, beyond gesturing vaguely to a rise in humanitarian sentiment.[20] Nor has the working population's allegiance to the sport in the face of opposition been questioned. If bull-baiting was nothing more than an occasion to indulge in brutalities, then it goes without saying that brutalised miners and metal-workers would be its chief votaries.

We need to recognise that this is exactly the story that reformers themselves liked to tell. This narrative has been derived from individuals who, if not campaigning for a specific programme of reform, were at least in sympathy with it; and consolidated through the endless repetitions of a second generation who approved of their actions. Understanding popular behaviour through stereotypes formulated by elites with a political agenda is arguably a sterile approach. We should be aware that there can be as much rebellion and dissent in a bull-baiting as there is cruelty and degradation. It is time to explore the different meanings that may have lain behind the actions critics were quick to label atavistic, to abandon the tired cliché of a degraded, brutalised populace, and think more carefully about the politics of recreation. And the struggles over bull-baiting in the west Midlands indicate most forcefully that popular recreation involves politics as much as culture.

How far can this struggle be understood in terms of a split between the respectable and unrespectable? There has been a trend recently in the historiography of popular culture to deny the usefulness, or even validity, of distinctions between elite and popular, the patricians and the plebs, the rulers and ruled, or however they are styled. It is suggested that exploring popular culture in terms of an elite/popular dichotomy is unhelpful, and we are urged to abandon the old 'bi-polar' model of social analysis, associated with such pioneers in the history of popular culture as Peter Burke and Edward Thompson, and to make our analyses of popular culture more sensitive to the complex social gradations of early modern England.[21] Yet though this advice may be helpful when considering certain elements of plebeian culture, its value for the study of bull-baiting in the west Midlands is less certain. The battles waged over bull-baiting were an essentially dichotomous conflict between rulers and ruled, and the fact of this social division should not be obscured.

The terse newspaper reports of prosecutions for bull-baiting contain little detail on who was responsible for bringing the actions. There were a few instances of individuals from outside the region spearheading the attack on bull-baiting – prosecutions at West Bromwich and Sedgley brought by the London based Animals Friend Society; and Charles Wheeler, an agent of the Ladies Society for the more effectual Suppression of Cruelty to Animals, hastening from London to the Black Country on the information that bull-baiting was planned at Walsall, Bilston and Wednesbury.[22] But in the great majority of cases, it was local people who were taking the initiative. In November 1827, the South Staffordshire Association for the Suppression of Bull-Baiting was established at Wednesbury, its object being to prevent bull-baiting within a twelve mile radius of the town. There are no records of the society's activities, but 'the clergy and principal inhabitants of West Bromwich and adjoining parishes' were apparently active members.[23] The society no doubt played a part in at least some of the prosecutions.

The role of clergy has been well documented, owing largely to the labours of local historians. For example, at Darlaston, John Waltham, rector and magistrate, displayed 'indomitable courage' in his attempts to suppress bull-baiting. At Tutbury, the vicar, Mr Dixon, led the campaign to suppress the ancient custom of bull-running in the manor. At Bilston, the rector William Leigh, though he opposed legislative interference in the recreations of the poor, nevertheless, whilst acting as a magistrate, convicted three men for baiting a bull on a turnpike road in 1828. And according to the local historian of Eccleshall, it was the vicar, Mr Moore, who 'personally put a stop to the outrageous practice' in that town.[24]

There has no doubt been some exaggeration in the heroic role played by the local clergy. At Rowley Regis, for example, it was claimed for the parish curate, George Barrs, that he had had his teeth knocked out attempting to prevent a bull-baiting. His personal journal contains a reference to bull-baiting in the neighbourhood one wakes Monday. He apparently felt 'very much grieved, and in some degree angry' when he saw his neighbours engaged in bull-baiting. However, though 'they made [his] heart bleed, and drew tears from [his] eyes', the journal gives no hint that he stepped outside and attempted direct interference. He remained safely indoors, where 'God kept my mind, and suffered not their noise to disturb my thoughts'.[25]

Results in most townships appear to have been achieved through an alliance of principal inhabitants and lower parish officials, rather than through the heroic actions of men of the cloth. In Rowley Regis,

Smethwick, Stone and West Bromwich, action against bull-baiting was led by the parish vestry; and at Willenhall a handbill, dated 1837, prohibiting bull-baiting, cockfighting, dog-fighting and badger-baiting at the wake bore the names of the vicar, two churchwardens, two overseers and two constables, suggesting a very similar alliance of parish officials.[26] This was clearly not a matter that divided local leaders, but one which all those holding official positions were ready to support. Furthermore, these examples suggest a fairly marked fault line running through these communities, with those above the bottom rung of parish officers ranged against those below. There is very little evidence of any participation in bull-baiting from those above this level, and certainly none of such people offering any resistance to attempts to suppress the sport. Taken together, those involved in the suppression of bull-baiting comprise a very heterogeneous social group, running from Sir Oswald Mosley, member of Parliament and local Staffordshire magnate, down to the humble parish constables, so frequently being assaulted in the course of the duties. The term 'patrician' is an inaccurate label for this group, but 'respectable' is not.

Solidarity was no less in evidence amongst those who continued to patronise the sport. Local histories and *Notes and Queries* were unanimous that the sport had become confined to the labouring population by the early nineteenth century. Those prosecuted for organising bull-baitings (in the few instances where occupations were given), were always working men – mostly labourers, though a carter, iron-worker, gun-barrel-maker and few butchers and colliers were also convicted. Those convicted for bull-baiting in Wolverhampton 1815, for example, were a miner, screw-filer, snuffer-maker, carpenter, latch-forger and a tin-plate-worker – a not untypical range of occupations in such cases.[27]

It has been suggested by Douglas Reid that the upper sections of the working class were retreating from the wakes in the first half of the nineteenth century, and that this was one factor hastening their decline in Birmingham. Although it is quite plausible that more respectable artisans disdained such events, it should be stressed that we have in fact very little evidence that this was the case. Any evidence on the views of respectable artisans would of course be hard to find; however, even if it could be demonstrated that labour elites were now absent from bull-baitings, this left a large section of the working community firmly united in favour of bull-baiting – and in clear conflict with those who ruled them. As was noted by a researcher in Shropshire, 'colliers and bargemen, who, though they fought each other every market day, were ready to make common cause against the disturbers of their cruel sport'.[28] Searching for conflicts within the working population seems to miss the point of these struggles, a point which was so clearly understood by those involved. The battle was not between working people, but between workers and their betters.

The social divisions engendered by the attack on bull-baiting were neatly summarised by an inhabitant of Blythemarsh, a village in northern Staffordshire. After a bull-baiting which continued, the reader is asked to believe, unabated for three days, one resident eventually went to the magistrate at Lane End with the names of nine of the participants. The magistrate dismissed the case, and once freed, the nine men returned home 'collected their abettors, got drunk, hoisted their colours, pressed a rustic piper into their services, rolled, and roared, and shouted, and piped up and down the village in true style. But their rage fell chiefly upon their worthy neighbours'.[29] The writer concluded that this must be stopped – though whether he was referring to the bull-baiting or to the rabble's insubordination was not made clear. Attacks on bull-baiting were capable of dividing communities into two, with the rulers and the ruled ranged against each other. It is no doubt unhelpful and ideologically loaded to present this conflict as one between the 'respectable' and the 'unrespectable', yet it is fitting to understand this conflict in dichotomous terms. And this crude social division was more significant to those involved than any more subtle or nuanced social conflicts within social strata that assiduous historians might be able to find.

Let us in conclusion, consider the significance of bull-baiting to the two sides in this conflict. Those involved in suppressing the sport liked to claim that concern about the consequences of bull-baiting for the morality of its participants underpinned their interference in the sport. For example, when inhabitants from Wednesbury petitioned Parliament for the suppression of bull-baiting, they argued that 'a continuance of that savage sport must demoralise all who partake in it'; and a letter on the same subject sent to *Aris's Birmingham Gazette*, pontificated on the continuance of these 'debasing and demoralizing' exhibitions in Staffordshire.[30] In practice, however, concerns about morality do not appear to have been confined to the cruelty of baiting animals with dogs. Local leaders in the west Midlands were also faced with the problem of insubordination. Sir Oswald Mosley, a Staffordshire magistrate, recalled with disgust that during the annual Tutbury bull-running 'all authority was set at defiance'.[31] The exasperation of local elites is apparent in the letter of one resident from

> [one of] those places where the worst disposed people can, as respects bull-baiting, have everything their own way; and where, as in the dense populations of our manufactories in this neighbourhood, they can always collect a numerous mob in support of them. But, in the meantime, is the better, and it is to be hoped, the larger portion of the inhabitants of West Bromwich, Dudley, Wednesbury, Darlaston &c, to have

their feelings outraged, and be doomed from year to year to witness such brutalities as I dare not repeat, because a few debased individuals chose publicly to perpetrate or encourage cruelties?[32]

The critique of bull-baiting may have originated in discussions about popular manners, but as attempts to suppress the sport in the west Midlands gathered pace, the refusal of the populace to obey their orders raised the stakes considerably. The continuation of bull-baiting was interpreted by local leaders as a challenge to their authority, and they responded by redoubling their attempts to eliminate the sport.

There is little written testimony by working people to indicate what the defence of bull-baiting meant to them. There are no clear statements from those involved about their motivation in the struggle to preserve bull-baiting at wakes. It is hardly fanciful, however, to suggest that accusations of barbarity miss the point. Bull-baiting was more than an expression or outburst of blood lust, it was an organised and structured way of disobeying authority – a powerful statement of the right of self determination.

Numerous bull-baitings were organised in defiance of the authorities' orders, and the patchy reporting of such events implies many more occurred. The organiser of a bull-baiting at the wakes in Leek had no time for the constables who came to prevent the bull-baiting; he persisted 'in defiance of all authority';[33] in a Shropshire mining town, Madeley, the population 'offered the most determined resistance', when a Methodist clergyman attempted to 'put a check' upon their customary amusements.[34] Resistance often involved physical violence: at Eccleshall, for example, the vicar, having freed the bull, found himself 'surrounded by a crowd of roughs, who tore his gown off his back, and otherwise maltreated him, until he was rescued by more sensible parishioners'.[35] But less aggressive ways to undermine the authorities' actions were also found. Following a set of successful prosecutions for bull-baiting at Handsworth, the *Birmingham Journal* lamented that the neighbourhood was nonetheless determined to protect the practice of bull-baiting, raising a considerable subscription for the purpose of paying the fines imposed.

Bull-baiting was perceived by local people as an integral part of a traditional festivity, all aspects of which had long been organised and determined by working people themselves, and official attempts to interfere with this culture during the first half of the nineteenth century were deeply resented. The numerous acts of defiance indicate not simply degradation, brutality and backwardness; they also reveal a community which had a clear sense of its own autonomy. The working community in this industrial region had established its own sporting and festive traditions, independent of elite guidance and control, and was prepared to go to considerable length to defend these local customs.

Endnotes

[1] *Birmingham Weekly Post Notes and Queries*, no.1639 (hereafter *BWP*). Birmingham Reference Library, [J. Jaffray], 'Hints for a History of Birmingham', 174534, chapter .16.

[2] Frederick W. Hackwood, *Old English Sports* (London, 1907), 319.

[3] *BWP Notes and Queries*, no.34.

[4] Francis Redfern, *History of the Town of Uttoxeter; with Notices of Places in its Neighbourhood* (London, 1865), 354. See also *BWP Notes and Queries*, no.2037.

[5] *Morning Chronicle*, 3 March 1851.

[6] *Aris's Birmingham Gazette*, 13 October 1828.

[7] For going as children see *BWP Notes and Queries*, nos.34, 1485, 1542, 2037 and 2086; no.2585. For the presence of women, see ibid., no.34, 384, 1543, 2037, 3303, 3315.

[8] *Morning Chronicle*, 27 January 1851.

[9] *Warwick Advertizer*, 19 February 1814, 6 March 1824.

[10] *Birmingham Gazette and Express*, 9 October. 1908; *BWP Notes and Queries*, no.1921.

[11] Birmingham Reference Library, 'Newspaper cuttings', 302127, 183.

[12] *BWP Notes and Queries*, no.3332, no.3319.

[13] Birmingham Reference Library 'Newspaper cuttings', 302135, 119.

[14] Walsall Archive Service 'Newspaper cuttings', vol.6, 86; Birmingham Reference Library, 'Newspaper cuttings', 302127, 183.

[15] Sandwell Community History and Archive Service, Wednesbury Notes and Queries, vol.3, no.379; *BWP Notes and Queries*, no.3368.

[16] Ibid., no.384. *Morning Chronicle*, 3 March 1851. See also *BWP Notes and Queries*, no. 3287.

[17] A full account of the suppression of bull-baiting is given in my PhD thesis; Griffin, 'Popular sports and celebrations in England, 1660-1840', PhD dissertation, Cambridge, 2000, 152-164.

[18] Charles William Hatfield, *Historical Notices of Doncaster*, 3 vols. (Doncaster, n.d), 72.

[19] Douglas Reid, 'Brutes and beasts: popular blood sports c.1780-1860', in Richard Holt, ed., *Sport and the Working Class in Modern Britain* (Manchester, 1990), 14. See also Jon Raven, *The Urban and Industrial Songs of the Black Country and Birmingham* (Wolverhampton, 1977), 131; J.F. Ede, *History of Wednesbury* (Birmingham, 1962), 156.

[20] Ronald Hutton, *The Stations of the Sun. A History of the Ritual Year in Britain* (Oxford, 1996), 357-358; R.J.R. Poole, 'Wakes, holidays and fairs in the Lancashire cotton district, c.1790-1890', PhD dissertation, Lancaster, 1895, 128-129.

[21] Harris, 'Problematising Popular Culture', in idem., ed., *Popular Culture in England, 1500-1850* (Hampshire, 1995), 4-5, 14-20; Reay, *Popular Cultures in England, 1550-1750* (Harlow, 1998), 126-45.

[22] *Staffordshire Advertizer*, 21 November 1835; William Salt Library, Broughton's Scrap Book, 41-2.
[23] *Staffordshire Advertizer*, 8 December 1827.
[24] J.F.W. Hackwood, *History of Darlaston* (Wednesbury, 1887), 87; Sir Oswald Mosley, *History of the Castle, Priory and Town of Tutbury* (London, 1832), 90; Rev William Leigh, *An Authentic Account of the Melancholy Occurrences at Bilston, in the Country of Stafford during the Awful Visitation in that Town by Cholera* (Wolverhampton, 1832), 6; *Aris's Birmingham Gazette*, 17 November 1828; Weston E. Vernon Yonge, *Bye-Paths of Staffordshire* (Market Drayton, 1911; 4th edn., Stafford, 1991), 104.
[25] *BWP Notes and Queries*, no.2076. Cf., George Barrs, *Four Sermons by the Late Reverend George Barrs... together with copious Extracts from his private Manuscript Journals* (Birmingham, 2nd edn., 1897), 82-3.
[26] *BWP Notes and Queries*, no.2055.
[27] *Wolverhampton Chronicle*, 29 November 1815.
[28] Charlotte S. Bume, *Shropshire Folklore. A Sheaf of Gleanings from the Collections of Georgina Jackson*, 2 vols. (London, 1883), vol.2, 448.
[29] *Staffordshire Advertizer*, 6 December 1828.
[30] *Journal of Commons*, vol.83, 1826, 407; *Aris's Birmingham Gazette*, 24 March 1828.
[31] Moseley, *History of Tutbury*, 89.
[32] *Times*, 31 October 1828.
[33] Ibid., 2 November 1822.
[34] John Randall, *The History of Madeley* (Madeley, 1880), 128.
[35] Yonge, *Bye-Paths of Staffordshire*, 105.

The Cheek of the Young Person: Sexualized Popular Discourse as Subtext in Dickens

Caroline Jackson-Houlston
School of Humanities
Oxford Brookes University
Headington
Oxford, OX3 0BP
cmjackson-houlston@brookes.ac.uk

For Mr Podsnap, 'the question about everything was, would it bring a blush into the cheek of the young person'.[1]*Everything*, therefore, has this potential, or, as R.B. Yeazell put it, Podsnappery is 'implicitly to convert all knowledge into sexual knowledge'.[2] And Podsnap blushes all the time, in seeking to police the experience of the young person. Dickens' most famous prude offers us a model of the split audience(s) of Victorian fiction, where patriarchal self-interest complicitly acknowledges certain kinds of knowledge in the process of preventing others from acquiring it. Dickens both derides and imitates Podsnap in this. This paper seeks to demonstrate that Dickens creates subtexts to his fiction, for both comic and serious purposes, that undermine the apparent proprieties of the overt meanings, and that some of these subtexts rely on sexual double meanings derived from more popular and more oral forms of discourse.

Previous commentators have, severally, made similar suggestions, but usually in a limited or tentative way. Thus, in discussing *Martin Chuzzlewit*, S.J. Newman notes the use of 'gravy' for sexual secretions. Yet although Newman's book is called *Dickens at Play*, this aspect of Dickens' play is not developed. Indeed, Newman claims that 'it is a condition of the civilisation [Dickens] is depicting that sex is masked and mutilated rather than celebrated by slang'.[3] Kelsie B. Harder proposes that the references to the pickpocket Charley, a member of Fagin's homosocial gang of trainee thieves, as *Master* Bates, cannot be accidental, but only while discussing a list of much more general names.[4] Monica Feinberg notes of *The Old Curiosity Shop* that 'Dick' is equivalent to 'penis' and 'swive' to 'fornicate' but this is in the course of an investigation into the effects of literary citation.[5] Most perceptively,

Michael Steig discusses at length in two articles[6] how we are to read Chapter 24 of *Martin Chuzzlewit*, where Mary Graham touches Tom Pinch's organ and is surprised to find it capable of elevation. Dickens, he concludes, 'would no doubt have expunged this last sentence had he been consciously aware of its extended sexual pun'; 'the subsequent passage of mawkish rhetoric ... may be seen as an unconscious attempt to subdue the organ that has just been elevated'.[7]

Indeed we *may* see these passages as the work of Dickens' unconscious, but why need we make this assumption? Steig discusses the implications of various interpretive strategies in his lucid and moderate essay 'The Intentional Phallus'.[8] One approach is to regard such *double entendres* as an inappropriate privileging of the modern reader, 'something twentieth-century academic lechers can giggle over but which has no importance for the novel'. A less condemnatory version of this is Ian Watt's assumption that Pecksniff's wish to see Mrs Todgers' idea of a wooden leg involves a 'phallic substitution [which] is child's play to a normally contaminated mind'.[9]

This leads to Steig's own more moderate position that Dickens described Tom's musical hobby as he did 'because of a *subconscious* [my italics] perception that Tom was experiencing a kind of sexual awakening'.[10] In critics who touch on such matters at all, this is the commonest response. Indeed, there are some substantial studies along these lines, including Arthur Washburn Brown's engaging and intermittently persuasive *Sexual Analysis of Dickens' Props*.[11] By and large, such studies analyse Dickens the writer or the texts of the novels rather than the ideological discourses of his age, and seek to reveal 'meaning in Charles Dickens' fiction which one might not ordinarily know was there'.[12] As Steig points out, 'few Dickensians would accept that Dickens was fully conscious of the pun, but assumed that his average reader would not notice it'.[13]

Critics, he notes, tend 'to view such double meanings as inherently improbable in an early or mid-Victorian English novelist'.[14] We need to ask why this should be the case. It may have something to do with our own desire to define ourselves as less repressed and inhibited than our predecessors. Steig asks how we limit 'the horizon of possible meaning'. He argues that 'the least problematic means is to ascertain the lexical meanings of individual words and expressions in the historical context of the work'[15] and considers the argument that 'since we do not find similar puns elsewhere in Dickens the intentionality of this one is unlikely'.[16] For any one occurrence – Tom's organ, Mrs Todgers' gravy, Dick Swiveller – this may seem an appropriate common-sense reaction. However, once one starts adding the instances up, the circumstantial evidence becomes stronger, as Steig admits, while still holding that 'an awareness of sexual innuendoes' was 'not fully conscious in Dickens'.[17] I contend that we *do* find similar puns elsewhere in Dickens, and that he was acquainted with a discourse in which ribald metaphorical substitution for everyday objects is a defining feature.

If we are to establish the lexical meanings current at the time Dickens produced his text, what lexicons are we to use? Here the process of historicisation becomes more problematic. The standard reference work for sexual *double entendres* is Eric Partridge's *Dictionary of Slang and Unconventional English* but even this is by no means comprehensive, for reasons of both inclusiveness and dating, as Partridge admits in his introduction.[18] For example, he omits some standard words where a primary denotative meaning is connected with sexual activity, such as the verb 'tup'. This appears even in older versions of the *Oxford English Dictionary*. By its very nature, sexual slang is more likely to occur in informal spoken rather than written language, and, if written, more likely to occur in texts of an ephemeral kind. Its currency is usually limited socially, geographically and temporally, though not necessarily at the same time. This makes the task of recording sexual slang usage more than usually onerous to the lexicographer, and makes dating yet more problematic. Partridge used a number of Victorian slang dictionaries, notably that by J.S. Farmer and W.E. Henley, to establish usage.[19] Unfortunately these are seldom specific about dating, and some are more limited than Partridge by the bounds of propriety, so they often focus on occupational, sporting and criminal rather than sexual slang. One example of this would be Ducange Anglicus' *The Vulgar Tongue: a Glossary of Slang, Cant, and Flash Words and Phrases, used in London, from 1839 to 1859*. The second edition of 1859 omits sexual senses of 'bob', 'dick', 'fanny', 'gravy', 'meat' and 'pudding' (all discussed below). Where more comprehensive, they often date from late in the century. They leave unrecorded many meanings which are quite apparent from some of the less respectable and consequently more ephemeral kinds of text, such as songsters containing pieces performed in the almost entirely masculine milieu of the song-and-supper clubs from the 1830s onwards.[20] Thus, the use of 'fanny' to mean what Partridge usually refers to as 'the female pudend' is formally dated by him as from 1860. Putting aside its apparently knowing usage in Cleland's novel *Memoirs of Fanny Hill* (abridged with this title, 1750) and assuming the usage is not derived from Cleland, this meaning is obviously current in nineteenth-century songsters of the 1830s.[21] It is demonstrable, then, that the dictionaries are not entirely reliable in terms of usage or dates, and it is reasonable to assume some leeway both pre- and post- the dates given.

Songsters demonstrate three main kinds of sexually subversive language. They may use terms not regarded as generally fit for print because of their referents. They may use puns. A title in 'The Flash Chaunter' illustrates both these points: 'With Mike Hunt I Have Travelled Over the Town'. The point of the joke is frequently reiterated in the text: 'Many a bright shilling with Mike Hunt I have got/By playing at the game of – you know what'.[22] Slang is usually metaphorical, either conventional personification ('fanny') or more inventively derived from a wide range of semantic fields, especially the occupational.[23] These may be formulaic, and used from song to song, or *ad hoc*, for example, a song praising the generous sexual endowments of the Hippopotamus newly arrived at London Zoo (1850), which also makes fun of Victorian double standards of sexual knowledge. Some ladies enquire of the keeper what the stiff round thing trailing underneath the Hippopotamus is, and are told it is his 'electric telegraph' for communicating to Mrs Hippopotamus.[24] Steven Marcus identifies 'at least two different kinds of language' to describe sexuality in Victorian times, that of literature, and that of pornography; 'one is elaborate, genteel, and periphrastic; the other is "plain", direct and violent'.[25] Here is another, periphrastic without being genteel, or, if direct, by no means always violent. For although some of these songs create outlandish circumstances that offend the reader's credulity purely for the sake of a sexual reference, some also use metaphor with a geniality and inventiveness that are not what we associate with pornography. I am going to suggest that there are occasions when Dickens seems to be conjuring up this sort of discourse.

More than the mere occurrence of *double entendre* in other forms of discourse would be needed to establish a belief in Dickens' intention. We would need to assess a) the probability of Dickens' having encountered these meanings, and b) their presence in a context in his fiction that would seem to activate them. Dickens is not a man whose surviving letters suggest he habitually wrote racy notes to male friends, even friends with equivocal reputations like Wilkie Collins with whom he enjoyed rackety evenings. A mild example of occasional suggestiveness would be his letter to C.C. Felton on March 14, 1842, which ends with a sly recommendation to try British oysters to check that they 'are not devoid of the refreshing influence which that species of fish is supposed to exercise in these latitudes' (i.e. aphrodisiac).[26] Moreover, he certainly acted in a Podsnap-like capacity himself, editing Sala's first *Household Words* paper 'so as not to shock young and lady readers'.[27] John Carey notes how 'in successive editions of *Sketches by Boz* the language was cleaned up, the "legs" of the young lady in "The Dancing Academy" becoming "ankles", and allusion to the aphrodisiac effect of oysters being toned down'.[28] Indeed, Marcus argues that in *Our Mutual Friend* (1865), Dickens' tactic was to 'suppress any references to prostitutes and to censor his report on the language of the dockside'.[29]

Nevertheless, it is also Marcus who argues that a younger Dickens, creating Major Bagstock in *Dombey and Son* (1848), 'uses a variety of means to communicate to the reader the intense, disturbed and corrupted sexuality of the Major'.[30] These means include what Marcus claims is a concealed sexual pun in Bagstock's name.[31] He implies what I am arguing for more strongly, audiences for Dickens' fiction divided along gender lines.

As a child, Dickens sang in public houses, as did his sister. Later in life he visited song-and-supper rooms, including Evans', as did Thackeray and other members of Dickens' circle, Jerrold, Mayhew, and Sala.[32] (The much younger Sala was responsible for writing part of a sadistic text, *The Mysteries of Verbena House*).[33] Dickens certainly had more than enough opportunity in his youth and early manhood to encounter the raffish discourse of masculine sexual *double entendre*.

Is consciousness of subversive linguistic potential activated by the context in which it might be said to occur in Dickens' fiction? Steig asks how we limit meaning; we can also ask how we liberate it, since the theoretical free play of the signifier manifestly does not operate in most contexts. I am not proposing that a Victorian *pater familias* had to suppress paroxysms of subversive inner laughter every time he was introduced to a character called Richard or Frances, or, for that matter, one wearing an old hat.[34] Dickens' sister was called Fanny. However, just as a sequence of mixed metaphors reanimates dead ones, so clusters of apparently sexual subtexts may suggest intention in the writer. Moreover, the metaphoric features of popular songs may suggest a discourse with a variety of dimensions beyond the mere use of a word suggestive in itself.

Is such potential for punning or metaphoric subversion present in many of Dickens' texts, or in other canonical Victorian texts? If the latter, conversion to my thesis would involve a radical rethinking of Victorian values. To test this, I decided to check out the potential in the names of Dickens' first and last completed novels. The members of the Pickwick Club do seem to have a suspicious similarity of name, even though some of the firm dating for the slang involved post-dates the novel (1837). 'Wick' itself is recorded by Partridge as meaning 'penis' by 1860, but it obviously occurs in 'Dip the Tallow Chandler' in the songster 'The Flash Chaunter' dating from the mid 1830s or 1840s. (This might set one wondering about George Eliot's use of Lowick as the home for Casaubon in *Middlemarch*. Had she really been associating for too long with Lewes' male friends, or, given the rest of the imagery used to suggest Casaubon's physical as well as emotional impotence, was she re-inventing the wheel here?) The 'tup' of the ladies' man Tupman does not even need Partridge. 'Winkle', as slang for 'penis' is listed as late nineteenth-century. It may be familiar to modern readers from the later song, 'I Can't Get my Winkle Out' but a similar usage occurs in a song of c. 1837, 'The Periwinkle: or, Harry's Wickey-icky', about a man with an undersized penis.[35] Even Dingley Dell has suspicious connotations. Apart from the obviously 'Freudian' ones, 'dell' meant 'mistress' from the seventeenth to the nineteenth centuries, and 'dingle' could be used for 'penis' at least by the end of the nineteenth century. This suggestive potential for such important names in the novel starts to look like more than coincidence.

Our Mutual Friend, however, the literary home of Mr Podsnap, appears to offer less room for conjecture. Notwithstanding Marcus' praise of Dickens' civilising influence in self-policing his description of waterfront life in Abbey Potterson's pub, 'abbess' was widespread and current slang for a madam. Moreover, Jenny Wren's real name is Fanny Cleaver. Perhaps 'wren' as a term for a whore frequenting Curragh army camp (1869) is too local to be likely. Apart from 'Fanny', 'cleaver' meant a wanton, certainly early in the nineteenth century. This reading does not seem to illuminate the novel – it lacks Steig's criterion of consistency with the overt meaning of the novel[36] – but it needs to be registered. However, the principals in the action (who are not, unlike the Pickwick Club, comic) have names that seem less open to question. Names like Veneering, Lightwood, Headstone bear implicit metaphors, but ones based on different and more serious principles.

This might suggest that further enquiries into material that is either earlier or comic, or both, would be more fruitful. Certainly some of the more spectacular suspicions raised in passing by other critics belong in these areas. Thus, Fagin's gang of adolescent boys includes the quite unnecessarily-titled Master Bates.[37] In *The Old Curiosity Shop* (1841) we have a character whose flute-playing has been interpreted as masturbatory activity and called Dick Swiveller. Although the use of 'Dick' in the modern slang sense is not recorded until about twenty years later a double meaning here is a possibility. 'Swiveller', then, would not need a derivation from 'swive' to gain its effect.[38]

Potentially subversive material seems therefore to be more common in Dickens' earlier work. *Martin Chuzzlewit* (1844) is the last of Dickens' major comic novels before he engages more deeply with social issues, and his most linguistically high-spirited. It seems to have noticeable clusters of this sort of material. Here too names are significant. Pecksniff's daughters are, formally, Charity and Mercy. However, they are given significant nicknames. 'Merry' had the sub-meaning of wanton or sexually available in the nineteenth century (rather like 'gay'). Cherry is a man-hungry spinster. The *Bloomsbury Dictionary of Contemporary Slang* says that the use of 'cherry' meaning virginity, as in 'to lose one's cherry' is at least as old as the late nineteenth century.[39] If it was not current earlier, this seems an odd coincidence. Another member of the Pecksniff household, for the first part of the book, is Tom Pinch, whose main pleasure in an otherwise frustrated life is playing the organ. This propensity has been commented on at some length by Steig.[40] The key passage here is in Chapter 24, and it summarizes Tom's past experience of Mary Graham's friendship for him in an exaggerated and sentimentalized tone of unrequited love:

> when she spoke, Tom held his breath, so eagerly he listened; when she sang, he sat like one entranced. She touched his organ, and from that bright epoch, even it, the old companion of his happiest hours, incapable as he had thought of elevation, began a new and deified existence.[41]

At the end of the novel Mary marries Martin Chuzzlewit, and Tom is left without a partner. He is not allowed to console Charity or Mercy Pecksniff, but consoles himself with his role as foster-uncle and his organ. Dickens hijacks the organ at this point for some elaborate rhetoric about music and memory with which to close the novel, but he cannot eliminate the earlier suggestion.

Steig concludes that the earlier passage is generated by a 'subconscious perception' in Dickens that 'Tom was experiencing a kind of sexual awakening'. He admits that '"organ" at the very least has as one of its meanings in Dickens's time as in ours a functioning part of the body'.[42] However, these implications are bolstered by Dickens' physical description of Tom's appearance and character, and backed up too by the illustrations, which show a spotty, thin, youngish man with a downcast look.[43] Compare this Victorian psychologist's advice:

> If ... one perceives in a young man a certain shyness, and an evasive and cast-down look, a dull irresolute character, which are soon accompanied by stupidity and confusion of head, and weakness of memory, then one must be mindful of this sad vice.[44]

The sad vice is, of course, masturbation. Although this summary is from the 1860s it only repeats points raised again and again from the 1840s onwards. Marcus quotes Acton to make a similar point about Uriah Heep:

> The frame is stunted and weak, the muscles undeveloped, the eye is sunken and heavy, the complexion is sallow, pasty, or covered with spots of acne, the hands are damp and cold, and the skin moist. The boy shuns the society of others ... he cannot look anyone in the face, and becomes careless in dress.[45]

Of itself this similarity would not be overwhelmingly compelling, partly because of Tom's rapid if unconvincing character change half way through the book, and more especially because there would be an undistributed middle in the argument – not that this prevented Victorian doctors from diagnosing masturbation as the root of a young man's troubles even if unaccompanied by the other symptoms not quoted here. However, together with the other evidence, it tends to strengthen the case that Dickens has created a character who is both comic and pathetic because of his inability to find a partner who could afford him sexual satisfaction.

Certainly neither Cherry nor Merry is going to be allowed to take pity on him. From the beginning of the book they have tantalized his search for even a modicum of physical satisfaction of any sort and always refuse to give him any gravy. 'Gravy' is standard Victorian slang for 'the sexual discharge male or female', as Newman has noted. The man-hungry widow, Mrs Todgers, is constantly perplexed by the demands of her all-male boarders for gravy:

> there is no such passion in human nature, as the passion for gravy among commercial gentlemen. It's nothing to say a joint won't yield – a whole animal wouldn't yield – the amount of gravy they expect each day at dinner. And what I have undergone in consequence ... no one would believe (189-90).

The modern reader will have no difficulty in recognizing 'todger' as slang for penis. This is a possibility, though by no means a certainty, here. The *Bloomsbury Dictionary of Contemporary Slang* calls it 'a vulgarism of unknown origin (probably from a lost dialect verb) used for many years in the North of England'. Partridge gives a nineteenth-century sense of the verb 'todge' as 'to smash to a pulp'. This type of metaphor is a common one for sexual intercourse (c.f. 'fuck'). There is also a similarity with the noun and verb 'ro(d)ger', meaning both penis and copulate, and one of the very commonest of slang terms for both in the mid-nineteenth century.

The conflation of gustatory and sexual appetites is one of the most frequent kinds of subversive metaphor. It increases still further the suspicions of Ruth Pinch's pudding-making made by Freudians.[46] This passage in Chapter 39 displays an authorial persona quite embarrassingly excited by Ruth's domestic arrangements. Ruth does have a lover, John Westlock, and when he is in the offing in Chapter 45 we are told 'the Temple fountain might have leaped up twenty feet to greet the spring of hopeful maidenhood' (763). Here, though, the imagery is more obviously related to the sexual slang of the songsters. There are two elements here, each one focused on one of the two sexually innocent siblings. With Tom, the emphasis is on the meat, which the butcher eases into his pocket for him (674). 'Meat' has signified 'the human body as an instrument of sexual pleasure' and the male or female genitals since the turn of the seventeenth century. Examples from songs of the 1830s are common, as in 'Mutton Fresh; or the Female Butcher', or 'The Butcher's Steel'.[47] 'I Will be a Mot' celebrates the desires of a young woman determined not 'to die for want of meat' and recalling her enjoyment of it from a variety of young men (William, Roger and Robert).[48] It is Ruth who is more associated with the actual pudding. 'Pudding' can mean either coition, or the penis, or (like gravy, also involved here) seminal fluid, from the Restoration onwards. For examples, see 'The Bellyful, a Comic Recitation' ('my daughter's fond of pudding') or 'The New Rolling Pin', which features a heroine whose puddings general favour will win and the lover who kneaded her dough with a new rolling pin.[49]

Several stylistic features in this chapter appear to be signals inviting subversive interpretation. Dickens' extraordinary concentration here on the meat and the pudding seems excessive even in an author notorious for his celebrations of food. He is often exclamatory, but usually suggests plenitude by means of lists rather than by concentration on a few points. He initially lulls suspicion by constructing a household based on sibling rather than sexual affection (John Westlock's invitation to share the pudding is an afterthought which embarrasses Ruth). However, the fulsome second-person address to Ruth, and to individual items of her clothing and body, suggest a fervent fascination with Ruth as sexual object on the part of the narrator:

> Oh, heaven, what a wicked little stomacher! and to be gathered up into little plaits by the strings before it could be tied, and to be tapped, rebuked, and wheedled, at the pockets, before it would set right, which at last it did, and when it did – but never mind; this is a sober chronicle. And then, there were her cuffs to be tucked up, for fear of flour; and she had a little ring to pull off her finger, which wouldn't come off (foolish little ring) (676).

What is more, the discourse here almost exactly mimics that of Pecksniff when, in real earnest, he becomes a sexual threat to Mary Graham in Chapter 30.[50] He

> repeated the Todgers performance on a comfortable scale, as if he intended it to last some time; and in his disengaged hand, catching hers, employed himself in separating the fingers with his own, and sometimes kissing them ... examining the rings upon her fingers, and tracing the course

of one delicate blue vein with his fat thumb ... 'Ah, naughty Hand!' said Mr Pecksniff, apostrophising the reluctant prize, 'why did you take me prisoner! Go, go!'

He slapped the hand to punish it; but relenting, folded it into his waistcoat to comfort it again (551-2).

It is obvious that Mary is being subjected to a very unpleasant sexual assault here, and that the blame lies squarely with Pecksniff, not the narrator, who is exposing him.

However, Dickens is also taking a sly dig at Pecksniff's sexual abilities. The subtitle for this chapter announces that 'Mr Pecksniff was a special hand at a Triple-bob-major'. Most readers do not pause to ask why Dickens should use this phrase when campanology never features in the text, and take it to be merely a metaphor about ringing changes, because this chapter is on the dissensions in the Pecksniff household. However, a bob (or dry bob) was a current term for attempted coition. It made a notorious appearance in a literary text in the suppressed Dedication to Byron's *Don Juan*. Byron comments on Robert Southey's creative powers:

> You overstrain yourself, or so,
> And tumble downward like the flying fish
> Gasping on deck, because you soar too high, Bob,
> And fall, for lack of moisture quite a-dry Bob.[51]

It is also found in 'New Version of the Amiable Family' (a pertinent title here):

> May your fingers so tickle his bob man,
> In the hope he don't come a dry bob-man
> May your c – at half cock, go off 'gainst his smock.
> And knock his p – and b – slap off marm.[52]

To confirm the likelihood of a subversive pun here, it would be worth noting a toast in 'Fanny Hill's Bang-up Reciter': 'Success to Fencer's Wharf, luck to major bob ringing, and prime grapps for the stiff kiddies'.[53]

These comments would not exhaust the bawdy potential of *Martin Chuzzlewit*; Poll Sweedlepipe and Young Bailey would bear more investigation for a start.[54] However, the argument that the joke about Tom's organ is unique no longer seems plausible. I would like to end with a brief discussion of the possible use of a sexual *double entendre* in a more serious context.

What conclusions would you come to if you were told the following story? A man enlists, after his sweetheart has renounced him for a deliberately unspecified action ('in an evil hour, he had given her cause to say to him' that she would never speak to him again). He becomes dissipated and reckless, and indeed spends much of his time in a 'Black hole'. The only person whose opinion he values is his commanding officer, Taunton, of whose physical presence he is always aware: Taunton has 'bright, handsome, dark eyes – what are called laughing eyes generally, and were serious rather steady than severe ... He had but to know that those eyes looked at him for a moment, and he felt ashamed'. When he feels guilty his desire is always to avid having to face 'those two handsome, dark, bright eyes'. Indeed, Taunton's gaze bring tears to the hero's eyes and makes his breast swell. Taunton's kind rebuke makes him kiss Taunton's hand and go out 'of the light of the dark bright eyes, an altered man'. The pair even achieve a reputation in the army: 'wherever Captain Taunton with the dark bright eyes, led, there, close to him ever at his side, firm as a rock, true as the sun, and brave as Mars, would be certain to be found, while life beat in their hearts, that famous soldier'. Taunton dies with the hero's arms around him and his own hand on Richard's breast. The hero becomes a 'lone, bereaved man' and carries a lock of Taunton's hair next to his heart for two years.[55] One might legitimately conclude that a love 'passin' the love of women', to use Kipling's phrase about army relationships, is being depicted here.[56]

What is more, the pseudonym adopted by this hero – the only name used for him – is Doubledick. It seems legitimate to suspect that the homosocial bond Dickens is celebrating here has a homosexual element to it. Partridge lists the usage of 'dick' for penis as army slang from c. 1860. Dickens' story is in the Christmas number for 1854. This is a pairing in which both partners are male. If 'a gay text is one which lends itself to the hypothesis of a gay reading, regardless of where the author's genitals were wont to keep house' then this is certainly a gay text.[57]

Whatever Dickens' intentions were, he did not of course openly present it as a gay love story. There is a formal heterosexual love interest in Mary, the sweetheart who is *never* physically described, and who finally marries Doubledick when he is so gravely wounded as to be thought dying. It takes several months before he is sufficiently conscious to remember what he has done, and even then he needs prompting by Mary. The story interestingly conflates the three male characters. Doubledick is treated as a son by the mother of his old commander. Taunton's death at Badajos was caused by a French officer who is his duplicate in being 'courageous, handsome, gallant, and who also has a 'bright, sudden look'.[58] Taunton dies at forty. In 1818, Doubledick, who has been bent on vengeance on the French officer, whom Taunton's mother has innocently befriended, remeets him. Both are forty one (Dickens was forty two when he wrote the story). The Frenchman does not recognize him. Mrs Taunton refers to her dead son using a capital letter for He. Doubledick feels it is the spiritual influence of the dead man that leads him to keep silence and forgive the man without revealing the story. The 'bright, sudden look' of the French officer at this point could, though, be taken as a contributory factor. The story has a homosocial coda. Doubledick, now a Major (Taunton's final rank) has a son who follows him into the army. This son and the French officer's son team up to fight together 'like long-divided brothers', presumably in the Crimean War, which was going on at the time of publication.

Dickens is firing on all cylinders to activate cultural codes of religion (this is a Christmas story), patriotism, family relationships, and heterosexual models of desire, to make this an acceptable story. It was one of Dickens' favourites. He wrote that it moved him to tears in writing. The number sold well and was dramatized many times in the succeeding twenty years.[59] What is going on here is exactly the situation identified by J. Michael Léger in *David Copperfield* and *Great Expectations*: 'incomplete transformations of these situations and characters into heterocentric situations Dickens' culture can approve. Dickens leaves traces of homocentrism and even of homoeroticism in the final configurations he elevates for approval'.[60] One of these traces is the self-naming of the character.[61]

What is the significance of all this? I am not claiming that we need radically to rethink Dickens' work in this light. There is certainly material for a gender-oriented psychopathological investigation of some of the more lurid of the songster texts, such the 'New Version of the Amiable Family' quoted above. However, many are genial and witty. And the portions of Dickens' work in which this discourse can be identified are small. Moreover, in Dickens' own writing the vehicles of the metaphors are sufficiently well-rooted in daily experience to offer a substantial literal meaning for which a subversive reading is not necessary. On the other hand, I hope to have demonstrated that it is sometimes not only possible, but plausible, given the occurrence of suitable clues to a *double entendre*, to add a subversive meaning which would have been available to at least some of the adult males among Dickens' readers. If this subversive reading generates a rush of blood to the superego in modern critics, so that they feel a need to isolate it and sanitize it in layers of academic analysis, perhaps we need to ask why. Though bawdry is but a small proportion of Dickens' writing, and that mostly early on, in the aftermath of the Regency, it is there. It is not *innocent* fun because the point of this carnivalesque species of fun is precisely that it does subvert standards of propriety. But it may be harmless. If we deny it, what are we preserving? Our sense of ourselves as more knowing, and hence more liberated and more humane than the Victorians? Or are we avoiding the fear that we ourselves might be seen as contaminated by enjoying the trivial and unrespectable aspects of the ludic?

Endnotes

[1] Because of the multiplicity of editions, references to Dickens's works will be given as chapter numbers, using continuous numbering. This is from *Our Mutual Friend*, Chapter 11.

[2] R.B. Yeazell, 'Podsnappery, Sexuality and the English Novel', *Critical Inquiry*, IX.2 (1982): 340.

[3] S.J. Newman, *Dickens at Play* (London: Macmillan, 1981), 110.

[4] K.B. Harder, 'Dickens and his Lists of Names', *A Journal of Onomastics*, XXX.1 (1982): 41.

[5] M.L. Feinberg, 'Reading Curiosity: Does Dick's Shop Deliver?' *Dickens Quarterly*, VII:1 (1990): 206.

[6] M. Steig, '*Martin Chuzzlewit*: Pinch and Pecksniff', *Studies in the Novel*, I:2 (1969): 181-88, and 'The Intentional Phallus: Determining Verbal Meanings in Literature', *Journal of Aesthetics and Art Criticism*, XXXVI (1977): 51-61.

[7] Steig,'*Martin Chuzzlewit*', 184.

[8] Steig,'The Intentional Phallus', 54.

[9] I. Watt, 'Oral Dickens', *Dickens Studies Annual*, III (1974): 168.

[10] Steig,'The Intentional Phallus', 54.

[11] A.W. Brown, *Sexual Analysis of Dickens' Props* (New York: Emerson Books, 1971).

[12] Brown, 8.

[13] Steig, 'The Intentional Phallus', 54.

[14] Steig, 'The Intentional Phallus', 54.

[15] Steig, 'The Intentional Phallus', 52.

[16] Steig, 'The Intentional Phallus', 54.

[17] Steig, 'The Intentional Phallus', 54.

[18] The edition used here is Eric Partridge, *A Dictionary of Slang and Unconventional English* (London: Bibliophile Books, 1982). This has two parts, the original and a large supplement. References to Partridge hereafter may refer to either part, but since entries are otherwise alphabetical no pages are given. Definitions and datings not otherwise ascribed in the text are to Partridge.

[19] J.S. Farmer and W.E. Henley, *Slang and its Analogues, Past and Present* (printed for subscribers only, VII vols, 1890-1903).

[20] Ducange Anglicus, *The Vulgar Tongue: a Glossary of Slang, Cant, and Flash Words and Phrases, Used in London, from 1839 to 1859: Flash Songs, Essay on Slang, and a Bibliography of Canting and Slang Literature* (London: Bernard Quaritch, 2nd ed., 1859). A selection from songsters c. 1835-50 (mostly late 1830s), predicated on *double entendre*, is available in George Speaight, *Bawdy Songs of the Early Music Hall* (Devon: David & Charles, 1975).

[21] E.g. Speaight, *Bawdy Songs*, 39, 46, 48, 76, and songsters such as 'The Swell, or, Slap-up Chaunter. An Out and Out Collection of Flash Songs, Rum Ditties, and Slang Chaunts' (London: Melford, n.d. but between 1835 and 1850), 48.

[22] 'The Flash Chaunter. A slashing, dashing, friskey and delecious [sic] collection of Gentleman's Songs, now singing at Offley's, Cider Cellers [sic], Coal Hole, &c, &c' ([London]: W. West, n.d., but between 1835 and 1850), 39. This, like other songsters,

was reissued in the 1860s. In this, and the songster in the previous note, mark the key adjectives, and the insistence on an exclusive, gender-defined audience.

[23] This kind of metaphoric treatment of sexual activity, is, of course, well-known in folk song, and these days much of it is treated as both serious and artful, as long as it is seen as dead enough to need revival in folk clubs and not sung in rugby-club showers. See A.L. Lloyd, *Folk Song in England* (St Albans: Paladin, 1967), 187-201.

[24] 'The Hippopotamus' (Birmingham: William Pratt, n.d.). The animal's arrival was celebrated by *Household Words* on August 3, 1850 (I, 445-9); the telegraph had been invented in 1837.

[25] S. Marcus, *The Other Victorians: a Study of Sexuality and Pornography in Mid-Nineteenth-Century England* (London: Weidenfeld and Nicholson, 1966), 227.

[26] H. House, G. Storey and K. Tillotson, eds, *The Pilgrim Edition of the Letters of Charles Dickens* (Oxford: Clarendon Press, 1965-) III, 131. The editors make a specific case for the sexual interpretation here.

[27] *Letters*, VI, 458.

[28] J. Carey, *The Violent Effigy* (London: Faber and Faber, 1979), 166.

[29] Marcus, *The Other Victorians*, 104.

[30] Marcus, *The Other Victorians*, 110.

[31] This is now widely accepted and is plausible, but a search in Partridge under 'bag' and 'stock' will reveal that this pun is concealed a good deal more elaborately than any of the more obvious ones I am arguing for. The claim is repeated in a more wide-ranging study of double meanings in the novel in J.L. Marsh, 'Good Mrs Brown's Connections: Sexuality and Story-Telling in Dealings with the Firm of Dombey and Son', *English Literary History*, LVIII:2 (1991): 405-26.

[32] For a discussion of this milieu and its representation in fiction, see Speaight, *Bawdy Songs*, 5-13, and C.M. Jackson-Houlston, *Ballads, Songs and Snatches: the Appropriation of Folk Song and Popular Culture in British Nineteenth-century Realist Prose* (Aldershot: Ashgate, 1999), Chapter 6.

[33] Marcus, *The Other Victorians*, 264.

[34] Widespread for female genitals. See Partridge, who also quotes Grose's early nineteenth century suggestion that this is because they are often felt.

[35] In 'The Cuckold's Nest' (London: W. West, c. 1837), 5-8.

[36] Steig, 'The Intentional Phallus', 59.

[37] Harder, 'Dickens and his list of names', 41. Those wishing to make much of this pun should, however, remember that the *Oxford English Dictionary* dates the verb from 1857, though the noun was in use from 1766.

[38] As suggested by Feinberg, 'Ready Curiosity', 206.

[39] T. Thorne, *The Bloomsbury Dictionary of Contemporary Slang* (London: Bloomsbury, 1994).

[40] Steig, 'The Intentional Phallus', 53-55.

[41] C. Dickens, *Martin Chuzzlewit*, ed. P.N. Furbank (Harmondsworth: Penguin, 1968), 462. Further page references will be to this edition.

[42] Steig, 'The Intentional Phallus', 55.

[43] Original illustration *Martin Chuzzlewit*, 69, and text 68-70. Dickens gave Phiz elaborate instructions about illustrative details.

[44] Schroeder van der Kolk, quoted in J.C. Bucknill and D.H. Tuke, *A Manual of Psychological Medicine* (London: J. and A. Churchill, 4th ed. 1879), 347.

[45] Marcus, *The Other Victorians*, 19.

[46] E.g. Brown's long and enthusiastic discussion, *Sexual Analysis of Dickens' Props*, 122-5. Brown examines some words for their punning potential but has nothing to say about the slang meanings.

[47] Both these are in 'The Flash Chaunter', 28, 43-5. See also, for one of many more, 'The Butcher' in 'The Corinthian; an Extensive Collection of Flash Songs ...' (London: Duncombe, c. 1833), 148-50.

[48] Speaight, *Bawdy Songs*, 76.

[49] 'The Flash Chaunter', 21-4; Speaight, *Bawdy Songs*, 51.

[50] This resemblance in tone is also noted by A.J. Guerard, '*Martin Chuzzlewit:* the Novel as Comic Entertainment', *Mosaic*, IX.4 (1976): 125.

[51] These lines were still reproduced in some Victorian editions of Byron's work; see *The Poetical Works of Lord Byron* (London: John Murray, 1870), 588.

[52] 'The Flash Chaunter', last verse of first song.

[53] 'Fanny Hill's Bang-up Reciter, Frisky Songster, and Amarous [sic] Toast Master' (London: G.K. Edwards, 1830s), 47.

[54] Barbers are often the subject of bawdy songs, though Poll's epicene appearance and manners suggest something different from the usual stress on the barber's pole. Young Bailey's injunction to go 'gently over the stones ... go a tip-toe over the pimples!' (530) implies he may have been frequenting song-and- supper rooms with toasts such as 'The female coachman – gently over the stones' ('Fanny Hill's Bang-up Reciter', 46).

[55] C. Dickens, 'The Seven Poor Travellers', *The Christmas Stories*, ed. R. Glancy (London: Dent, 1996), 65-70.

[56] 'Follow Me 'Ome', *The Definitive Edition of Rudyard Kipling's Verse* (London: Hodder and Stoughton, repr. 1969), 447.

[57] G. Woods, *Articulate Flesh: Male Homo-eroticism and Modern Poetry* (New Haven and London: Yale University Press, 1987), 4.

[58] *Christmas Stories*, 69, 76.

[59] *Christmas Stories*, 55.

[60] J. Michael Léger, 'The Scrooge in the Closet: Homo-erotic Tropes in the Novels of Charles Dickens' (Doctoral thesis, University of Notre Dame, Indiana, 1991), abstract.

[61] Since this is a Christmas number there are also references to pudding and gravy in the introduction to the stories, but without other contextual keys I take these to refer solely to food.

Acknowledgements
I would like to thank those colleagues and students with whom I have discussed some of the ideas above, especially Paul O'Flinn and Margery Hanson, for their combination of scholarly respect and occasional healthy irreverence for canonical texts.

The Joy of Sex?: Paradoxes of representation in the Age of Photography

Nicholas Jagger
3 Bell Lane
Rawcliffe
Goole
E. Yorks, DN14 8RP
NMJagger@art-historian.demon.co.uk

Introduction

Although it would be tempting to correlate the political events of the nineteenth century with visual representation, this would yield only partially successful results, since the domains of the discursive and non-discursive are not neatly tied together. The language of the visual is complex and often paradoxical, despite what some art historians continue to write. What can be said is that visual representation provides clues to the kinds of tensions and anxieties prevalent at key (political) moments in the period, though the clues can be read in different ways.

Visual language is, like any language, inherently labile, and the ways in which individuals responded to imagery was profoundly personal. Thus to describe the illicit pleasure taken with visual representation in the Victorian period is best approached through a twin analysis, both of reading, and of the resistance of sexuality to denial and codification.

A phenomenon as complex as sexual identity does not coalesce into anything like a tangible form, and frequently images deny what concerns them the most. I suggest that at the core of debates surrounding the female nude in art are tensions about definitions of male sexuality: the subjects depicted are open to reversals both in meaning and implied gender.

In a wider view, (at some level) unintended exchanges of meaning were common in the large salon (female) nudes painted by figures such as Leighton which, though accomplished, lacked entirely the kind of contact and relation to the physical that (male) sculptures such as *The Sluggard* epitomized. Quite often, direct confrontations with the norms of female depiction, representations of a sexualized female, collapsed into their other and their subjects were reversed: images which emerged from a crisis in male sexual identity spoke volumes about it, in fact they were garrulous.

It is an extraordinary period in which all kinds of reversals took place. Paintings could be profoundly unaesthetic, pornographic images unrelated to sexuality; illustrative photographs the most sexual, and overt representation of given female sexuality far more concerned with male identity, purpose, role and function.

The chronological focus of this essay is the period from the twilight of the Pre-Raphaelite painters to the First World War, a moment which for many heralds the end of the Victorian. Its subject is the relation of photography to the body in art, or at any rate, to the body as a prepossessed site, particularly in sexual terms. Although I take as my subject the tense relation between representations of the body and accepted taste, pornography as such features only slightly in this essay. My focus is the ways in which images of the nude, publicly displayed (or published), could be read, despite the ways in which representation was managed, and the complex ways in which denials of sexuality emphasized rather that surpressed it. I argue that there is much more to this subject than concrete power relations between the progressives and the repressives, though – clearly – punitive measures against transgressors were serious, and reaction to male domination could be violent, as with the case of suffragette activity (see below), to say nothing of the lives eked out in such a society.

My principal subject is *A Handbook of Anatomy for Art Students*, (Oxford: Clarendon Press, 1906). In many ways it typifies its period. It contains a chapter by chapter account of the regions of the body, accompanied by a description written as a useful anatomical guide to art students, probably studying in one of the chief London art establishments. The relation of musculature to movement, the visual effects of the organization of the body, and the forms created by movement are emphasized. There are the usual kinds of detailed and labelled line-drawings, but the book contains a series of photographic plates, which add a dimension of the real to the handbook. Rather than passively accepting the mild stimulation of draughtsmanship, the reader is confronted by the actuality of human form; images which feature people occupying the same space and time as the viewers, the same cultural moment. Its author, Arthur Thomson, was an anatomist who held several important academic posts, including Professor of Human Anatomy at Oxford, Professor of Anatomy at the Royal Academy of Arts, and Anatomy Lecturer at the Royal College of Art, South Kensington. My copy, the third edition, was bought from Lamley & Co., Exhibition Road,

South Kensington and given as a gift to V.E. Corbett in 1910. The *Preface to the First Edition* (dated 10 August 1896) states Thomson's belief that the art student does not require exhaustive description of

> every bone, muscle, and joint, but only such an account as will enable him to appreciate their influence on the modelling of the figure. Names convey little to his mind, forms alone interest him [...] In the following pages, which are based on the lectures which I have had the honour of giving at the Royal College of Art, South Kensington, I have endeavoured to carry out as far as possible these principles.[1]

He later suggests that

> In order to carry out such an idea it was necessary that the descriptions given should be supplemented by frequent reference to the model or by copious illustration. In the present work photography has been employed for this purpose. I am well aware of the drawbacks of such a method, yet it seems to me that these are counterbalanced by the truth of the resulting figures. The plates lay no claim to artistic excellence; their value depends on their fidelity to nature [...] Apart from the professional models employed, I am largely indebted to some of the better known athletes of this University for the facilities which have enabled me to take the photographs.[2]

One quickly notes the reference to the 'better known athletes of this University'; a biographical aside that does much to emphasize the physicality and presence of the figures in the plates. Yet, to some extent, the book is a surrogate or supplement to the life class experience. It allows the reader a privacy in examining the body normally denied to the student in the life class. This creates a different kind of potential audience for the book, and a different range of possible readings, which can also be understood as a metaphor for a wide range of similarly vicarious literature. It bespeaks of a modernity which is impatient, and that demands information: for all Thomson's words, it is the plates that speak.

What the plates provide is an unimpeded view of the figure; the one singular view which the photograph can transmit, chosen for its exemplary description of the area of the body under discussion. Yet historically, access to the life class was hard-won, and denied to many. In the traditional schools of the Royal Academy, students would spend an extended period working from plaster casts taken from some of the most famous Antique sculptures found in European collections. Once they had graduated to the life class, students would have found easels arranged in roughly circular fashion around a model. Students would draw lots for places. Only the drawing master had direct access to the model, touching, and arranging the pose as was necessary. Women had always been denied access to the life room on the grounds of moral impropriety, and had in any case only lowly status as aspiring, or emergent professional artists, which, they argued, could only improve if they had the same opportunities as their male counterparts. Under the aegis of the Society of Female Artists, 38 signed a petition in 1859 to the Royal Academy demanding to be accepted to study from the Antique. Laura Herford made the bold move of using only her initials on her application to the R.A. Schools, her gender only becoming known once her application had been approved. Twelve others also took the same step between 1861-63 at which date the Academy denied further numbers on the grounds of a lack of space. So during most of the nineteenth century, women had no access to the life room of the Royal Academy,[3] and male students access only to an impersonal and physically distant body, posed according to the rather stagnant prescripts of the Pre-Raphaelite aesthetic.

One can position Thomson's handbook very precisely. It adjoins the age of academic conventionalism in terms of its attitude to the kinds of depiction considered pertinent to serious art, yet these ideas were becoming exhausted. The major exponents were old men, if not already dead. At another level, modernity was at the heels of academic training more generally. For one, younger artists were keen to spend time in France acquiring the skills of *plein-air* painting; a change of taste which eventually produced a different outlook at the Royal Academy. After the deaths of Leighton and Millais, John Poynter was appointed President in 1896; an establishment figure he was also the first Slade Professor at University College (1871-75) and became Director of the South Kensington Museum and Principal of the National Art Training School. In 1894 (until 1904) he was Director of the National Gallery. Though overshadowed as an artist by Leighton, Poynter's work included similarly monumental scenes, much influenced by the French classical tradition, which enjoyed a final flourish in state-funded reaction to more modern salon work in the mid-nineteenth century. Poynter was succeeded as Slade Professor at South Kensington by Alphonse Legros, a member of Courbet's circle, and student at the Ecole des Beaux-Arts until 1855. He contributed to the first Salon des Refusés in 1863, and knew Fantin-Latour, Manet and Whistler.

On another front, having demanded a thorough and unexpurgated art education, women were outnumbering men in institutions such as the Slade (opened in 1871), where they were allowed to work from the draped nude. Yet further, the development of technology, such as photography, led to different relationships to space and time, and forever changed the potentials of the compositional space. Degas' reaction to photography led to the creation of markedly distinct paintings, at once both diagrammatic and naturalistic. By the end of the First World War, the mythologies of monarchy, wise leadership (both political and military), heroism, femininity and female conduct were all subject to renegotiation. The Europe-wide discovery of the Freudian unconscious was perhaps the end of the beginning of modernity, and its significance could not be undone. Thomson's book arrived at the last point before it would be rendered useless by changing agendas both as to morality, and as to depiction.

The Nude

The rigorous control of the photographic plates in Thomson's book is also a potent reminder of the tensions surrounding the nude throughout the mid- to late nineteenth century. One notes that the male genitals have been placed *sous-rature*. Excavated from the photographic plate, yet present as a lack, a space marking the location of sex, the boundary between the erased genitals and the rest of the body neatly delineated as if marking a necessary amputation. No fig leaf prettifies the emasculation, no pictorial narrative provides an easy compositional solution. One wonders why the academic convention of the draped nude could not have been employed, yet for whatever reason, the genitals have been got rid of. For the female figure, there is a kind of obfuscation, certainly the figure lacks pubic hair, and there is no detail, yet the breasts remain intact. Despite the potentials of photography, or perhaps because of them, photography itself, its powers of depiction, have been denied. The photographic space is policed with the eye of a censor. I do not use the vocabulary lightly, since Thomson's book can also be placed accurately within the history of debates concerning sexuality. By no means were the debates over by 1896 (the date of the book's first publication), or even 1910 (the year in which my copy was first bought).

One cannot discuss sexuality without making reference to the debates through which the discourse of sexuality has been framed; particularly the themes of pornography and censorship. This in itself forms the basis of a perennial contradiction, if frequently remaining implicit, for whilst the urge to look is almost universal, public discourse tends to recognize as a good the state's intervention in the production, supply and distribution of sexually explicit texts and images. For more recent commentators, the perspective has often been that of liberalization as a social good; the removing of shackles from the imagination of progressive authors. Anyone who comments on the historical debate is therefore implicated, and should consider this situation, because it is easier to caricature than to understand the nature of state intervention in matters of public morality. Even an oblique Foucaldian approach which restricts itself to considering discursive fields can still privilege individual voices as a kind of authorial ventriloquism, and what may appear to offer a study of legal apparatus can sometimes be speaking from a liberal platform, giving voice to otherwise forgotten figures. The point can also be made that the Victorians knew their society better than we, and that the social, age and professional distinctions at use in definitions of obscenity in the period were useful and directed at preventing harm: practical measures had to be taken against dangerous materials in order to protect the young and the vulnerable. Geoffrey Robertson's *Obscenity*[4] takes the view that liberalization is a good, whilst *On Pornography*, by Ian Hunter, David Saunders and Dugald Williamson argues that the objective of protecting citizens against harm is more important, as they argue that

> The important task now is to sketch [the] career [of obscenity legislation] without collapsing the historical variations of obscenity law and the policing of pornography into a single story of personal right, human sexuality and literary expression struggling against the dark forces of law and censorship. That would be a story of repression, not a history of legal regulation and policing.[5]

Whilst historians and literature specialists might quibble over the supposed distinction between 'story' and 'history', the point remains that to focus on the producers, let alone to idealize them, does little to analyse the idea of obscenity, real or imagined, within society. Neither does it allow for a comment on the general social climate in which these historically determined constructions emerged.

Though it may seem a difficult gap to bridge, debates on obscenity were also carried on directly through the medium of images, particularly painting. Rather than regard obscenity as an isolated category, a more useful approach is to consider what were thought to be the possible effects of obscene publications on various elements found within the 'demographics of moral vulnerability', a phrase developed by Hunter, et al, to describe the categories into which Victorian society could be divided, and onto which (the working class, women and children etc) ideas of moral vulnerability were projected. It is no surprise to consider that women were thought to be at serious risk from explicit kinds of material. Lynda Nead's essay on *Past and Present*, a series of three paintings by Augustus Leopold Egg, exhibited at the Royal Academy in 1858, points to the fact that the iconography of downfall within painting could be very precise. Contained within a single frame, the images tell the tale of the demise of a family and the death of a husband caused by the moral collapse of a wife, occurring as the result of the wife's infidelity. In one of the images is a house of cards, which is founded on a novel by Balzac. As Nead states

> The French novel is an important element of the narrative because it indicates the source of the woman's deviancy and the cause of her fall from virtue. French society was regarded as unstable and dangerous, its literature was believed to be a source of corruption and immorality and many contemporaries were concerned about the harmful reverberations of French morality in England.[6]

One could also argue that rather than a source of deviancy, the book signalled a susceptibility to temptation, a modernized iconographical element standing as metaphor for Eve's apple. This reading would place Egg arguing in favour of suppression if only to take some of the temptations beyond woman's reach: almost a call for purdah.

Yet the place of French literature within English culture was indeed an area of contention, and formed the basis of many hours of legal debate. The Obscene Publications Act of 1857 retained the earlier common law offence of obscene libel, which stated that a work which libelled no one specifically corrupted the morality of everybody. Because of its basis in common law, it allowed a defendant a chance for trial by jury at the Quarter Session, which could produce public spectacle and did not preclude moral pronouncements on behalf of the public against obscene material. However, much more 'obscene' material was dealt with summarily. I use the inverted commas advisedly, since the same material, say a novel by Balzac in translation, could be treated differently depending on the conditions of its publication and sale. Produced as a work of literature, for a discerning audience, the novel could pass inspection, yet sold on a street corner as a penny edition, it could be seized as an obscene publication, and everyone connected with it prosecuted. There is ample evidence to show that many decisions were made by individual police officers on patrol, and were not tested at law. Many decisions regarding obscenity were based on context, the police taking the responsibility for decision making in routine street policing. They also had specific tests for assessing the nature of imagery: in Thomson's handbook, the female model was shorn of pubic hair and would have passed the test which many officers applied to the material before them, pubic hair being regarded as rendering an image obscene if present. Whilst its lack might alleviate the risk of an image's definition as obscene, it could still have been considered indecent: though material may have been within the law, this did not mean that it was approved of.

The pubic hair test was applied by the police as late as 1908, in the middle of the period in which Arthur Thomson's book on anatomy was part of the culture. Though the test may seem odd, the same criterion was applied in high art and helped maintain, or police, the binary opposition of the artistic nude and pornographic image. In terms of the photographic manipulation at work in Thomson's book, it had the effect of neutering the models, redefining their evident nakedness and recasting them as nudes in the accepted sense. Yet the technique of retouching stimulates questions about the nature of self-censorship, and the potentials of photography. What connects the presence or absence of pubic hair, and a work of foreign literature are the shades, or taints, of meaning laid over the sign 'woman'. Both add an air of moral questionability to the idea of woman, yet point to the rigorously policed nature of the accepted image, since women naturally had pubic hair, and were also at liberty to read. Such a disjunction between sign and reality could only cause confusion. A useful phrase that Nead develops is 'moral panic', a scenario in which a public or national concern creates unease which results in some form of governmental action, which then eases the panic. Of course it is cyclical, yet it accounts for the considerable legislation which was added to the statutes in order to combat public immorality, or supposed threats to public health. In terms of general action against obscenity, waves of inaction followed periods of profound unease. The nineteenth century was not a single uniform historical moment, and many things were possible in one period which at others were not.

Defining Masculinities

By 'defining masculinities' I intend to capture both the means by which a basically male discourse sought to define masculinity, and also those masculinities which were produced. One can turn to the silent other in this debate, and examine ideas of femininity for the ways in which that discourse is utilised, perhaps even created, to negotiate a space for the masculine.

Seen as shocking at its exhibition in the 1870s, Millais' *The Errant Knight* is interesting for the ways in which masculinity is put beyond the agenda; yet it is so tightly patrolled an identity that it begins to collapse of its own accord. The figure of the female is clearly nearer the life room than an idealized, or academic, figure pose. Her fleshiness, the dimpled skin, signal the real. To a contemporary audience, the presence of warm flesh tones would have caused unease, moving thoughts away from cool sculptural perfection, closer to the corporeal. She is also placed within a wood, far from the safety of hearth and home (what Freud would later label the *heimlich*, the homely space which also contains elements of the disturbing and discomforting). Yet if this seems to focus thoughts on the vulnerability of the female (in all the senses described above), what of masculinity?

It is here that the painting begins to break down. The female's nakedness acts as a kind of brutal camouflage, masking the questionable status of the male, and definitions of heroic masculinity in general. Tied to the largest silver birch on record, she is rescued by a knight in full armour, heavily sheathed, of whom so little is disclosed. He wields a ferocious sword, and attempts to cut the lady's bonds. I need add nothing to the work already carried out by Millais in calling into doubt the idea of a certain kind of masculinity. By packing the image with multiple signifiers the sign itself breaks down. One can place this image within discourses which sought to deny female autonomy (including sexuality) through a whole variety of languages, from the visual to the medico-moral. Simply on the subject of sexuality, views were based in complex mythologies, yet these too were directed by contributions from professional men: the voices of authority. Auguste Debay stated that 'a reasonable woman should always be contented with what her husband is able to do and should never demand more'. Yet an over-indulgent husband should be warned that sexual excess will exhaust him, and any children produced from this excess will suffer 'deadly' consequences. Speaking on behalf of 'most medical men' William Acton stated that 'what men are habitually, women are only exceptionally'.[7] In exactly the same way as with Millais' painting, the deflection away from male sexuality, the denial of anxiety concerning masculinity creates a tension that refuses to go away. Yet the question remains in what ways was masculine sexual identity affected by the denial of an autonomous female sexuality? Since the male was seen as the initiator of sexual activity which demanded a response from the female, what was the range of sexual selves available to men? Even in such works as Thomson's handbook, because a male and female model are present, they are regulated as in any other kind of social space. In the more academic poses, the bodies are placed in their respective roles, with due regard to ideas of masculine physical strength and woman as suited to the home and a general passivity. The female model may occasionally be allowed to carry a pitcher for visual variety, though it is the male who is given the task of striking heroic poses.

Recoding the Real

Yet one can also look to incidental material, to the private archives of images built by artists at this period in order to shed light on the varieties of masculinity of which they had experience, if not transmitting this personal experience directly into the public sphere. It is here that the disjunction between periods causes the largest of problems, since whilst I want to examine varieties of masculinity, I do not want to establish a space often determined as 'gay' (affirmative) or 'homosexual' (neutral or condemnatory), since this is to replicate the kinds of tensions which always occur when dealing with defined sexualities, and which I have discussed above.

One of the fascinating aspects of later nineteenth-century art is the relation of photography to traditional practice, and the ways in which photography makes itself useful. Rodin's collection of photographs is quite wide-ranging, including a number of nude professional child models, and others of babies, plus the more familiar photographs of posed models, and famous sitters. One of the most interesting processes is the transformation which takes place between the model's corporeal uniqueness and the finished piece. Pignatelli, one of the models who worked at the Beaux-Arts, posed for *John the Baptist*. The photographs show an adequately nourished form, not particularly well-formed in terms of muscular development, but very expressive in terms of facial expression, and physical gesture. The shift from studio model to finished work reveals a transformation by way of the codes and conventions of the depiction of biblical saints. The sculptor creates a tense musculature, emphasizing the muscles of the torso, neck, shoulders and arms, and Rodin imbues the facial expression with an earnestness, thereby modifying Pignatelli's slightly vacant look as he held the pose for the photograph. A similar treatment is meted out in the production of *The Age of Bronze*. A heavier framed model, Auguste Neyt, is transformed into the more classical sculpture. In contrast to Pignatelli, Neyt's frame is more athletic to begin with; the arms and chest muscles well developed. The sculpture reduced this to a lighter more lithe body, also reducing Neyt's genitals to a less distracting scale. It is an important point, for the denial of sexuality cannot be so easily made, and what Rodin denies to Neyt's genitals, he reinvests in the sculpture's buttock region, which must be one of the most stroked in sculpture. So the process is not simply a matter of denying overt male sexuality, since the repressed always finds a form of expression.

The kinds of control artists carry out in policing their public works sometimes breaks down, and the representation does not quite speak the same language in other pieces. One need only compare Leighton's formal and distant female figures with the dramatic sculptures *Athlete Struggling with a Python*, (*c.* 1874-7) and more particularly *The Sluggard*, (1882-5). Whilst the former is a restrained treatment of a deeply fraught (and Freudian) subject, the latter is a much more spontaneous response to a particular moment and musculature, a work which was admired for its treatment of the nude. Leighton makes use of his natural corporeal knowledge and know-how *vis-à-vis* the male, whereas his females are rendered more like sculpture and remain distant. Only very rarely do his female figures break away from a standardized depiction such as the *Standing Nude Figure, Seen from Behind*, this produced in an era where the buttocks could be read in terms of belonging to either sex, and where the gender of personnel involved in flagellation pornography was open to the reimaginative capacities of the reader.[8]

A further use of photography was in the production of exotic material. A small number of men began to legitimate a sexual interest in the young male via the language of classicism, and an appeal to authenticity by focusing on the Mediterranean body. Figures such as Wilhelm von Gloeden made a career for themselves by selling photographs of local youth, generally unclothed, though artfully posed in groups or with the staffage of terracotta pots and local scenery. Whilst there is no overt sexual activity in the images, some of them attempt to mimic passionate friendship between the boys. Whilst it is difficult to cross cultural boundaries, it is interesting to note that in England during the moral panic of the Regency period, and moment of Napoleonic threat, executions for sodomy increased, and suspects were regularly pilloried. Whilst the specific offence of buggery was defined, the condition, or state, from which it emerged was not. It is literally a nameless or unspeakable condition. The several decades that separate this moment from the second half of the nineteenth century do little to change the potentials of discourse, which allow von Gloeden's images into the photographic salons and magazines of the period simply because there is no well-formed vocabulary for highlighting the nature of von Gloeden's work, or for isolating them. Paradoxically, what the images mimic, they also deny precisely by the act of mimicry, which conventionalizes and condifies same-sex desire as a discourse of marriage-like power relations and normality. They strip out sexual desire and leave the images totally empty.

Whilst many other archives of images exist which point to a much less rigidly defined sexuality within the people producing imagery, the renegotiation of appearance and the adherence to conventions of depiction for publically displayed work allowed the continued policing of diverse sexuality, and its disapprobation within medico-moral vocabularies. Yet just as artists' attempts to police the boundaries of their works produced anxiety and ridiculous over-emphasis in the government of representation, the ways in which works were read by audiences somewhat undercut attempts to deny adults their sexuality. In parenthesis, I am not suggesting that a repressive force was set against a liberal majority, but that confusion and anxiety on a personal level could produce incompatible beliefs within individuals when compared side by side, though these beliefs were maintained as aspects of social and private practices and were therefore distinct from one another in thought and deed.

Modes of Reading: a conclusion

I have already argued that idealization of the masculine and feminine relied on the presence of the other in order to produce the polarization of meaning through which identities were produced and maintained. Yet unsurprisingly, over-emphasis tended to force the breakdown of identity, and often, a general sense of crisis, or panic, emerges. In relation to this I have suggested that some artists, quite deliberately, maintained a rigorous check on the distinction between public and private work. Yet even in the public work, there is a natural response to subjects of genuine interest, such as Leighton's young males, who provoke an entirely different kind of work from his more laboured and formulaic female forms.

When it comes to the matter of photography, the visual field is changed forever. If nothing else it adds an almost viral confusion to traditional work. If going no further than the material discussed above, in Degas' hands it alters his perception of space, and can be demonstrated to affect his decision-making in terms of where the pictorial boundary is placed, and makes him aware of the kinds of clutter which occupies domestic space and invades the visual field. Rodin adopts a different approach and uses photographs to deliver information which is then modified in the production of a re-classicised body. Overt sexuality is held very much at arms' length and the physical signs of the model's sexualities are re-modelled along Greek lines (to employ a euphemism). Von Gloeden appropriates the trappings of a classical frame of reference, yet for him there is no further translation of the body: the photograph is the finished article.

Which returns my argument to Thomson's handbook in which photography and attitudes to the body join together. In the final analysis the plates can be seen to be shot through with tension, if not exactly panic. Clearly Thomson's interest is didactic, and most of the plates have a hand-drawn twin, traced from the plates and filled with the anatomical detail below the surface of the flesh. The over-seeing discourse in this respect is medical. Yet the areas in which the anatomical gaze should not flinch finds erasure, in that the male genitals are lacking, replaced with nothing more than a mid-grey tone. Yet one answer to this was hinted earlier, in which it was stated that similar works could be treated differently depending on context and readership. Clearly defined genitals in a book with a student audience, some of whom were young women, were out of the question. Yet though the models' sexuality may be compromised, their gender roles remain firmly those of established social and academic values. It is the male that can carry a spear and is athletic,

58

whereas the female is restricted to virginal poses of contriteness, or given a pitcher to carry. The female model's very demeanour speaks from a tradition of the statuesque and other-worldly, which is the opposite of the much more dynamic and physically active male. In many of the plates featuring the male there is an implied narrative, and an easier relation between photographer and subject; the viewer and the viewed. Yet what the retoucher has painted out cannot be denied, destined always to be re-touched in the sense of a revisitation. Though Thomson's intention may be anatomical, the subject is sexuality, perhaps the return of sexuality, not only this, but the photographs themselves, even though explicitly secondary images, are poetic and extraordinarily beautiful, marking the futile denial of an aesthetic identity to photography, of photography itself.

Even at the turn of the century, one which would shortly witness a German incendiary bomb damaging the Royal Academy, and London would observe a series of hatchet attacks in galleries made by suffragettes, the public aspects of sexuality were tightly controlled: the anatomical detail of athletes of London University replaced by the aporias of a tired, yet still tense, art academy and still largely 'Victorian' public and legislative body.

Endnotes

[1] Arthur Thomson, *A Handbook of Anatomy for Art Students* (Oxford: Clarendon Press, 1906), vii.

[2] Thomson, *Handbook of Anatomy*, viii.

[3] Though this was the case, a number of private classes took place, and women were far more readily accepted at the Slade, when it was opened in 1871.

[4] Geoffrey Robertson, *Obscenity* (London: Weidenfeld & Nicolson, 1971).

[5] Ian Hunter, David Saunderds, Dugald Williamson, *On Pornography* (Basingstoke: Macmillan, 1993), 73.

[6] Lynda Nead, *Myths of Sexuality: Represemtations of women in Victorian Britain* (Oxford: Basil Blackwell, 1988), 73.

[7] *Victorian Women*, ed. Erna Olafson Hellerstein et al, (Stanford: Stanford University Press, 1981), 175-177.

[8] 'we must conclude, I believe, that the entire immense literature of flagellation produced during the Victorian period, along with the fantasies it embodied and the practices it depicted, represents a kind of last-ditch compromise with and defence against homosexuality'. Steven Marcus, *The Other Victorians* (London: Weidenfeld & Nicolson, 1964), 260.

'... one of the most mischievous Acts that ever passed the British legislature'. The 1830 Beerhouse Act and its consequences.

Paul Jennings
7 Valley Road
Harrogate
N. Yorks, HG2 0IQ

The words quoted are those of Alderman Thomas Beaumont of Bradford, a campaigner in the cause of temperance, spoken in May of 1849 in support of a resolution which he moved be adopted by the town Council in support of proposed legislation for the 'gradual and ultimate suppression' of the creation of the Act of 1830 – the beerhouse or beershop. More than anything else, he claimed, the Act tended to 'the demoralization, the pauperization, the social, personal, and domestic wretchedness of thousands and tens of thousands in this country'.[1] Such words are entirely typical of what must amount to millions spoken and written about the eponymous drinking place during the almost 40 years of its particular legal existence and beyond. For, without doubt, the Act and its progeny have had an 'appalling press'.[2] Sidney and Beatrice Webb, in their history of liquor licensing to 1830, provided a comprehensive indictment: 'So instantaneous and dramatic a transformation as occurred in October 1830 has seldom been effected by any Act of Parliament'. 'It is hard to find a redeeming feature of this debauch'.[3] In similar vein wrote George B. Wilson in his massive 'contribution' to the study of the liquor problem, likening the country when it came into force to 'a proclaimed American territory ... thrown open to the drink adventurers'.[4] Their views, coloured though they avowedly were by their temperance sympathies, nonetheless helped shape the judgements of later historians. To cite just one example here, that of S.G. Checkland in a survey of public policy making from the eighteenth to the twentieth centuries, describing it emphatically as a 'disastrous step'.[5]

To what extent does the beerhouse deserve this condemnation? It is the purpose of this paper to explore some aspects of this question. In so doing it does not claim the status of pioneer. Brian Harrison posed the question almost 30 years ago in his *Drink and the Victorians*, which remains the best account of the Act, in particular of its origins which space precludes dealing with here.[6] One is bound to say 'some aspects', not simply from the customary modesty of a short paper such as this, but because this huge and complex subject has still to receive a successor study to that of the Webbs' disarmingly slim volume. Towards that project this paper represents work in progress.

First, briefly, the Act itself.[7] Passed in the summer of 1830, its 32 sections took effect in October. The key feature was that any householder who was assessed to the poor rate was permitted to sell beer by purchasing a licence from the Excise, without the necessity of obtaining prior authorisation from the magistrates. This licence cost two guineas, was valid for one year and renewable. The conditions attaching to the new licence were substantially as for existing publicans, save that hours of opening were more restricted. Within just three months of the Act coming into force over 26,000 such licences had been issued throughout England and Wales, representing more than half the corresponding figure for full justices' licences.[8] By the close of the first year of its operation the figure had risen to almost 32,000, or almost two-thirds the figure of existing justices' licences. Thereafter beer on-licences continued to represent, to put it another way, around two-fifths of the total of both types of on-licence.[9] The overall number of beerhouses may thus fairly be viewed as significant. The impact of the numbers, however, is perhaps more effectively conveyed at the local level. It also needs to be placed in the much longer-term context of stability or limited growth in the number of justices' licences, which in consequence had failed to keep pace with the growth of the population.[10] In this situation the new beerhouse might represent a considerable change. Evidence of this from around the country can be found in the reports of the commissioners inquiring into the municipal corporations, which cover the initial years of their existence. They also show local variations. Looking for example at the West Country, the tiny borough of Camelford in Cornwall, with a population of around 600, had its four public houses augmented by five beershops. Penzance, with over 6,500 people, saw seven beershops added to 22 publics. In Plymouth, in neighbouring Devon, with a population of over 31,000 and where, as in the other two places, the magistrates had hitherto sought to limit the number of drinking places, 135 public houses now faced the competition of no fewer than 74 beershops.[11] In some of the industrial centres, where population growth had greatly outstripped the supply of drinking places, the new beerhouses became the more common of the two types, as was the case in Birmingham, Bradford and Manchester.[12]

It was in rural areas, however, where the new beerhouse might appear in a locality hitherto lacking a public drinking place, or in one supplied with a licensed public house which by definition was subject to closer regulation, that especial concern was evinced at the outset. This is certainly an impression to be gained from the 1833 Select Committee on the Sale of Beer, the first parliamentary inquiry into the new system, and which is significant in that the Webbs drew particularly upon it in framing their own conclusions. The first resolution of its report noted the 'considerable evils' which had arisen from the 'present management and conduct of Beer Houses'.[13] The very first witness before the Committee, the Reverend Robert Wright, a Hampshire magistrate of Itchen-Abbas near Winchester, noted that there was not a village around which had not got two or three beershops (or worse perhaps, those in little back lanes or on roadsides), and contrasted their conduct with the better order maintained in the older licensed public houses, which were kept generally by people of more respectable character, but which were also under the control of the magistrates.[14] In common with a disproportionate number of the 58 witnesses who gave evidence to the Committee, Wright came from the rural south of England, which had been affected by widespread and serious disturbances in the winter of 1830-1. As he claimed in remembering those disturbances, 'the blow that I got then I shall never recover', and he went on to implicate the new beerhouses firmly in their genesis. Asked if distress were not the real cause of the riots, he answered that people were led astray by false views and placards in beerhouses.[15] Yet it is difficult to evade the question so posed of their real cause, as Brian Harrison noted: beerhouses were a country-wide phenomenon, but the riots were largely concentrated in the south-eastern counties; furthermore, they had begun before the Beerhouse Act came into operation. 'It was absurd, though convenient', he concluded, 'to assume that drink or drinksellers had actually inspired the riots'.[16]

The Chartist movement produced in the minds of contemporaries a similar response. In South Wales, for example, one local paper was convinced that beerhouses were a major cause of the promotion of Chartist activity, with lodge meetings often held in them.[17] So too in the north of England were the beerhouses seen as providing special cover for subversion. During 1848, according to the clerk to the magistrates in Bradford, the scene that year of major disturbances, 'chartists and other disaffected persons held their meetings and concocted their plans in beerhouses. Not a single public-house was implicated. Not one beer-house keeper furnished any information of the chartist proceedings to the local authorities'.[18] More than that, two of the beerhouse keepers themselves were brought before the courts for their part in the riots.[19] Licensed houses were subjected to more immediate magisterial pressure not to permit Chartist gatherings, but despite that they were still so used and there were in addition examples of Chartist publicans.[20] The beerhouses though were more suspect. With the fading of Chartism, however, this specifically political threat from them would seem also to have receded in the minds of those in authority. Thereafter both types of house were used for meetings of all kinds.[21]

It would seem likely then that in the troubled decades of the 1830s and 1840s the perceived connection between the beerhouses and political subversion contributed to the intensity of the criticisms levelled against them. But what of the general charge of debauchery? This embraced, in the minds of contemporaries, a catalogue of evils. Witnesses to the 1833 Committee, for example, alleged drunkenness and disorder, 'demoralising' recreations from gambling to blood sports, sexual licence, the corruption of youth and honest labour and the provision of cover for criminal activity. In Leominster, Herefordshire, according to one – a magistrates' clerk – a beershop there had repeatedly been complained against where cock-fights and badger-baitings were staged and a four-corner alley was run. It was said to get through ten times the amount of beer as did the old public house, whose trade was now nearly destroyed. In Warwick, so testified another witness – the head police officer – beerhouse customers included boys, prostitutes and thieves, with the latter arranging their depredations and dividing the spoils there. Three beerhouse keepers had been transported for their crimes.[22] The reports of the commissioners on the municipal corporations referred to above add further similar testimony. Those 74 beershops in Plymouth were said to be 'more detrimental to the morals of the town than all other causes combined', sentiments echoed for Camelford and Penzance. Returning too to Thomas Beaumont's Bradford: the month after his resolution the Mayor, Titus Salt, called a town's meeting 'to confer as to the best means to be adopted to remove or suppress the immorality and vice which prevails to so great an extent among our population'. He cited in particular the connection between beerhouses and crime and prostitution, which he had observed from his position as chief magistrate, as well as on a Saturday-night tour of the town with the town clerk and the chief constable. The meeting's outcome was the formation of a committee to examine 'the moral condition' of the town and the best way to improve it. Its report, presented the following March to an invited meeting of gentlemen, began with the beerhouses and brothels. Many of the former, it claimed, were in fact brothels in all but name and almost all of them afforded 'facilities for dishonourable intercourse between the sexes'. All possible means should be tried, it concluded, to bring to an end a system 'so prolific of evil'.[23]

How is one to assess the weight of this evidence? It has already been suggested that the social and political unrest of the 1830s and 1840s might have influenced the views of some of those in authority. This point might apply equally to the southern rural interests overrepresented on the 1833 Committee and to the local elites in a rapidly expanding industrial centre like Bradford. But another important point is that not only might parliamentary inquiries listen to an unrepresentative selection of witnesses, but the final conclusions might not necessarily fairly reflect all the evidence which they did hear. Brian Harrison found this in an examination of the 1834 Select Committee on Drunkenness among the Labouring Classes and it is equally true of the Committee of 1833.[24] The Beer Act itself retained vocal supporters. Jasper Parrott, MP for Totnes, Devon and a magistrate, described it to the Committee as 'one of the greatest boons ever given to the landed interest, and to the consumers of beer'. The new beerhouse keepers he characterised as 'decent kind of labourers' and reported no complaints of them or their houses.[25] A number of beersellers themselves gave supportive evidence. The voice of the customer was also occasionally heard, mostly from London: Joseph Hogan, a watchmaker of Clerkenwell, frequented the Globe beershop in King Street in the morning to take a glass of ale and look at the paper, and sometimes too in the afternoon because he was 'dry'.[26] If one looks further at the evidence relating to the beerhouse keepers, the Webbs made much of that which pointed to 'all sorts and conditions of men': those who had been refused justices' licences on account of bad character, petty tradesmen afraid of hard work, 'poor widows set up in an easy business by the charity of their neighbours, or even by gift from the poor rate, unemployed labourers whose cottages happened to be rated, and all the nondescript class of those who combined a little poaching and gambling with the occasional receipt of stolen property'.[27] But again, evidence elsewhere in the Committee's report presented a picture of the beerseller as typically from the background of a skilled worker or small tradesmen. That was certainly the finding of a detailed study of the trade in Bradford.[28]

It may be that in the early years of the new trade some entrants *were* of relatively modest means, but a number of developments had the effect of making that less likely. The cost of a beer on-licence was raised to three guineas by an Act of 1834 which introduced a distinction between on and off sale, with the latter licence being cheaper at one guinea. The same statute increased the qualifying rateable value with effect from 1836, and this was raised again in 1840 on a scale up to a high of £15 a year in towns with over 10,000 population. Evidence of rateable values shows that whilst overall not as high as those of fully-licensed houses, they were considerably above mere cottages assessed to the poor rate. In Bradford in 1845 a sample of 42 beerhouses had an average rateable value of £16. In Birmingham in 1851 over 60 per cent were rated at £17 or above, whilst in 1867 the average rateable value of 37 beerhouses in the old part of Portsmouth was £20.[29] Premises thus became more substantial and represented a greater investment, either to the individual beerseller or to beerseller and brewing company (an important development, but one on which space precludes discussion here). This investment was a fact to which the more articulate and organised members of the trade were keen to point. When petitioning the licensing magistrates for an extra hour opening time in 1838 the Beersellers' Association of Bradford drew attention to the sums 'large and small' which were invested in their businesses. Similarly in 1854, the secretary of the then Bradford Beersellers' Protection Society claimed that many of their houses were rated at substantially more than the £15 qualifying amount, the average being from £50 to a £100 per house and with sums of as much as £1,000 or £2,000 invested in them.[30] In addition to its role as pressure group the fact of organisation itself also suggests an increasing aspiration to respectability by beerhouse keepers. Thus the Leeds Licensed Beersellers' Association held their anniversary dinner in 1839 at the Crown in Roundhay Road, which was served, according to a newspaper account, 'in a manner which would have reflected credit on a first class hotel'.[31] A corollary of this increase in the scale of the business and aspiration to higher status was the desire by beerhouse keepers to obtain a full publican's licence. Indeed, they were dependent on each other, as only to substantial premises and respectable applicants would magistrates even contemplate the grant of a licence. Many were established expressly with that in mind. In Leeds, for example, in 1840, there were at the brewster (licensing) sessions that year 47 applications for a full on-licence, all but one of which were trading as beerhouses under a specific sign. Only three, however, were granted, a not untypical proportion.[32]

In addition to the foregoing evidence one can also point to contemporary witnesses to the orderly beerhouse, although by its very nature less likely to enter the historical record than evidence of debauch. Joseph Hogan's morning glass and a look at the paper come back to mind. In Bradford, writer and journalist James Burnley visited a beerhouse in the Silsbridge Lane district, the town's poorest, in the late 1860s. There he found a small but moderately clean room, in which were two men and two women seated at a table, one of the latter smoking a short pipe, while on a bench by the fire 'three or four young navvies sit fast asleep, their hands deep in their trousers' pockets, their heads hanging heavily over their breasts'.[33] In addition too, there are the frequent reports in newspapers of meetings held at beerhouses, which similarly present a more positive image. Those of friendly societies, for example, as when in June 1852 John Dobson, landlord of the Puddlers' Arms in Well Street, Bradford, was part of a group initiated into a new lodge of the Bolton Order of Oddfellows, and where the ceremony closed with an organ 'pealing forth the National Anthem'.[34]

If the foregoing begins to suggest a rather different picture of the beerhouse trade to that of the Webbs, what still of the specific debauchery charges? Brian Harrison looked at the connection of the new trade with any general increase in drinking and drunkenness, concluding that the available figures do not support a pejorative interpretation of the Act's effects.[35] But what of cases brought specifically against beerhouse keepers? A Return to Parliament of convictions for permitting disorderly conduct and of keeping open at unlawful hours between April 1831 and April 1833 showed that at London police offices over those two years 211 beerhouse keepers were convicted. Taking an annual average for the years 1831-3 of 1,283 beersellers in the metropolis produces a figure of one conviction for every twelve. In three of the offices the offences were specified separately, with 34 disorderly and 37 unlawful hours convictions. Given that beerhouse opening hours were stricter anyway, the disorderly figure alone of say 50 a year for the whole capital does not seem excessive.[36] A further Return of 1839 looked at those charged with breaches of the law between 1830 and 1838 and showed a ratio of charges to houses ranging from 1:3 to 1:7.4 (excluding 1830), with the comparable figures for publicans being 1:5.8 to 1:8.9. Over the whole period 2,551 beerhouse keepers were charged, of whom 1,272 were convicted. If a similar proportion of offences of selling in unlawful hours, to say nothing of other unstated minor offences as seen in the earlier Return, is assumed, then once again the number of cases coming to court, still less those resulting in a conviction, does not seem excessive.[37] Particular local evidence points to the same conclusion. Statistics of specific offences at beerhouses in Bradford for the years 1855-7 and 1861-3 together show similarly that opening in prohibited hours, especially on Sunday, accounted for almost two-thirds of the 237 offences in the six years. Permitting gaming covered another 36 cases, but since this could include playing dominoes itscarcely merits the title of serious disorder. Of offences which could merit the title – permitting drunk and disorderly conduct, harbouring notoriously bad characters and permitting prostitution – there were 42, or 18 per cent of the total.[38]

The foregoing evidence is of course offered with the caution due to statistics of crime. These are of course cases which came to court and one should certainly bear in mind, for example, the frequent complaint of witnesses to the 1833 Committee of the difficulty of securing evidence against beerhouse keepers. As one publican put it: 'There are not many people who like to turn informers in country places'.[39] This might include those responsible for policing, itself of course a crucial variable in the generation of statistics of crime.

Another point is that the publican as well as the beerhouse keeper might appear before the courts, if in general less frequently as is illustrated by the figures cited above for charges from 1830 to 1838, but the publican too can sometimes be found running a pretty disorderly establishment. For example, at the Leeds brewsters of 1837, whilst praising on the one hand the 'great improvement [which] had taken place in the public-houses in the borough' the Mayor and his fellow magistrates felt compelled to suspend 22 licences to an adjourned sessions for investigation into one or more of four classes of charge of varieties of disorderly conduct. Of the four the most serious was that of permitting 'lewd women' to drink in the dram shop attached to the premises, along with 'disorderly men', 'convicted thieves' and 'persons of notoriously bad character'. In three instances renewal of the licence was granted providing the dram shop was closed and just two licences were in the event refused.[40] These dram, gin or spirit shops, as they were variously named, were a great cause of concern in Leeds and in other towns. Licensed public houses were converted wholly or in part to such establishments, frequently fitted out in palatial style and specialising as the name suggests in the sale of spirits. In neighbouring Bradford they were said to be 'the regular resort of the vilest characters which infest the town', but frequent magisterial warnings and occasional sterner action had little effect on the growth in their numbers. There were some 50 such spirit vaults in the town by 1865.[41]

To return though to our beerhouses: despite correctives to an overly malign view of their general conduct there remains, as with some of the dram shops we just saw, at the extreme a minority of disorderly establishments. Detailed local studies make that clear. My own work on Bradford revealed a succession of landlords and houses earning especial notoriety. Men and places like David Brooksbank of the Leg of Mutton in Nelson Street, who made a string of court appearances from 1838, surviving the forfeiture of his licence after a constable found two women in one bed and two men undressing, but going on to face further charges of disorderly conduct, the stabbing of a waiter and the apprehension of three robbers on his premises.[42] In a study of a country market town, Horncastle in Lincolnshire, B.J. Davey found similar houses. A beerhouse run by one William Wople, who, though he apparently generally kept the place fairly quiet, allowed known criminals and poachers to drink there and kept prostitutes, whilst another run by William Daft functioned as lodging house and brothel. One should note, however, in support of the point above, that the worst house in Horncastle was in fact the Fleece, a fully licensed house.[43]

One can attempt an overview of the incidence of disorderly houses by looking finally at some evidence for the end of the period of their unrestricted existence. In July 1869 that was ended when legislation extended to beerhouses the requirement of a justices' licence. At the following brewster sessions magistrates were thus given the opportunity to either grant or refuse a licence to existing houses. Returns to Parliament[44] of the following year allow us to make some assessment of the extent to which the opportunity was taken up, particularly in the case of where refusal was on the grounds of the beerhouse keeper's unfitness of character. The other reasons for refusal were insufficient rating qualification, insufficient notice given of application or 'other grounds'. The returns cover petty sessional divisions in counties and boroughs throughout England and Wales. They also include reports from chief constables and superintendents of police on the working of the new legislation. Throughout the country 2,078 existing licences were refused on the grounds specifically of 'want of character' in the applicant. This represented 4.2 per cent of the beerhouse on-licences held that year.[45] If one takes this category as synonymous with disorderly houses then nationally it does not appear either that there was a massive problem or that magistrates particularly perceived there to be one. However, within the Return, when one compares in some instances the report of the police with the figure of licences refused for want of character, it is clear that the two were not always equivalent. That the category *was* sometimes synonymous is shown, for example, with the pair refused in Andover, Hampshire, which the police described as the worst houses there. Similarly in Blackburn, where a particularly zealous bench refused 73 beerhouses for the misconduct of the landlord and which appear as such in the statistics refused for want of character. Conversely in Reading, for example, the police reported that a number of houses had been suppressed which permitted thieves, prostitutes and 'suspected persons', but whilst eleven licences were refused, none were for want of character. Similarly in Plymouth, the police reported that certificates had been withheld from the keepers of all known badly conducted and immoral houses, but of the 42 then stated as having been refused, just four were apparently for reasons of the character of the applicant. In Portsmouth too 52 licences were refused, of which just two were for want of character. Here, however, one can look at the local study of public- and beerhouses already noted, which cites a newspaper account of the 1869 brewster sessions to the effect that some 41 disorderly beerhouses were closed. As one might expect in this particular town the connection between them and prostitution was the chief concern of the authorities.[46] If one fairly takes the 'want of character' category then as an understatement, that gives us perhaps roughly between one in twenty and one in ten beerhouses which could merit to some degree the characterisation 'disorderly'. Places like the Battle of Inkerman in Portsmouth run by William Newton, which earned the name of 'Infant School' from its association with child prostitution. Or in Bradford, among the 60 beerhouses which were closed there, 13 per cent of the total prior to the sessions, places like the White Horse in Adolphus Street, according to the police the haunt of dog-fighters, dog-runners, cock-fighters prostitutes and thieves, especially juveniles.[47] As Bradford's chief constable noted, drawing particular attention to the limitations on his powers with regard to beerhouses prior to the new Act, it had 'proved to be of immense public benefit'.[48]

What can one say then in conclusion? It is worth noting first the very difficult problems which the evidence presents and in its evaluation the crucial importance of detailed local study. Only a beginning has been made to that latter endeavour. But for the moment one can suggest the following. The view that the 1830 Beerhouse Act represented a 'disastrous step' is certainly an exaggeration. It most commonly represented an opportunity to enter the retail drink trade, a trade which had been hitherto relatively restricted by the operation of the licensing system. Although it may be the case that without the Act magistrates might have taken a more accommodating view of new applications for licences, it does not seem likely that this would have been other than limited and certainly not to the extent that the number of beerhouses in fact developed. As to the running of the beerhouses there is nothing to suggest that the majority were not well conducted, but there is evidence to suggest that a minority merited the disorderly charge. So too, however, did a small number of fully licensed public houses, but the limitations which police and magistrates had in their powers in relation to the beerhouses was one factor in the greater propensity to disorder in the latter type of house. Only to those possessed of particular views, such as those of temperance reformer Thomas Beaumont, and with opportunities to voice them, was it 'one of the most mischievous Acts that ever passed the British legislature'. It is in any event a title for which the competition must be fairly intense.

Endnotes

[1] *Bradford Observer*, 24 May 1849. Thanks to Dave Russell and George Sheeran for comments on an earlier draft of this paper.
[2] T.R. Gourvish and R.G. Wilson, *The British Brewing Industry 1830-1980* (Cambridge: Cambridge University Press, 1994), 15.
[3] S. and B. Webb, *The History of Liquor Licensing in England Principally from 1700 to 1830* (London: Frank Cass, 1963. First published 1903), 123-4 and 127.

[4] G.B. Wilson, *Alcohol and the Nation. A Contribution to the Study of the Liquor Problem in the United Kingdom from 1800 to 1935* (London: Nicholson and Watson, 1940), 101.

[5] S.G. Checkland, *British Public Policy 1776-1939. An Economic, Social and Political Perspective* (Cambridge: Cambridge University Press, 1983), 105.

[6] B. Harrison, *Drink and the Victorians. The Temperance Question in England 1815-1872* (Keele: Keele University Press, 1994. First published 1971), chapter 3.

[7] The Beerhouse Act is the title given to the legislation under the provisions of the Short Titles Act of 1892. It was also referred to at the time, and subsequently, as the Beer, or Sale of Beer, Act. Its full title is 'An Act to permit the general Sale of Beer and Cyder by Retail in England'. Whilst the particular legal entity was the product of the Act, the term itself had been in use for some time to denote a public house that served wholly or mainly beer, rather than doing a full beer, spirit and wine trade.

[8] Account of Quantity of Beer exported and brewed in G.B.; Number of Brewers, Victuallers and Retailers of Beer, 1830 (P)arliamentary (P)apers 1831 (60) XVII.67 No. 6.

[9] The statistics, inevitably, have their complications. The decennial figures for on-licences are usefully summarised by Wilson, *Alcohol*, 236, utilising the Annual Returns for Brewers' Licences which he felt probably approximated to the number of actual premises. .

[10] Webbs, *Liquor Licensing*, chapter 3. P. Clark, *The English Alehouse. A Social History 1200-1830* (London: Longman, 1983), 55-9.

[11] Royal Com. Of Inquiry into Municipal Corporations of Eng. And Wales. First Rep., Apps.: Pt.1 (Midlands, W. and S.W. Circuits) 1835 (116) XXIII.133.

[12] Comparative statistics cited in the *Bradford Observer*, 28 October 1852.

[13] Sel. Cttee. On Sale of Beer Rep., Mins of Ev. 1833 (416) XV.1, 3.

[14] 1833, QQ. 20, 67 and 73.

[15] 1833, QQ. 4, 11, 14-15, 118-19 and 217.

[16] Harrison, *Drink and the Victorians*, 83.

[17] W.R. Lambert, *Drink and Sobriety in Victorian Wales c.1820-c.1895* (Cardiff: University of Wales Press, 1983), 18.

[18] Sel. Cttee. of House of Lords to consider Operation of Acts for Sale of Beer Rep., Mins. of Ev., App., Index 1850 (398) XVIII.483, 844.

[19] *Bradford Observer*, 1 June and 3 Aug 1848.

[20] *Northern Star*, 7 September 1839. Lambert, *Drink and Sobriety*, 18.

[21] P. Jennings, *The Public House in Bradford, 1770-1970* (Keele: Keele University Press, 1995) 100.

[22] 1833, evidence of William Holmes Q. 685 and of Thomas Bellerby QQ. 3049, 3080 and 3090.

[23] *Bradford Observer*, 28 June 1849 and 7 March 1850.

[24] B. Harrison, 'Two roads to social reform: Francis Place and the "drunken Committee" of 1834', *Historical Journal*, XI (1968): 272-300.

[25] 1833, QQ. 844-7.

[26] 1833, evidence of George Bush, for example, on 206 and of Hogan on 224-5.

[27] Webbs, *Liquor Licensing*, 125.

[28] 1833, Q. 1592 for example. Jennings, *Public House in Bradford*, 88-9.

[29] Jennings, *Public House in Bradford*, 277 note 24. W.M. Bramwell, *Pubs and Localised Communities in Mid-Victorian Birmingham* (London: Queen Mary College,

1984), 10. R.C. Riley and P. Eley, *Public Houses and Beerhouses in Nineteenth Century Portsmouth* (Portsmouth: Portsmouth City Council, 1983), 9.

[30] *Bradford Observer*, 6 September 1838 and 7 December 1854.

[31] *Northern Star*, 19 October 1839.

[32] *Leeds Mercury*, 15 Aug and 5 September 1840.

[33] J. Burnley, *Phases of Bradford Life* (Bradford: Brear, 1870), 28.

[34] *Bradford Observer*, 17 June 1852.

[35] Harrison, *Drink and the Victorians,* 80.

[36] Return of Number of Publicans and Keepers of Beer-Houses convicted at London Police Offices, and before Magistrates, 1831-33 1833 (419) XXIX.399. For the number of beerhouse keepers in the capital see Return of note 37.

[37] Return of Number Of Licensed Victuallers and Keepers of Beer-Shops charged before Police Magistrates with Breaches of Laws, 1830-38 1839 (173) XXX.435.

[38] Jennings, *Public House in Bradford,* 106.

[39] 1833, QQ. 1560-1.

[40] *Leeds Mercury,* 9 and 23 September 1837.

[41] For this and the phenomenon generally see Jennings, *Public House in Bradford,* 114-19.

[42] Jennings, *Public House in Bradford,* 102-3.

[43] B.J. Davey, *Lawless and Immoral. Policing a Country Town 1838-1857* (Leicester: Leicester University Press, 1983), 69, 94-5 and 115.

[44] Return of Number of Licences for Sale of Beer and Cider in Eng. And Wales granted or refused in each County and Borough at Brewster Sessions of 1869 1870 (215) (215-I) LXI.177,261 and Return of Number of Licences for Sale of Beer and Cider in Middlesex and Surrey granted or refused at Brewster Sessions of March.1870 1870 (434) LXI.277. Both Returns present problems of interpretation in addition to the points in the text.

[45] Account of Number of Persons in U.K. licensed as Brewers and Victuallers, October. 1868-69 1870 (187) LXI.281.

[46] Riley and Eley, *Public Houses and Beerhouses in Nineteenth Century Portsmouth,* 12-13.

[47] *Bradford Observer*, 30 Aug 1869 and Jennings, *Public House in Bradford,* 108.

[48] 1870 (215) (215-I) LXI.177, 261

Ludicrous Politics: Nautical Melodrama and the Degradation of Law

Matthew Kaiser
Department of English
Rutgers University
510 George Street
Murray Hall
New Brunswick
NJ 08903
U.S.A.
mkaiser@eden.rutgers.edu

Theatre historians generally agree that the evolution of English melodrama in the nineteenth century consists of three overlapping yet relatively successive stages, distinguished not only by subject matter but by concomitant ideological and aesthetic objectives. With its focus on the supernatural and macabre, Gothic melodrama, against a backdrop of castles and storm clouds, dominated the first two decades of the century, supplanted only in the mid-twenties by nautical melodrama, which took as its arena the open sea, as its hero the British sailor. In the mid-thirties, the sailor was upstaged by family, factory and street, by the primarily working-class struggles depicted in domestic melodrama, which remained a fixture until late in the century. Due to its sentimentalization of the Royal Navy, the crown jewel in the British apparatus of colonial expansion and economic hegemony, as well as the working-class sailors and seamen who functioned in the popular imagination as synecdoche for British military supremacy – due, then, to its transparent jingoism, nautical melodrama has enjoyed scant critical attention, dismissed, with rare exception, on both political and aesthetic grounds as reactionary and heavy-handed, as amalgamating what critics deem the less savory attributes of its melodramatic siblings, the escapism of Gothic melodrama and the social conservatism of domestic melodrama. Replete with ideally masculine, zealously patriotic, sailor-heroes, dutiful brides, and diabolical villains, nautical melodramas by playwrights such as Douglas Jerrold, John Haines, and Edward Fitzball, unambiguously celebrated not only British militarism, but discipline and order in general, glorious self-sacrifice, recreating on elaborate sets – which included at times large water tanks – naval battles and shipwrecks, mutiny and piracy, to the accompaniment, of course, of contagious ditties and maudlin ballads. These plays would be nostalgically parodied four decades later in nautical farces and burlesques, which in turn would inspire the nautical operas of Gilbert and Sullivan. Occasionally, theatre historians suggest, as Marvin Carlson has, that nautical melodrama provided a site of proletarian identification, but any sense of solidarity, others argue, was necessarily subsumed in and conterminous with patriotic interpellation, an audience's capacity for docility, for identifying with those who embodied order.[1]

This paper offers an alternative vision of nautical melodrama and, by extension, of melodrama in general. The notion that nautical melodrama constitutes a straightforward endorsement of authority and the status quo rests upon the problematical assumption that acquiescence to law and order – even when enthusiastic – results necessarily in legitimation of law and order. Complicity and critique are not, however, mutually exclusive. I do not mean to suggest that this explicitly chauvinistic genre encourages in its audience active resistance or protest, nor that its chauvinism be construed as satirical or parodic, as it eventually became, to some degree, in the farces and burlesques of the sixties and seventies. This paper suggests, rather, that it is the genre's flagrant idealization of militarism, of its orderly ideal, of Law, wherein lies paradoxically a demystification of patriotism, a demythologization of its martial ethos, and ultimately a delegitimation of Law. Politically and aesthetically, then, nautical melodrama is neither radical, nor ironic, but *ludicrous*: the heavy-handedness, the excessiveness, of its chauvinism renders ludicrous, degrades, the very order it upholds, the patriotism it promulgates. This phenomenon is evidenced, to cite but one example, in the sailor-hero's peculiar lingo, an obsessive nautical metaphor, a direct reference to the often impenetrable argot of British sailors and seamen, some of whom were all but certain to be in the house on any given evening, at least in London, where Jack Tar sojourned in tavern, brothel, and music hall. This professional jargon – whereby everything from a woman's body to the sailor's own bodily functions is metaphorized as ship, crew, or equipment – not only reinforces the uniformity and rigidity of naval culture, but is symptomatic of the sailor's successful socialization, his subjection to and interpellation by authority, betraying, therefore, not only professional enthusiasm and hence patriotism, but laughable artificiality, comic automatism, as when William, in Jerrold's *Black-Ey'd Susan*, describes his own tears as 'standing in either eye like a marine at each gangway', and his impending death as 'the vessel of life ... get[ting] under way for the ocean of eternity'.[2] In nautical melodrama, Law is made ludicrous, both in the pedestrian sense of the word, in being made absurd, hyperbolic, untenable, and in the etymological sense of the word, in being made *ludic*, game-like, playful, functioning as a closed, autonomous set of rules. Rendering Law game-like, ludic, fundamentally delegitimizes it, deprives it not only of gravity but ultimately of the metaphysical foundation from which it derives its authority. This paper suggests, then, that it is neither radical resistance, nor ironic distance, whereby nautical melodrama renders Law ludicrous, exposes its inherent arbitrariness, but, rather, the genre's very acquiescence to and complicity with Law, its idealization of order. Before exploring how 'the politics of the ludicrous', as one might call it, degrades Law in two of the most popular and widely imitated nautical melodramas, Haines' *My Poll and My Partner Joe* and *Black-Ey'd Susan*, let us focus our attention first on the nature and function of the ludicrous.

Time has not been kind to the word 'ludicrous'. It greeted the nineteenth century rich with meaning, full of promise and frivolity, but by century's end, found itself impoverished, stripped of its positive denotations, clinging to just one bitter thought. Its only current meaning is decidedly derogatory, referring, of course, to that which is ridiculous or laughably absurd, to that which induces derisive laughter. There was a time, however, at the beginning of the nineteenth century, when 'ludicrous' also denoted playfulness and gaiety, sportiveness and jocularity, when calling an individual 'ludicrous' meant that he or she exuded wit, or wielded humor with skill. Gone, too, are its etymological cousins, the nouns, verbs and adjectives, which sought to describe, to illuminate, each facet of life's ludic complexity: gone, then, are 'ludicrosity' and 'ludible', 'ludibund' and 'ludicral', 'ludicrism' and 'ludify'. At the root of 'ludicrous', of course, is *ludus*, Latin for 'play', 'game' and 'sport', but also 'pastime', 'joke' and 'fun', as well as 'school', the place one grows strong by way of practice, by way of youthful contest. At one time, then, 'ludicrous' referred to that which brimmed with ludic spirit, that which appreciated the profundity of play. More than a mere attitude or personal aesthetic, the ludic represented, and still does to some degree, an ethical world view, which posited life as a game, as a play of surfaces, not only in the Platonic sense, in which the world is seen as *illusion*, which means literally 'in-play', as Johan Huizinga points out, but in the Spinozan-Nietzschean sense, in which morality, the metaphysical distinction between truth and falsity, hence right and wrong, is supplanted by an ethics of levity over gravity, joy over despair, and ultimately life over death.[3]

At first glance, game and Law appear diametrically opposed: under scrutiny, though, the chasm between them narrows. Whereas game evinces motion and illusion, Law strives for fixity and certainty. Both, however, stand in stark contrast to chaos and disorder, for both provide ethical bounds, a sense of definition. The rules of a game and the rule of Law, however, create different orders: whereas the former is illusory, lighthearted and ephemeral, the latter is moral, grave and enduring. To cheat at a game, or to refuse to play, is merely to shatter the illusion, to dispel levity, to prove a spoilsport. To break the Law, on the other hand, is to bring upon one's head moral condemnation, metaphysically sanctioned violence. This does not mean that games are not, at times, perilous or tragic, or that the ludic precludes pain or agony – at the root of which, after all, is the Greek *agon*, or contest. To treat a game, however, as a *moral* struggle, as a gauge of righteousness, in short, to take a game too seriously, is to fundamentally degrade it and the illusory life it celebrates, subordinating play to moral order, to a higher principle. Conversely, treating Law as a game, not taking it seriously enough, degrades it, deprives it of metaphysical referentiality, a legitimacy grounded in what Huizinga terms 'abstract righteousness'.[4] Frivolous lawsuits and sophistical trial lawyers are favorite targets of law-and-order politicians precisely because they embody in the paranoid eye of the public the ludic degradation of Law, the specter of Law collapsing into an amoral, arbitrary game, a closed, autonomous set of rules, grounded in nothing beyond itself. Yet, despite lawmakers' best efforts to deny it, Law *is* arbitrary; it *is* self-grounded. Law's legitimacy, its moral authority, depends, it turns out, upon its ability to mystify its ludic essence, to obfuscate the fact that justice is indeed arbitrary, self-grounded, that it functions as a game – a game, however, which refuses to acknowledge its own ludic nature. Rather than the antithesis of game, Law is best understood as a game which takes itself too seriously, which shatters it own illusion, and which erects in its stead an edifice of denial. Law is fundamentally depressive, for it constitutes a turning-away from life, from illusion, from its play of surfaces. Law defines itself against ludic self-groundedness, denouncing it as infantile and irresponsible, in order to distract its subjects from its own tyrannical arbitrariness. Its tyranny, however, derives not so much from its arbitrariness – for all games are self-grounded and hence arbitrary – but from its moralistic refusal to face its own chimerical legitimacy, to concede its arbitrariness. To render Law ludicrous, to degrade it, means, in essence, to betray it for what it is, to cause its ludic character to become perceptible, laying bare its arbitrary nature.

Typically set ten to thirty years in the past, during the Revolutionary and Napoleonic Wars, nautical melodramas such as *My Poll and My Partner Joe* and *Black-Ey'd Susan* mythologize military order and its concomitant imperial agenda in two distinct ways. First, they idealize the British sailor, present him as an *uber* sailor, the epitome of discipline, or, as one of William's shipmates describes him: 'The trimmest sailor as ever handled rope; the first on his watch, the last to leave the deck; ... he has the cleanest top, and the whitest hammock; ... give me taut Bill afore any able seaman in his Majesty's fleet'.[5] The sailor-hero is the pillar upon which the crew's morale rests, his sense of duty manifesting itself in small ways, when he sacrifices his grog to his fellow seaman, for instance, or when he 'play[s] upon the fiddle like an angel,' as William is said to do, as well as in more profound ways, when he saves the lives of his fellow sailors and even – in the case of the appropriately named Harry Hallyard in *My Poll and My Partner Joe* – the lives of his superiors. Second, the nautical melodrama provides an overtly revisionist account of the Royal Navy's contentious relationship during the Revolutionary-Napoleonic period with both the public and its own largely conscript population. Disgruntled and resentful, mistreated and malnourished, at times, openly seditious, many sailors, of course, served the Crown against their will, having fallen prey to the press gang, an universally hated institution all but abandoned after 1815, but nevertheless instrumental in supplying the requisite manpower for defeating France. Despite the fact that both William and Harry are 'pressed', that Harry's violent abduction is enacted within the play, both recruits thrive in their new milieu, Harry, in fact, within the space of a scene: indeed, so encoded is he by his new profession, when asked by his cynical captain if he is ungrateful for all that the Royal Navy has given him, he replies: 'May I spring a leak, and go down in the black sea of contempt, if ever I take such a villainous cargo on board!'.[6] Nautical melodrama's jingoism and militarism, then, provide a conservatively sanctioned space for the public to experience its own latent and overt anxieties about the tyrannical and unjust nature of Law, its ludicrousness, even as the public endorses through patriotic identification the institutions which perpetuate injustice and tyranny. Acquiescence and complicity, therefore, function as vehicles whereby the ludic nature of Law is betrayed, a critical stance vis-à-vis the Law enabled.

Both texts are concerned with issues of legality, justice, obligation, and discipline. In *Black-Ey'd Susan*, William's beautiful wife Susan awaits her husband's return from sea and his impending discharge from the Navy, but not before she repels the greedy advances of her landlord-uncle, who, it turns out, is responsible for William's impressment and subsequent three-year absence. Once in port, William foils the uncle's plans and helps to defeat a band of smugglers; a reunited William and Susan make their way to a public house, where his shipmates literally sing his praises. The lecherous Crosstree, William's intoxicated captain, mauls Susan in a darkened street and is struck by William, who fails to recognize his captain in the dark. The play's action then centres around William's arrest and court-martial for striking a superior officer. Despite the fact that the presiding officers at his trial feel that he was justified, despite the endless witnesses to his exemplary character, despite Crosstree's acknowledgement that he deserved to be struck, the Court is forced by inflexible naval law to sentence the beloved sailor to death. As a pall descends upon the fleet, 'true blue' William, employing his characteristic nautical metaphor, expresses his respect for the letter of the law, his fidelity to and enthusiasm for naval order, and his willingness to face his fate. He is saved from the scaffold, however, rescued in the waning moments of the play, when his discharge papers are discovered to be dated prior to the fateful scuffle, revealing that he is not subject to the Law he so idealizes.

My Poll and My Partner Joe is similar in theme as well as plot. In the first act, Harry is torn from the arms of his fiancée Mary Maybud by a press gang sent by Black Brandon, a slave ship captain, who seeks revenge against Harry for magnanimously paying the debts of an old man whom Brandon sought to bankrupt. Four years elapse. By now a sailor in His Majesty's Navy, Harry has been arrested for disobeying an order, ironically, out of his obsessive sense of duty, taking it upon himself in an ecstasy of heroism to sneak under enemy guns and almost single-handedly capture an enemy vessel. Before Harry's punishment can be carried out, however, a battle ensues between his ship and what turns out to be Black Brandon's approaching slaver. In the mayhem, Harry manages to free himself, invade the slave ship, free the slaves, defeat Brandon, and, amidst fiery explosions, invade the island fort of Brandon's pirate conspirators. A naval hero, Harry returns to London only to discover that Mary, thinking him dead, has married his best friend Joe. As a jealous Harry and a devastated Mary lament their fate, Joe conveniently dies, linking their hands in a final gesture.

I would like to outline three acquiescent and complicitous means by which Law is rendered ludicrous in these and other nautical melodramas. One might think of them as ludicrous technologies, political and aesthetic devices which function to degrade Law, to betray its tyrannical nature. The first means by which Law is made ludicrous, degraded, is fetishistic idealization, the literalness with which the naval hierarchy and the sailor-hero worship the letter of the Law, investing procedural and regulatory detail, and the order it purportedly creates, with hyperbolic significance, in effect, at the expense of justice. This phenomenon is evidenced most explicitly, of course, in both *Black-Ey'd Susan* and *My Poll and My Partner Joe*, in the sailor-hero's arrest for violating naval regulation, even though his transgression is clearly motivated by valiance, duty, and love of nation. Adherence to Law is idealized in nautical melodrama to the point where it becomes absurd, illogical, unjust, where heroism is criminalized. At Harry's trial, for instance, Captain Oakheart, faced with the dilemma of punishing a sailor for his bravery, navigates the troublesome discrepancy between ideal sailor and the naval ideal of order:

> To preserve the necessary discipline, we are compelled to reprimand a brave man for an act that confers honour on the British flag; yet, while obliged to condemn, we shall applaud and honour in our hearts one of the best seamen that ever trod a plank – one of the most fearless spirits that ever handled a cutlass: his very courage must be restricted with severity, or his example and extraordinary success will banish subordination from the fleet.[7]

So inflated in value are statutory and legalistic minutiae, that Law is reduced to a fetish, an empty signifier, grounded not in abstract righteousness but in itself.

The metaphysical legitimacy of Law, it turns out, derives from its referentiality, from the belief that it is neither self-grounded, nor self-justifying, nor, therefore, tyrannical, but grounded instead in a higher principle, the Good, the primary power from which Law draws its own secondary power, and to which it refers. Despite the fact that Kant and other late-eighteenth- and early-nineteenth-century philosophers had begun to problematize, and even to overturn, this Platonic, Judeo-Christian model of Law, nevertheless, throughout the nineteenth century (and even today) Law's legitimacy remained dependant in the popular imagination upon its purported metaphysical referentiality, which functioned to naturalize social hierarchy, mystifying with a veil of inevitability Law's tyrannical arbitrariness. According to Marx, of course, fetishism consists essentially of the repression of an entity's referentiality, in the case of the commodity, the devaluation of the labour which produced it and the magical investment of that entity with an autonomous value. Referring to nothing beyond itself, the fetish functions as an autonomous signifier, a thing-in-itself. To fetishize Law, therefore, that which derives its legitimacy, its justice, from its referentiality, is to endow it with a magical autonomy, as well as a tyrannical arbitrariness, a self-groundedness independent of the Good. Law is thus made ludicrous: it is not only made absurd, unreconcilable to a higher logic, but betrayed as ludic, game-like, as functioning as a closed, autonomous set of rules. In nautical melodrama, the more idealized and fetishized Law becomes, the more self-referential it becomes, hence the more unjust it becomes. When justice does eventually prevail in nautical melodrama, it is a necessarily arbitrary justice, manifesting itself somewhat disconcertingly in luck, chance, or coincidence. Degraded Law is little more than a ridiculous tyranny of rules.

The second acquiescent or complicitous means by which Law in nautical melodrama is rendered ludicrous, degraded, is masochistic submission, the sailor-hero's lack of resistance, his docility, in the face of Law's violence, his complicity in his own victimization by Law. Despite the fact that Harry characterizes naval law as 'cruel', acknowledging that he is forced to 'defend a country whose laws deprive him of his liberty', nevertheless, as the press gang closes around him, he announces to his tearful fiancée: 'I must submit ... without one thought of the green hills or the flowing rivers of a country that treats me as a slave!'.[8] Despite the fact that William characterizes Law as 'Beelzebub's ship', which 'founders in fair weather', which is 'provisioned with mouldy biscuit and bilge water', he succumbs willingly to the punishment it metes out, embracing with kamikaze enthusiasm its ideal of discipline, refusing, in fact, against the urging of his judges, to reconsider his guilty plea, to equivocate or to qualify his actions, claiming that 'it is beneath the honesty of a sailor ... to go upon the half tack of a lawyer'.[9] William goes so far as to bless profusely the men who are about to carry out his execution. According to Gilles Deleuze, masochism constitutes the philosophical and political strategy of capitulating, surrendering to Law so zealously, obeying the letter of the Law so literally, that the violent foundations of Law, its consequences, are betrayed, its purported nobility rendered ludicrous.[10] The masochist, who is motivated not by admiration but by contempt for Law, does not take pleasure in suffering, but endures the greatest pain in order to experience the pleasure of demystifying Law, forcing it to reveal itself for what it is: an apparatus of violence, in short, tyranny. Masochism, as Deleuze sees it, is a form of humor, a means of exposing Law's ludicrous underpinnings. History's most famous masochist is probably Socrates, who delivered his own death sentence with masochistic relish, the knowledge that with each bitter gulp the mask of nobility slipped further from the Law's face. To be sure, William and Harry, indeed, the sailor-heroes of nautical melodrama in general, lack the acuity and verbal elegance of a Socrates. It is the play itself and, by extension, its amused audience, then, which succumbs masochistically to Law, experiencing its tyranny through patriotic identification with submission: the sailor constitutes merely the submissive body, the docile flesh upon which the ludicrous consequences of one's total subjection to Law are dramatized. Indeed, William and Harry are constitutionally incapable of discerning Law's ludicrousness, or seeing the humor in Law's degradation. Through its patriotic identification with their submission, however, through a vicarious masochism, the audience *does* see it.

The third and final acquiescent or complicitous means by which Law in nautical melodrama is degraded, rendered ludicrous, is the sailor-hero's automatism, the machinic 'inelasticity', as Henri Bergson describes the phenomenon, 'of habit that has been contracted and maintained', 'something mechanical encrusted on the living'.[11] Bergson continues:

> We begin, then, to become imitable only when we cease to be ourselves. I mean our gestures can only be imitated in their mechanical uniformity, and therefore exactly in what is alien to our living personality. To imitate any one is to bring out the element of automatism he has allowed to creep into his person. And as this is the very essence of the ludicrous, it is no wonder that imitation gives rise to laughter.[12]

The stylized nature of the sailor's nautical speech and physicality, its rigidity and uniformity, functions ultimately to betray the unnatural, even violent, effects of successful socialization on body and psyche, the transformation of the individual into machine, a concatenation of verbal and physical gestures: in short, a type. The sailor's automatism, which bespeaks, as I've said, his professional enthusiasm, his acquiescence to the demands of Law, nevertheless degrades Law, renders it ludicrous by exposing its tyranny, its transformation of the human into a puppet. If colourful costume, garish makeup, and the melodramatic mugging of actors – the most legendary being T.P. Cooke, who immortalized the roles of both William and Harry – were instrumental in solidifying the sailor-hero as a recognizable physical type, then his obligatory nautical metaphoricity reminded audiences that subjection to typification is as intellectual as physical, that rigorous socialization renders mechanical not merely the human body but emotion and thought. The sailor-hero's humanity, his uniqueness, recedes, supplanted by the role he plays, by a set of rules, by habits, which govern his every thought, render his mind inflexible, his speech formulaic. The sailor-hero is imprisoned within his own self-imitation, marked simultaneously by an abundance of personality and by a loss of self: hyperbole and erasure. Encountering at one point an acquaintance from his pre-naval days, Harry barely recognizes the man through the distorted lens of his own sailorness: 'But – why, there's something about the build of your figurehead as strikes me – did you ever cross my latitude afore?'.[13] 'I don't know what you mean by your latitude', his friend replies, 'but I've crossed your door-way at Battersea many a time'. William, too, having docked with his shipmate Peter, fails to recognize his own wife among the other naval wives:

> *William.* A little more to larboard messmate. There's my Susan! Now pipe all hands for a royal salute; there she is, schooner-rigged – I'd swear to her canvas from a whole fleet. Now she makes more sail! – outs with her studding

booms – mounts her royals, moon-rakers and skyscrapers;
now she lies to! – now – eh? May I be put on six-water grog
for a lubber.

Peter. What's the matter?

William. 'Tisn't she – 'tisn't my craft.[14]

Fetishistic idealization, masochistic submission and automatism represent
three inherently political means – three acquiescent and complicitous
means – by which Law is degraded, not overturned, not subverted, so
much as denuded, seduced into exposing its tyrannical underbelly. The
politics of the ludicrous, then, is neither radical nor reactionary: the
ludicrous seeks not to change the rules, nor to do away with Law
altogether, but to set it in play, to unleash it from a debilitating gravity, to
provide for its subjects a ludic agency, literally, a game plan for surviving
tyranny. To perform, as I have sought to do, a revaluation of the
ludicrous, a reconstruction of its lost ethical and political potentiality, not
only enables nautical melodrama, the subject of this paper, to be viewed
through a less simplistic political frame than that of subversion and
recuperation, but provides a means of awakening the dormant seeds of the
ludicrous in all their myriad manifestations.

Endnotes

[1] See Marvin Carlson, 'He Never Should Bow Down to a Domineering Frown: Class
Tensions and Nautical Melodrama', *Melodrama: The Cultural Emergence of a Genre*,
eds. Michael Hays and Anastasia Nikolopoulu, (New York: St. Martin's, 1996), 147-
66.

[2] Douglas Jerrold, *Black-Ey'd Susan; or, 'All in the Downs'* (*Nineteenth-Century
Plays*, Ed. George Rowell, Oxford: Oxford University Press, 1972), 19, 39-40.

[3] Johan Huizinga, *Homo Ludens: A Study of the Play-Element in Culture* (Boston:
Beacon Press, 1950), 11.

[4] Huizinga, *Homo Ludens* 78.

[5] Jerrold, *Susan* 35.

[6] John Thomas Haines, *My Poll and My Partner Joe*, *Hiss the Villain: Six English and
American Melodramas*, ed. Michael Booth, (New York: Benjamin Blom, 1964), 111.

[7] Haines, *My Poll* 110.

[8] Haines, *My Poll* 111, 107-8.

[9] Jerrold, *Susan* 18, 34.

[10] See Gilles Deleuze, *Coldness and Cruelty* (*Masochism*, Trans. Jean McNeil, New
York: Zone, 1991), 81-90.

[11] Henri Bergson, *Laughter: An Essay on the Meaning of the Comic* (Trans.
Cloudesley Brereton and Fred Rothwell, Copenhagen and Los Angeles: Green
Integer, 1999), 28, 39.

[12] Bergson, *Laughter*, 34-35.

[13] Haines, *My Poll*, 122.

[14] Jerrold, *Susan*, 19.

Popular Sunday Newspapers, Class, and the Struggle for Respectability in Late Victorian Britain*

David Scott Kamper
309 Gregory Hall
810 South Wright Street
Urbana, IL 61801
U.S.A.

dkamper@uiuc.edu

By the end of the nineteenth century, the press critic Henry Sell could declare confidently that 'Sunday papers have established a precedent that no opposition can break down'.[1] Numbers alone proved his assertion: in 1890 some two million copies of popular Sunday papers like *Lloyd's Weekly Newspaper*, *People* and *News of the World* were sold every week. In terms of sheer magnitude, Sunday penny papers were the leading cultural products of late Victorian Britain, eclipsing music halls, cheap novels, and football in size, if not necessarily influence.

Size, however, did not guarantee cultural acceptance. To be sure, Sunday newspapers had shed their reputation as the mouthpieces of revolutionary anarchism, so prevalent in the 1840s and 1850s.[2] Even in the late Victorian years, though, it 'was not considered respectable to read a Sunday journal'.[3] Sunday newspapers were either ignored by their contemporaries, or, at best, disparaged and belittled as unworthy counterparts of the *Daily News* or *Standard*. Why were popular Sunday newspapers, so commercially successful, unable to attain the same status as their daily counterparts?

One reason was that the respectability of Sunday newspapers was inextricably linked with questions of class. Respectability was not the same thing as social class; there could be respectable labourers just as there were dissolute noblemen. However, in the case of Sunday newspapers, the connections were much closer. There was a general feeling, best expressed by an anonymous journalist for a Sunday newspaper, that they were 'low-class papers'.[4] The ambiguous meaning of 'low-class' helps illuminate the position of Sunday papers. For, not only did they fall below the horizontal dividing lines of social class, they also faced challenges along the vertical line of respectability.

This paper will examine how the cultural position of Sunday newspapers was influenced by these links between class and respectability. While Sunday newspapers were not purely working-class organs, they were *perceived* as being so. This class identification challenged the precarious respectability of Sunday newspapers in two ways. First, they were on the wrong side of a powerful discourse on how the respectable working classes were supposed to spend their Sundays. Second, they fell prey to existing stereotypes about the sensational nature of working-class reading habits. This paper will conclude with a case study of how the interaction between class and respectability affected one groups' relationship with Sunday newspapers: the newsagents. In the 1890s, retail newsagents across Britain organized to improve not only their working conditions, but also their status in society. Their ambiguous attitudes about Sunday newspapers demonstrate the insecure cultural position occupied by the largest cultural products of Victorian Britain.

This paper will, hopefully, begin to touch upon several important aspects of Victorian social and cultural history. Many historians have examined the development of popular and working-class cultures in late Victorian Britain, but so far empirical studies have tended to focus on specific locales and small populations; as Sunday papers reached much of the country and millions of people, this might offer a new perspective on class, culture and politics.[5] This paper also can help contribute to the literature on the construction of working-class and lower-middle-class respectability in Victorian Britain, which is in need of further case studies.[6] Finally, I hope this paper will encourage a renewed look at the role of Sunday newspapers in the development of Victorian popular press, a role often marginalized by modern historians.[7]

Who read Sunday newspapers? They had enormous circulations in the late Victorian years. *Lloyd's Weekly Newspaper* was in every respect the head of the pack. In 1870, it was already claiming circulation above half a million, and in 1896, under the editorship of Thomas Catling, it became Britain's first paper to reach the million sales mark.[8] *People*, founded in 1881 as the only major Conservative Sunday, reached 360,000 by 1890.[9] Four others – *News of the World*, the *Weekly Dispatch*, the *Weekly Times and Echo*, and *Reynolds's Newspaper* – were smaller, but at least one of them 'guaranteed' advertisers a circulation of 150,000 a week in 1895.[10]

With so many being sold, therefore, it would be foolish to assume the readership was drawn exclusively from the working class. Yet, this is precisely what the Victorians did, whenever they deigned to discuss Sunday newspapers at all, which was rare. The 1856 opinion that the readers of Sunday papers included a 'man who has passed six days in the week on carting parcels from one railway station to another, in unloading ships, in watching the wheels of the machine', echoes that of a newsagent in 1899, who characterized them as 'carpenters, bricklayers, plumbers, smiths, navvies, labourers, carters, gardeners and so forth'.[11]

This impression was reinforced by the rigid dividing line set up between readers of daily papers, and readers of Sunday newspapers. They were seen as two completely distinct sets of people. Robert Donald, Managing Editor of the *Daily Chronicle* (also owned by the Lloyd family), was certain that Sunday papers were for 'the multitude ... a class who do not buy a daily paper regularly'.[12] To the Reverend H.R. Haweis, 'there are daily papers that are not Sundays, and there should continue to be Sunday papers that are not dailies'.[13] When T.P. O'Connor started the *Sunday Sun* in 1891, he made a deliberate effort to disassociate his venture from the existing Sunday papers. 'Our Journal will be', he claimed, 'to use a conscious contradiction – a daily paper published once a week'.[14] Even with his energetic effort at rhetorical distance, however, he soon felt it necessary to change the name of the paper to the *Weekly Sun*.

This dividing line was never more accurately demonstrated than in the uproar over 'Seven-Day Journalism' in 1889, and again in 1899.[15] In 1889, the London edition of the *New York Herald* began, promising a paper every day of the week, including Sundays. In 1899 it was no foreign paper, but London's two biggest dailies, the *Telegraph* and the *Mail*, that decided to introduce Sunday editions. Massive protests took place both times, the first led by William Thomas Stead, editor of the *Pall Mall Gazette*, and the Archbishop of Canterbury, and in 1899 involving almost every bishop of the Church of England, prominent labour leaders like John Burns, and over 50 MPs. Both protests were successful: the London edition of the *New York Herald* survived less than two years, and the Sunday editions of the *Mail* and *Telegraph* in 1899 just seven weeks.

While the controversies were primarily about seven-days' labour, there was a strong feeling that daily papers had no business alongside Sunday papers. When the *New York Herald* defensively pointed to the existing Sunday papers, they were told by Reverend Newman Hall of Christ Church, 'it is not the same', because the existing Sunday papers 'do not distract the mind by ... the ordinary contents of a newspaper'.[16] In 1899, meeting a deputation, the Home Secretary acknowledged 'it is quite true that at the present moment there are a very large number of papers distributed throughout the metropolis on Sunday ... but those papers [e.g., *Lloyd's*] are not, as I understand it ... *pari passu* with the new issues. (Hear, hear.)'.[17] *Pari passu* means 'equally' or 'side-by-side'; there was consensus among opponents of seven-day journalism that a

Sunday edition of a daily paper was fundamentally different than existing Sunday papers. They were culturally segregated; there was not a popular press, but, rather, popular presses.

In short, while the *News of the World* could claim in advertisements that 'its general news and information fits it alike for the aristocracy and middle classes, as well as mechanics', Sunday newspapers were seen as papers for the lower-middle and working classes.[18] How did this identification affect their status? Respectability was, as Brian Harrison puts it, 'always a process, a dialogue ... never a fixed position', and there is a danger of oversimplifying a complex dialogue.[19] There were Victorians who saw nothing unrespectable in Sunday papers. And a small taint of unrespectability does not mean Victorians hated or despised Sunday papers. Despite these caveats, however, the evidence suggests that two significant discourses of respectability were used to challenge Sunday newspapers specifically because they were identified with the working classes.

The first is Sunday observance. 'The weekly holiday', observed future bishop H.H. Henson, 'must be kept under lock and key until the working-classes have learned how to use it'.[20] Late Victorian discussions of the proper place for Sunday frequently treated it primarily as a question of what to do about the working classes.[21] The middle classes and the elites, it was assumed, did not need protection from Sunday labour, or instruction as to why Sunday observance was beneficial. The lower orders, however, were lost souls in need of special attention; they could not be trusted to look after their best interests. 'The working classes are not awake to the value of Sunday', wrote a commentator during the seven-day journalism protests of 1889; 'they see that there is no foundation for its theoretical sanction, but they do not see what an intensely human value it possesses'.[22] The support of existing legislation, therefore, was vital in the eyes of Sabbatarians. The most relevant statute was the Lord's Day Observance Act, which dated back to the reign of Charles II, though it was amended in 1871. The Earl of Shaftesbury, who presided over the Working Men's Lord's Day Rest Association, described the Act as 'the working-man's charter, securing to him the right to a suspension of toil for one day in seven'.[23]

While it is true that, in the eyes of some, in this case the Radical P.A. Taylor, Sabbatarians 'seemed to think that they could never serve God unless they were prosecuting men', we should not assume only extreme Sabbatarians held strong views on Sunday observance.[24] While few Victorians were vociferous, most felt that Sunday was a special day, and its infringement was tolerable at best. John Burns, in 1889 still describing himself as a 'Socialist', felt Sunday labour was 'a desire of the capitalists' vanguard to extend the period of labour's exploitation'.[25] The

W.M.L.D.R.A. claimed the support of 2,412 'working-class societies', totalling 501,705 members, in their fight against the Sunday opening of the British Museum.[26] Even the Sunday League, and other groups pushing for relaxed Sabbath restrictions, felt the need to qualify their positions, stressing utility and necessity, instead of insisting openly on a free and open Sunday. Support for the Sabbath, the evidence suggests, was the respectable position to take, for elites and for members of the lower-middle and working classes.

The second challenge to Sunday newspapers was the prevalence of stereotypes about working-class reading habits. By no means were the stereotypes universal. 'It is certain that there is a general impression abroad' wrote J.F. Stephen in 1856, 'that they [Sunday papers] are unfailing sources of furious political incendiarism, and pander to all kinds of prurient curiosity ... nothing can be more unlike the impressions which we get from the papers themselves than the expectations'.[27] Few, however, followed Stephen's lead and examined Sunday newspapers before condemning them.

The main charge was the printing of indecent or sensational material. While Thomas Catling maintained that a 'murder mystery has always been of great service to every newspaper', Sundays were singled out for special attention.[28] The *Saturday Review*, which had been so complimentary in 1856, by 1870 could hardly be too critical of Sunday papers. While railing against 'indecent' advertisements in the daily press, it nevertheless did 'not propose to attempt the reformation of the weekly press. The newspapers that lay themselves out for the work of public corruption – the *Reynolds* and the *Lloyds* – the buzzflies of dirt who stink and sting – are beyond indignation'.[29] An article reprinted with evident approval in *The Newspaper Press* called Sunday papers 'a catalogue of all the villainies of the week'.[30] It mocked the contents of *Lloyd's* with a fake bill of contents: 'Trial of a Burglar and a Murderer – Shocking Suicide of a Girl and Her Betrayal – A Woman Murders Her Five Children – Brutal Treatment of a Pauper – An M.P. Garotted in the Seven Dials – Thrilling Death of a Drunkard'.[31]

This picture continued through the Victorian years. Mr. White, of the retail giant W.H. Smith & Son, thought the 'majority' of Sunday papers were 'simply summaries of the week's accidents, murders, police-court cases, and that sort of thing; and are read by servants, or those whom you see sitting at their windows in their shirt sleeves, with pipes in their mouths, instead of going to church' (What Mr. White had against pipes is not clear).[32] At the height of the 1899 controversy over seven-day newspapers, the *Sun* (forgetting its foray into Sunday journalism a few years before), published a cartoon entitled 'Going to Church in the Near Future'.[33] It showed a respectably dressed couple, surrounded by a score of handbills of various (fictitious) Sunday newspapers, all advertising vicious murders, horrible scandals, and indecent revelations. 'There is a special charm about the Sunday morning's paper', wrote a newsagent, 'because special attention is devoted to the collection of sensational news on Saturday, and this class of thing suits the taste of the majority of working man'.[34]

This is not the time, unfortunately, for a defence of the content of Sunday newspapers. Few seemed to pay attention, for example, to the regular dramatic and literary reviews in the Sunday papers. Few noted the political news, even though Ashton Dilke, brother of Charles, owned the *Weekly Dispatch*. One of T.P. O'Connor's first jobs was as the Parliamentary reporter for *Lloyd's*.[35] They did print a lot of police news. Indeed, the memoirs of *Lloyd's* editor Thomas Catling show he was proud of the quality of his paper's crime reporting. Regardless, the point is the *perception* of Sunday newspapers was that their content was sensational and scandalous. Sunday newspapers were less respectable not only because their content was suspect, but because the content so neatly accorded with stereotypes about working-class reading habits.

From at least two angles, then, Sabbath-breaking and sensationalism, the respectability of Sunday newspapers was attacked using discourses of class. It is not enough, however, to lay out Victorians' broad, generic views of Sunday papers and leave matters to rest. Rather, it is important to descend to the particular, to see not what Victorians *thought* about Sunday newspapers, but how they *acted* when confronted with the uncertain status of (purportedly) working-class newspapers. The remainder of this paper will look at the tensions between the commercial success of Sunday newspapers and their shaky respectability experiences by one important segment of the Victorian mass media network: newsagents.

While W.H. Smith & Son had a near-monopoly on the railway station trade, independent newsagents still supplied the vast majority of newspapers throughout the country. The Retail Newsagent's and Bookseller's Union (R.N.&B.U.) was founded at the beginning of the 1890s to unite independent newsagents to address their many grievances. Their first General Secretary, E.C. Gowing-Scopes was, it appears, a very active organiser, and soon the R.N.&B.U. had branches across the country. The official organ of the R.N.&B.U. was the *Newsagent and Bookseller's Review*, which claimed a weekly circulation of over 10,000.[36] The *Newsagent* printed minutes of the Union's Executive Committee, quarterly Council, and annual meetings, as well as branch meetings across the country. It is, therefore, an excellent public record of the activities and thoughts of 1890s newsagents.

The main activity of the R.N.&B.U. was agitating newspaper publishers over practical grievances. Thus, we read about the folding of newspapers, payment for inserts, and postal rates. Much of this activity was simply economic, but what is noteworthy is how often they employed the language of respectability. Responding to the charge newsagents were an 'illiterate class', the *Newsagent* was quick to reply that 'retailers of newspapers are, without exception, far above the average in both knowledge and intelligence'.[37] One of the union's ongoing campaigns was to regulate independent news hawkers (who worked irregularly, but cut into the income of newsagents' shops), by licensing them all to work with 'established' newsagents. Far from pleading the fear of competition, however, the newsagents made the scheme sound like benevolence on their part: 'The idea was to secure respectable lads ... to make them responsible to and employed by a respectable tradesman, to have them respectably dressed; ... and to pay them a respectable wage, and if possible, to see that they spent it respectably'.[38] Like other Victorian trade unions, collective organising was not seen as class conflict, but as part of the process of improving the status of newsagents. Such a move required not just money. It required respectability.

Sunday newspapers proved a challenge to respectability, but also increased incomes. In the opinion of E.W. Hickox, President of the North London branch of the R.N.&B.U., 'Sunday trade has done more than anything else to bring the newsvending trade into disrepute'.[39] The Executive Committee, who ought to have known, thought that perhaps one-fourth of the 20,000 newsagents traded on Sundays.[40] They were quite aware of their predicament: many newsagents 'derive the better part of their weekly income' from Sunday sales, yet 'the feeling of even those who are Sunday sellers is entirely opposed to the system'.[41] In their efforts to salvage both respectability and profits, newsagents went to great lengths to distance themselves rhetorically from Sunday newspapers, but never went far enough to threaten their business.

Their first challenge was to justify their existing Sunday trading. One technique was to blame the readers. One newsagent, while supporting 'Sunday as a day of rest for the workers', wondered 'how these same workers show their gratitude for our consideration'. 'The fact remains', he contended, 'that those who cater for these classes are compelled to work on Sunday, and the 'hardly treated' working man, who ... will not work a minute after half-past five at night without being paid one-and-a-half times his usual rate of wage, is responsible for practically every scrap of the Sunday opening of shops'.[42] A regular stream of letters in the following weeks supported him. The working-class buyers of Sunday papers were 'the greatest tyrants under the sun, and make the worst masters. I believe they are patted on the back as the poor, suffering working man too much'.[43] 'When the toiler open his paper on Sunday morning it must be piping hot from the press' wrote another.[44] Even those not so disparaging agreed with Mr. Pratt of the Executive Committee that 'the Sunday paper was an institution in the land. The working man had always been used to it', and would not easily abandon it.[45]

The problem with blaming Sunday papers on the readers, however, was it did not explain why newsagents couldn't close on Sundays. To do that, newsagents made it clear that the alternatives to Sunday trading were worse. A stream of undesirables would swarm the streets if they closed. 'Under present conditions', said Mr. Miller, a member of the Executive Committee and staunch opponent of Sunday trading, the Sunday trade 'must be turned over to street loafers unless the retailers worked seven days a week (Applause.)'.[46] Closing on Sunday would 'create a street sale by a class of people who can and will make themselves so obnoxious that the respectable inhabitants of each town will petition to have the [Lord's Day] act repealed'.[47] Street sellers, Mr. Jones of the Executive Committee believed, 'did not as a rule want [need] money, and instanced cases of men in regular work, earning good money, going out in this way'.[48] One newsagent wondered of street sellers: 'are they Jews ... or is it possible he is too idle to work on other days and would rather do his bit on Sunday'?[49] All agreed with Mr. Curtice, that 'all the scum went into the trade on Sunday ... much to the annoyance of the respectable trade'.[50]

And, if that wasn't enough, Sunday sales also would have corrupted wayward youth. An alderman in Southampton contacted the R.N.&B.U., concerned that Sunday School 'scholars' were truant, selling papers instead; he urged the newsagents to stay open on Sundays so the newsboys would have no trade.[51] One of *Newsagent*'s regular columnists, writing from Southsea, marvelled, in wonder and disgust, at the 'pack of boys and lads of all ages, from about ten years old to twenty', who 'were scrambling like hungry wolves over a carcase [sic]' to sell their papers. 'I will only say ... that the newsagents' shops are open on Sunday ... and ought to be able to do this trade in a respectable manner'.[52]

Still, justifying Sunday trading was not enough for many newsagents; they wanted to find a solution to the burden of selling Sunday newspapers. However, they could not accomplish this without upsetting those who depended on Sunday newspapers for their livelihood. A letter from 'Newsman' wondered, 'if I were to go to my opposite neighbour, whom I know depends on his Sunday business ... and try to persuade him to join the Union, telling him that the Union is going to compel him to close on Sunday ... what would he think of me? He would think I was a lunatic'.[53] The R.N.&B.U., unable to reconcile simultaneously the demands of profit and respectability, ended up passing the buck – letting the opponents of Sunday newspaper claim the moral high ground, but never giving them enough support for success.

The newsagents most actively opposed to Sunday newspapers were not all rigid Sabbatarians. The two members of the Executive Committee who led the first push in 1893 to end Sunday newspapers, Mr. T. Chismon and Mr. J.W. Miller (one looks in vain for first names in the R.N.&B.U.), were ardent trade unionists and political Radicals. Miller, who became a newsagent in part to sell newspapers 'of an advanced character', and had been interested in trades unionism 'from boyhood', insisted that the way to end Sunday papers was collective union action to secure one day's rest in seven.[54] Chismon warned, in classic union language, that 'there is a mighty struggle in the paper trade coming ... in a very little while, in which trade unionists will have all the advantage on their side, and the rich publisher, with all his wealth will be powerless ... They will find themselves face to face with a power they have not had to face before ... then, perhaps, they will see that the shekels they are so eager to scrape in on Sunday' are not worth the price of a labour struggle.[55]

The first concrete proposal, made by Miller at an R.N.&B.U. Executive Committee Meeting in January, 1893, was to ask Sunday newspaper publishers to print a late Saturday edition in addition to their Sunday edition, that could be sold late Saturday evening, thus allowing newsagents to close on Sunday. The proposal was enthusiastically received. It passed unanimously, and the Chairman, Charles Roberts, said 'I don't think any resolution put before the Executive has ever given me greater pleasure (Applause.)'.[56] Almost immediately, however, differences appeared. When the Stepney branch endorsed the scheme on the proviso that there be no Sunday editions whatsoever, the General Secretary, E.C. Gowing-Scopes, urged the branches not to tack on 'impossible conditions'.[57] Yet, two weeks later, in an open letter, Scopes suggested an Act of Parliament against Sunday selling 'would prove an immense blessing to the newsagent'.[58] Two weeks later, in response to a stream of letters from members opposed to the scheme, he backtracked again, claiming 'it is quite useless to think of stopping Sunday papers – we could never do it if we wanted to (Applause.)'.[59] In his report to the Annual meeting the next month, he cleared everything up: the Sunday issue was a 'bone of contention' between members; 'we have had to approach the subject very delicately'.[60] 'Delicately' might have meant 'not at all', because, while Scopes wrote to Sunday newspaper publishers, asking them to publish late Saturday editions, no further action was taken once he had received their (unsupportive) replies.

The members of the Executive Committee found themselves waffling back and forth, unable to avoid contradictions. When Mr.

Chismon announced at a May, 1893 meeting that he had got nearly all his customers to sign a petition opposing Sunday papers, he was greeted with applause. A few minutes later, though, when Mr. Legg (who had supported the original plan for late Saturday papers), argued that 'their agitation on the question showed a great deal of the dog in the manger business. Those who wished to give up Sunday papers should do so and not try to make others follow suit', he too was applauded.[61] At the same meeting, Chismon urged the Executive Committee to pass a resolution, commending the towns of Birmingham and Southampton for restricting Sunday selling, but by a 10-7 vote the Committee refused. Two weeks later, however, in a purely symbolic gesture, they voted to expurgate that vote from the minutes, on the grounds that it looked bad for them to refuse to congratulate others whose actions supported their cause.[62]

This went on for more than a year. In 1894, Mr. Chismon persuaded the General Secretary to ask every branch their opinion on Sunday newspapers, but it took a month for the Executive Committee to agree on the wording of the letter. All but two of the branches supported a ban of some sort. Acting on that information, Chismon arranged for the Archbishop of Canterbury to receive a deputation from the Union on the subject of Sunday newspapers. However, days before the meeting, the chair of the Executive Committee suddenly decided that 'it was deemed inadvisable to continue the matter, as it was a question of considerable difference of opinion'.[63] A serious debate ensued, as many members of the Committee were afraid a deputation to Archbishop would give the appearance of a unanimity that did not exist. Yet, Mr. Diprose added that 'we should keep in touch with the question and not *appear* to want to shelve it'.[64] In the end, Miller, Chismon and a third member of the Committee went to see the Archbishop, but in a private capacity, and received a lukewarm reception.[65]

When the controversy over seven-day journalism erupted in 1899, once again the newsagents showed themselves desirous of respectability, but unwilling to make the financial sacrifices to obtain it. The R.N.&B.U. quickly joined the protests against the *Sunday Daily Telegraph* and *Daily Mail (Sunday Edition)*. Unity was maintained during the seven weeks' struggle. Gowing-Scopes became the secretary of the National Protest Committee, rubbing elbows with bishops and MPs. A petition circulated through the pages of *Newsagent* garnered nearly 250,000 signatures. A great many newsagents boycotted all publications affiliated with either of the seven-day papers.

The 1899 attempt to mix respectable daily and unrespectable Sunday newspapers crossed a strong cultural dividing line. When that dividing line was restored after the withdrawal of the seven-day editions, the newsagent's unanimity collapsed. At the Annual Meeting of the

R.N.&B.U., in Liverpool, just weeks after the defeat of seven-day journalism, there was, it appeared, a strong anti-Sunday mood. Mr. Fletcher's speech declaring that 'he wished to see them band together in such a way as it could be said "the newsagents are altogether opposed to Sunday trading"' drew loud applause from the assembled newsagents.[66] Speaker after speaker followed him in agreeing with Fletcher, and with Mr. Chismon's characteristically aggressive cry that 'the time had arrived for whipping away the thing at once'.[67] One member even urged those who traded Sunday papers should be expelled from the Union. However, despite apparent unity, the newsagents found reasons to avoid action. They agreed that 'the working man could not be aroused to take action ... he was a bit selfish'. Others warned that their allies in Parliament and the Church might not support a step this far. Having thus excused themselves from taking any substantive steps, a face-saving motion was introduced (seconded by the most ardent anti-Sunday newspaper man among them, Mr. Chismon) to direct the Executive Committee to 'carry the matter out to the best of their ability'.[68] The Executive Committee never discussed the subject again.

It is not surprising that newsagents were unwilling to deprive themselves of the profits from the sale of thousands of Sunday newspapers. What is surprising is the lengths to which they went to give the appearance of wanting to do so. In all the records of the R.N.&B.U. examined for this paper, not once did a newsagent admit to *reading* a Sunday newspaper. Very few claimed to like doing Sunday business, and even those who took a pro-Sunday position did so on the grounds that it was a necessary evil to keep the trade in respectable hands. Being seen to oppose Sunday newspapers was perceived as a necessary step to achieving respectability.

We can conclude, therefore, by suggesting that the Sunday newspapers' struggle for respectability was neither an empty intellectual debate nor a pitched battle for survival, but something more subtle and far-reaching. Because they were seen as 'low-class' publications, Sunday newspapers opened themselves up to criticism by Sabbatarians and by cultural critics. The existence of popular Sunday newspapers was never in doubt in late Victorian Britain, but endurance and respectability were not the same. Even if they could not themselves be eliminated, *Lloyd's*, *People*, *Reynolds's* and the others were able, by association, to challenge the respectability of working-class and lower-middle-class society. The case of the newsagents shows how far some in that society were willing to go to be seen as respectable. The history of Sunday newspapers in the late nineteenth century needs to be more closely integrated into the history of popular culture and working-class respectability. Sunday newspapers helped define the terms of a class-based cultural debate in

92

which claims to respectability could be articulated and accepted. Britain's lower-middle-class and working-class newsagents might have found Sunday newspapers unrespectable, but without them they would scarcely have had the opportunity to claim respectability for themselves.

Endnotes

* I would like to thank Professor Walter L. Arnstein for his years of support and advice, the US/UK Fulbright Commission for supporting my doctoral research, Dr Roland Quinault for his service as my mentor on this side of the Atlantic, and the staff of the British Library Newspaper Library, who were unfailingly helpful and polite.

[1] Henry Sell, 'The World's Press and its Developments', *Sell's Dictionary of the World's Press* (1900), 22.

[2] See Virginia Berridge, 'Popular Journalism and Working-Class Attitudes: A Study of *Reynolds's Newspaper, Lloyd's Weekly Newspaper* and the *Weekly Times*, 1854-1886' (Ph.D. dissertation University of London, 1976) and Michael W. Shirley, '"On Wings of Everlasting Power": G.W.M. Reynolds and *Reynolds's Newspaper*, 1848-1876' (Ph.D. dissertation University of Illinois, 1997).

[3] Harold Herd, *The March of Journalism* (London: Allen & Unwin, 1952), 186.

[4] *Pall Mall Gazette*, 9 February 1889, 2.

[5] See, for example, Gareth Stedman Jones, 'Working-Class Culture and Working-Class Politics in London, 1870-1900: Notes on the Remaking of a Working Class' in Jones, *Languages of Class* (Cambridge: Cambridge University Press, 1983); Ross McKibbin, *Ideologies of Class* (Oxford: Clarendon Press, 1990); T.G. Ashplant, 'London Working Men's Clubs, 1870-1914' in Eileen Yeo and Stephen Yeo, eds., *Popular Culture and Class Conflict, 1590-1914* (New Jersey: Humanities Press, 1981); J. Cornford, 'The Transformation of Conservatism in the Late Nineteenth Century', *Victorian Studies*, 7, (1963): 35-66; A. Davies, *Leisure, Gender and Poverty: Working-Class Culture in Salford and Manchester, 1900-1939* (Buckingham: Open University Press, 1992); Mike Savage, *The Dynamics of Working Class Politics: the Labour Movement in Preston, 1880-1914* (Cambridge: Cambridge University Press, 1987) and Judith Walkowitz, *City of Dreadful Delight* (London: Virago, 1992).

[6] See, for example, Brian Harrison, 'Traditions of Respectability in British Labour History' in Harrison, *Peaceable Kingdom* (Oxford: Clarendon Press, 1992); F.M.L. Thompson, *The Rise of Respectable Society* (Cambridge, Mass.: Harvard University Press, 1988); Gertrude Himmelfarb, *Victorian Minds* (New York: Alfred A. Knopf, 1968); Asa Briggs, 'Victorian Values' in Eric M. Sigsworth, ed., *In Search of Victorian Values* (New York: Manchester University Press, 1988) and Peter Bailey, "Will the Real Bill Banks Please Stand Up?": Towards a Role Analysis of Mid-Victorian Working-Class Respectability', *Journal of Social History*, 12 (Spring 1979): 336-353.

[7] For example, G.A. Cranfield *The Press and Society: From Caxton to Northcliffe* (New York: Longman, 1978); Alan Lee, *The Origins of the Popular Press in England, 1855-1914* (London: Croom Helm, 1976); Lucy D. Brown, *Victorian News and Newspapers* (Oxford: Clarendon Press, 1985); R.D. Altick, *The English Common Reader* (Chicago: University of Chicago Press, 1957); Stephen Koss, *The Rise and Fall of the Political Press in Britain: The Nineteenth Century* (Chapel Hill: University of North Carolina Press, 1981); Aled Jones, *Powers of the Press* (London, 1996), Joel

Wiener, ed., *Papers for the Millions: The New Journalism in Britain, 1880s-1914* (New York: Greenwood Press, 1988) and George Boyce, James Curran and Pauline Wingate, eds, *Newspaper History: From the Seventeenth Century to the Present Day* (Beverly Hills: Sage Publications, 1978).

[8] *Newspaper Press Directory* (1870) ,138; Thomas Catling, *My Life's Pilgrimage* (London, John Murray, 1911), 231.

[9] *Newsagent and Advertisers' Record*, (January 1890): 51.

[10] *Sell's Dictionary of the World's Press* (1895), 360.

[11] J.F. Stephen, 'The Sunday Papers', *Saturday Review*, 19 April 1856, 493; *Newsagent and Bookseller's Review*, 3 June 1899, 642.

[12] Robert Donald, 'How Seven-Day Journalism Was Killed in London', *Outlook*, LXIII (1899): 262.

[13] *Pall Mall Gazette*, 5 February 1889, 1.

[14] Quoted in *Sell's Dictionary of the World's Press* (1892), 150. This was quite similar to the claim of the *Sunday Times* (with the *Observer*, one of a small number of low-circulation middle-class Sunday papers) to be a daily paper published on Sundays.

[15] I have examined the second incident in "An Evil of Untold Magnitude': The Seven-Day Journalism Controversy of 1899 and Late Victorian Attitudes Towards Sunday Newspapers', Presented at the Annual Conference of the Research Society for Victorian Periodicals, 1997.

[16] *New York Herald* (London edition), 4 February 1889, 5.

[17] *Newsagent and Bookseller's Review*, 20 May 1899, 604.

[18] *Newspaper Press Directory* (1870), 139.

[19] Harrison, 'Traditions of Respectability', 161.

[20] H.H. Henson, 'The British Sunday', *National Review* (July 1899): 767-768.

[21] The only full-length study of Victorian Sabbatarianism is John Wigley, *The Rise and Fall of the Victorian Sunday* (Manchester: Manchester University Press, 1980), which is rather brief and uncritical. See also Brian Harrison, 'Religion and Recreation in Nineteenth-Century England' in Harrison, *Peaceable Kingdom*, 123-156.

[22] *Pall Mall Gazette*, 15 February 1889, 2.

[23] *The Times*, 19 July 1871, 12

[24] *Parliamentary Debates*, 3rd. ser., vol. 208 (1871), 254.

[25] *Pall Mall Gazette*, 12 February 1889, 1.

[26] *The Times*, 1 January 1884, 6.

[27] Stephen, 'The Sunday Papers', 493.

[28] Catling, *My Life's Pilgrimage*, 202.

[29] 'Newspaper Cleansing' *Saturday Review* 9 July 1870, 39.

[30] *Newspaper Press*, 1 September 1870, 209.

[31] Ibid., 209.

[32] *Newsagent and Bookseller's Review*, 25 February 1893, 209.

[33] *The Sun*, 28 March 1899, 1.

[34] *Newsagent and Bookseller's Review*, 8 July 1899, 16.

[35] Catling, *My Life's Pilgrimage*, 118.

[36] It was the *Newsagent and Advertisers' Record*, a monthly publication, from 1889 to January 1891.

[37] *Newsagent and Advertiser's Record*, (October 1889): 3.

[38] *Newsagent and Bookseller's Review*, 25 March 1893, 300.

[39] *Newsagent and Bookseller's Review*, 30 September 1893, 327.

[40] *Newsagent and Bookseller's Review*, 15 April 1899, 437.

[41] *Newsagent and Bookseller's Review*, 28 January 1893, 108.

[42] *Newsagent and Bookseller's Review*, 3 June 1899, 642.

[43] *Newsagent and Bookseller's Review*, 10 June 1899, 665.

[44] *Newsagent and Bookseller's Review*, 8 July 1899, 16.

[45] *Newsagent and Bookseller's Review*, 11 March 1893, 246.

[46] *Newsagent and Bookseller's Review*, 28 January 1893, 102.

[47] *Newsagent and Bookseller's Review*, 13 May 1893, 482.

[48] *Newsagent and Bookseller's Review*, 11 February 1893, 149.

[49] *Newsagent and Bookseller's Review*, 10 June 1899, 665.

[50] *Newsagent and Bookseller's Review*, 28 January 1893, 102.

[51] *Newsagent and Bookseller's Review*, 4 February 1893, 197.

[52] *Newsagent and Bookseller's Review*, 28 July 1893, 104.

[53] *Newsagent and Bookseller's Review*, 10 March 1894, 234.

[54] *Newsagent and Bookseller's Review*, 9 September 1893, 254.

[55] Ibid., 248.

[56] *Newsagent and Bookseller's Review*, 28 January 1893, 102.

[57] *Newsagent and Bookseller's Review*, 11 February 1893, 150.

[58] *Newsagent and Bookseller's Review*, 25 February 1893, 209.

[59] *Newsagent and Bookseller's Review*, 11 March 1893, 246.

[60] *Newsagent and Bookseller's Review*, 22 April 1893, 402.

[61] *Newsagent and Bookseller's Review*, 6 May 1893, 446.

[62] *Newsagent and Bookseller's Review*, 20 May 1893, 493.

[63] *Newsagent and Bookseller's Review*, 28 June 1894, 58.

[64] *Newsagent and Bookseller's Review*, 28 June 1894, 59. Emphasis added.

[65] The relevant issues of the *Newsagent* describing the meeting have been lost. See *The Times*, 21 August 1894, 9.

[66] *Newsagent and Bookseller's Review*, 24 June 1899, 722.

[67] *Newsagent and Bookseller's Review*, 24 June 1899, 724.

[68] *Newsagent and Bookseller's Review*, 24 June 1899, 724.

Circumambulatory; or, The Adventures of Three Gentlemen and a Lady in Search of a British Public
Mary Elizabeth Braddon (circa 1860)

Gabrielle Malcolm
Drama Department
Edge Hill College
Ormskirk
Lancashire L39 4QP
malcolmg@edgehill.ac.uk

Dramatis Personae
The 'talking jellyfish' nicknamed the 'Zoophyte,' worships Carlyle.
Hypatia, the lady, not given to female maladies or complaints. 'She can make an omelet [*sic*], a dish of macaroni.'
Dougal, 'The Creature,' 'good in tragedy.'
Volage, husband to Hypatia, 'indifferent to an empty purse, a bad dinner, a crying wife.'[1]

The members of the company discuss their preferences for performance, in anticipation of finding their public.

'If 'twere done, when 'twas done, then 'twere well it were done quickly,' said the Dougal Creature.
'Will you let that wearisome Scotchman alone?' said The Zoophyte. 'If you can't keep Inverness-shire out of your conversation I wish you'd hold your tongue.'
'Shakespear [*sic*] wasn't a Scotchman,' said the maligned Creature.[2]

There is a week's gap in the programme at their London theatre and so, as a small Vaudeville Company, they embark on a journey to find a public to tide them over the lean spell. Braddon addresses her readers directly in this short story. Her characters describe their theatrical world and articulate their attitudes in a form of self-conscious dialect, even a patois-style speech of mixed references, quotations and insults, hence their names.

This story has rarely come to light in the past, in fact only critically and briefly referred to once before.[3] There is the mystique of the theatre and the intimacy of domesticity in this account, if we take away the surface picturesque, and picaresque, qualities. Undoubtedly, she is offering the telling of a tale imitative of Dickens,[4] but Braddon, almost in spite of herself, is proffering more than that in this piece which never saw the light of day or emerged, transformed into a more extensive, polished form. *Lady Audley's Secret* eclipsed it, as it did much of the Braddon Familyh Collection that marks her early years.

Folded and stored carefully in her study and finally in the family collection in the bank at her death, *Circumambulatory* is evidence of Braddon's whispered past. In her own lifetime it was a past that could be referred to, but discreetly. Since her death, it is a past that was thought to bear little relevance to her position as a mediocre lady novelist; a little colour here, a little sensation there and, of course, that eye for detail that Sadleir and other critics found noteworthy. Inescapable, however, is the interest and the glamour of her 'unrespectable' past profession. This story is the material evidence that she carefully and deliberately preserved of the life that she had known and loved.

If we take her to be the lady Hypatia in this story, as Wolff does, then she casts herself more clearly than anywhere else as that determined, unorthodox young Victorian, who resisted all her life any attempts to be categorised or boxed in.

> Our heroes are of a hybrid class, half actor, half author, half dramatic artist, half three pence a liner ...[5]

All of these halves, make up more than one whole. In fact, they make double the ordinary person. Braddon is scaling herself up to function in all these capacities. There is the author alongside the actor, the 'three pence a liner'[6] coexisting with the dramatic artist, all in one.

When, in 1876, Braddon returned to the stage for one night only[7] we can only surmise how she must have felt at finally topping the bill. Having styled herself Mary Seyton throughout her stage career, 20 years before, she had managed to remain relatively incognito once her name became associated with writing. However, to compound her situation there was the scandal of Maxwell's marriage and this dogged the couple throughout the early years of their relationship. The year 1876, then, could be seen to mark a triumphant rise from scandal, when she allowed herself to be recognised as Braddon the 'eminent novelist' on the bill at Jersey, and as Maxwell's wife. She was now respectable, both she and her children could claim the name and identity that suited them. The

1870s were in sharp contrast to the preceding decade for Braddon and Max.

It is perhaps typical of her that once she achieved the status of wife and renowned author, she should mark the event with a fleeting nostalgic return to her old life. She had covered her tracks too well, as the reviewers of her performance in 1876 were convinced that 'Miss Braddon ... has never appeared on a public stage before, but has on one or two occasions taken part in private theatricals at her own residence'.[8] Once respectable, for recreation, she decided to revisit her unrespectable self. Instead of the circuitous journey her characters undergo, 'in search of a British Public,' the public came to her. Unknown to the majority of the audience on that night in 1876, Braddon was 'recreating' a part of her old life. How much more ungenerous might the critics' response have been if they had known she was more than the celebrity amateur they took her for?

In *Circumambulatory*, Braddon adopts a narrative style inspired by the affectations and self-consciously refined 'patter' of theatrical types.

> That London Theatre to which our friends appertain being shut for a weeks vacation, the question that is mooted in the opening of this work, is, as to how the four compatriots are to employ themselves, or vulgarly speaking, get their living.[9]

They debate the various merits of performing Shakespeare or a varied bill of entertainment, arguing the point of what their, as yet, non-existent audience will want.

> 'What can we do? We can't act Shakespear [sic], with four people.'
> 'And I hate Shakespear [sic],' said the Zoophyte, 'I believe he devoted himself to literature with a special view towards my torment. I can see him writing in a prophetic fury, and saying, "Aha! this will tie him up I think, I flatter myself this will twist his eyebrows!"'
> 'Bah! Shakespear [sic] never thought of such small deer as you. He saw a line of ..., Garricks, Macreadys, Keans *pere et fils*, stretching into futurity, and helping to fill the measure of his greatness, as telescopes glorify the stars by bringing them nearer to common folk.'
> 'Shall we read Shakespear [sic] then?' said Volage. 'I will take the comic scenes, the Creature is good in tragedy, and that Zoophyte could come in when we were tired, and send the audience to sleep.'
> 'If there were any audience, and if I weren't asleep myself,' interjected that person.

'But readings are stale,' said Volage. 'I've a better idea.
Let's form ourselves into a Vaudeville company. We can get
up two or three light pieces, we shan't want any orchestra;
Hypatia can play the piano behind a green curtain, and the
Zoophyte can take the money at the doors.'
'Ah, my genius is adapted to a sinecure.'[10]

Their debate illuminates the issue of whether to offer high or low art to an
audience of the day, and what might constitute the popular draw. As
Volage iterates, the audience 'might just not happen to care for a feast of
Thespis, with three performers and a piano behind a green curtain'.[11]

What their debate also highlights, as Braddon carefully proceeds to
demonstrate, are the differences between Volage and The Zoophyte, the
former Hypatia's husband. Implicitly, Braddon establishes the feelings
the 'human jellyfish' has for the lady, that he might be spineless but not
without passion. The Zoophyte (the reader never discovers his given
name) adopts a demeanour of affected boredom. Volage 'was so named
from that ethereal gaiety which made him alike indifferent to an empty
purse, a bad dinner, a crying wife or an angry creditor'.[12] Indifference to
'a crying wife' opens up the tension between the two leading men in the
company. The Zoophyte hides behind his manner and actually offers a
forlorn sympathy to Hypatia, who must adapt herself to the majority male
members of the company, sharing meals and quarters with them, but
respectably so as the wife of their leader. In making Hypatia 'respectable'
Braddon also allows for the possibility of an unrequited love interest.

Our heroine is the wife of Volage, and has been honoured by
her husband with the high sounding nickname of Hypatia,
out of admiration for the romance of that name by Mr.
Kingsley, renowned author of Alton Locke and renowned
preacher of sermons that do not send me to sleep. She is, as
heroines should be, charming – she is only moderately given
to crinoline,[13] and has been seen with a bonnet *on* her head.
She has not long been married to the bewitching Volage, and
she entertains the belief (quite orthodox in his eyes) that
there never has been, and never will be, any man in the
world so great, so good, or so delightful. She entertains a
ladylike indifference for her husband's bosom friends, and
the Dougal and the Zoophyte. She doesn't mind cigars in the
drawing room. She never has headache or hysterics. She can
make an omelet[*sic*], a dish of macaroni, an Irish stew, and
rum punch ... she can correct a proof, and play the piano;
and she has a soul not above buttons *id est* the sewing of

them on. She is a charming travelling companion, a good sailor, and doesn't mind being chaffed.[14]

It is confirmed that Braddon was an actor for some years, that she could play the piano, and that she enjoyed travelling. It is therefore not too extreme to assume that she is describing her other attributes of simple cooking, correcting proofs and sewing on buttons. These are valuable skills to bring to a small theatre company.

Hypatia finds it hard to impress her husband. It is easier to remain ladylike and in awe of him and agree to wear short petticoats in the performances of 'Swiss Cottage' and 'Love in humble life'. The latter piece, reasons Volage, is 'rather like "Swiss Cottage" over again, but then of course the audience will have forgotten the plot of that work of art. Hypatia in another short petticoat, another gold cross ... Oh it will be refreshingly delicious and can't offend the Lord Chamberlain, as that naughty Jack Sheppard has done'.[15]

They resolve to embark on their weeklong tour in fictional Sussex, beginning with the town of Rofant, and moving on to Piddinghoo. Volage feels certain that this mini tour will succeed in the provinces because he doubts whether 'the inhabitants of Piddinghoo are likely to have seen Mr. Charles Kean, Madame Celeste or the talking fish, ergo they'll appreciate us'. Instead of booking ahead they simply look up the train times and set off from London Bridge early the next morning, laden with baggage. Braddon reads our minds, and addresses 'Mr and Mrs Reader' and 'my gentle reader', urging us not to dismiss them for their folly of lack of common sense. Her appeal is for us to understand the creative, impulsive sensibilities of theatrical folk, who, 'from the high ground of common sense' appear 'deficient in that ... one qualification'. Common sense, she argues, has no place in theatre, if so 'you would have Claude Melnotte back among his cabbages, and Mademoiselle Deschappelles in her father's counting house learning book keeping by double entry. You would have Sir Lancelot married and settled, and Queen Guinevere running the heels of King Arthur's stockings that they might not come to want premature darning'.[16]

Braddon launches into the description of the departure for the tour with vigour, clearly drawing upon her own experience, and that of male company members. The urgency of the dawn awakening, with rapid ablutions and toilette ('you fall asleep while you are doing your hair and put the pomade in your mouth, and even Atkinson's pomade isn't nice before breakfast'), followed by packing, breakfast, loading the cab, before finally arriving at the station, unloading and sinking into a vacant carriage. The luggage itself, of Volage and company, takes on a life of its own as the cabman struggles to pile it into a teetering 'pyramid' on the roof of the cab. Their pile of band boxes and trunks is treated as a character in its own right, requiring attention to shunt it on and off the train, loading on and off trolleys, and finally creating a castellated construction of baggage on the remote platform at Rofant, from behind the 'rampart' of which The Zoophyte peers.

Upon reaching Rofant they make the terrible discovery that it is not a town, simply a station built for the convenience of 'two or three gentlemen' whose country villas are in the vicinity. This elicits dramatic responses from The Zoophyte.

> 'It is too dreadful! It must be a horrid dream!' said The Zoophyte. 'Have the goodness to punch me hard, someone; I am lying on my back I daresay; or I have eaten cold pork, or taken a little too much punch. I *cannot* be real!' But alas it was only too real; and the disconsolate trio returned to the butcher's tray on which Hypatia was seated.[17]

The Zoophyte likens their plight to 'Pilgrim's Progress', wondering if they will rise from the Slough of Despond, up the Hill of Difficulty to the Delectable Mountains; in other words whether there is a public house in the area as he has missed his dinner, the ultimate sacrifice. He takes refuge in peppering his speech throughout with literary, historical and theatrical allusion, a practice Braddon pursued in her writing career to demonstrate her own and her characters' erudition. As a juvenile writer in this context, she uses allusions to romances and plays to reinforce the structure of her story and signify her 'higher' ambition of novel writing. Her plot in this instance is generated from Tennyson's 'Idylls of the King' loosely framing the dynamic between The Zoophyte, Hypatia and Volage.

Volage is the picture of noble Anglo-Saxon gentlemanliness, compared to Tennyson's Arthur. The Zoophyte is a self-indulgent, melancholy figure: 'You might ... take him from his speculative eyes and turn down collar, for a poet ... (or) a lotus-eater'. Hypatia is the gentle, useful, uncomplaining wife, kind to her poodle, Punch, and her canary bird. Both she and the Zoophyte, at the end of their arduous and fruitless day, sit together and discuss Tennyson, whilst Volage and The Creature play dominoes. On failing to find an audience, stranded on the platform at Rofant in the company of the 'nebulous boy' who assists travellers from dawn until late night, they had resolved to return to London, fearful of being stranded any longer. The Zoophyte teased the pleasingly plump Hypatia, threatening to make a meal of her if he had to wait any longer for his dinner.

The company console themselves with rump steak and oysters on their return and The Zoophyte perks up considerably, whilst the domino game proceeds. Hypatia and he remain apart, discussing poetry and breeding. Their adventure of the day, their humorous, pathetic quest has left The Zoophyte, after steak and oysters, in a contemplative, philosophical mood. He wants to sit in Hypatia's company, listening to her voice, and they find their kindred love of poetry draws them together whilst the husband, of whom she is in awe, and The Creature sit puffing on their pipes and playing dominoes.

A young, gentle wife easily grows bored in the evenings. A slight whiff of what might be to come emerges here, with the gentle implications Braddon inserts into the conversation between Hypatia and The Zoophyte as they discuss the 'unrespectable' intrigue of Lancelot and Guinevere. It is, however, with Elaine and her unrequited love that Hypatia identifies most strongly. A solemn note is struck during this exchange and the characters unburden themselves of their private frustrations.

> 'Ah how much can be said in ten syllables when a great poet strings them together,' says Hypatia. 'Is not Elaine's whole life shut up in those little words,
> "I have gone mad, I love you, let me die"?
> Poor little broken hearted hopeless thing, she knew as well as possible that the answer would be death, but she was compelled, her soul and her love got the better of her reason, and she cried out despite her in the bitterness of their agony. Madness, the cruel effect, love, the womanly cause, and the bitter remedy, death! Exquisite, exquisite poetry that can compress a life into a line!'[18]

The Zoophyte follows this with a taunt, underlined with jealousy for her relationship with her husband. He is jealous of Volage – who coldly lacks appreciation for his obedient faithful Elaine – and of their situation; that they have had the confidence to wed.

> The Zoophyte elevated his eyebrows. 'Did you propose to Volage after that manner? Did you march straight up to him telling him that you were a subject for a lunatic asylum, inasmuch as you were so smitten by his attractions as to as to wish to be allowed to die?'[19]

Hypatia understands this to be derisory of her relationship, which she is trying to sustain as an ideal of perfect married bliss. She is fighting against the odds in this, as Braddon has shown the kind of strain put upon the relationship by the priority of the company. As a 'lady' she is also appalled and indignant at The Zoophyte's suggestion that she has pursued her husband.

'You know he proposed to me,' said the young lady indignantly, 'And if he hadn't-'

'Well if he had not? Is the poet true to nature? Should you have done as Elaine did?'

'I was not brought up like Elaine, with no more worldly teacher than my own simple heart. I never nursed Volage through a long illness or watched him day after day through the troubled phases of danger and convalescence. I think the situation and the words are truth itself, and that in spite of crinoline French governesses [sic], (and) Rotten Row ... women feel pretty much the same today as they did in that old Saxon time. Tennyson does not go to Utopia in search of his heroines, you might meet them every day if you had the eye of the poet to discover beauty and virtue.'[20]

This striving to find the beauty and poetry in life, amidst fashion and affectation, resurfaces in Braddon's characters throughout her career. The pragmatic heroines; who work, travel or attempt murder, are one sort. Then there are the Hypatias, who must work but seek the beauty of true, honest love as their ideal; such as Florence Sandford in *A Lost Eden* (1904), from the latter part of Braddon's career. Perhaps this type is the closest to Braddon herself, with their experiences mirroring hers. She also experiments with the truly fantastical mind of an Isabel Sleaford in *The Doctor's Wife* (1864). Isabel's ideal is that described by Hypatia here, wishing to be an Arthurian or melodramatic heroine, the lines between fantasy and reality blurring for her as she craves the real opportunity to nurse a wounded hero, Lancelot or Napoleon, or sit at the feet of a poet in the manner of Byron's lovers.

Hypatia wants to find the extraordinary in the mundane of everyday existence. Because her career is composed of acting as extraordinary women in extreme situations of melodrama she wants to find the genuinely profound in her marriage to Volage. He appears to resist that and so she consoles herself with talking poetry with The Zoophyte, whilst Volage is absorbed in his game with The Creature.

'Poor little Elaine,' murmured the Zoophyte, in a somnambulistic reverie. 'I'm really sorry for her, it can't be pleasant to be in love with a person who doesn't care twopence for you. It must be something like beating one's life out against a stone wall. You may dash out your brains against the soul-less fabric, you may spatter it with your heart's best blood, but you cannot move it from its pitiless serenity, because you see it *is* a stone wall.

'Poor little Elaine, and so she died and cold Sir Lancelot was sorry. Oh did she ever know of that sorrow? Does she know it now? If I took laudanum tomorrow and the woman I loved came and wept and howled over me, should I know of her anguish and take comfort from her tears? Oh mysteries of life and death when, when shall our souls be pure enough to fathom you? Poor little Elaine! I think the worst of all human sorrows is to have to put a cheerful face upon your sorrows. Oh how I envy those jolly old Israelitish kings who used to turn their faces to the wall and neither eat nor drink for days. They fought out that terrible and silent battle of the breaking heart at least in solitude. They didn't go out with gaudy waistcoats over their wounds and choke their sobs with ... tobacco smoke as we moderns do. Sackcloth is bad wearing no doubt, and ashes scarcely an agreeable cosmetic, but better those than that miserable comedy of grins and smirks with which we act the great lie of everyday life.'[21]

This is quite a speech from a boneless sponge, a 'human jellyfish', who is supposed to think of no one but himself and nothing but his stomach. He has suffered the pain of undeclared and unrequited love, and his refrain of 'poor little Elaine' emphasises his feelings for Hypatia and how he has read the situation of her relationship with Volage. They use Tennyson and biblical allusion to iterate their own feelings, an interesting choice for people whose career was commonly seen as 'unrespectable' and so close to immorality. This speech puts the events of the day in a new light and actually finishes this simple tale of theatre folk. Although unpublished, this story is far from being unfinished.

The Zoophyte's conclusions here remind the reader of the façade of everyday fashionable existence and the hypocrisy innate in society. Actors might perform the 'lie' on stage every night, but living it is altogether different and more 'miserable'. They are looked down upon for their itinerant and supposed immoral existence, but it allows them the chance to empathise with others and investigate their own feelings. By showing actors at their hearth and table Braddon represents them as a moral, sympathetic breed. They might be driven by commercial concerns, and the women amongst them might be compelled to wear short petticoats, but they are, in her experience, as aware of acceptable morality as the most respectable members of society, from the structured lessons of the plays they perform in public and the poetry they read in private.

In many senses this is a story of innocents abroad, and simple people with ordinary concerns in their lives – where their next meal is coming from most especially. They are also people capable of profound feeling in her depiction of them, who treat the characters they play and read about in a human fashion. They strive to understand them in order to portray them, or attempt to fathom the intentions of Shakespeare or Maddison Morton in creating such characters. It is the job of the acting profession to comprehend as well as portray human characteristics, such as those described by Tennyson.

Braddon is sentimental in her description of her characters, fellow actors. At the time of writing she was still fully professional in the theatre and dependent upon the income from it for herself and her mother. Her friends from this period comprise actors, managers and fellow writers: H Nye Chart, Wybert Rousby and William Sawyer amongst them, whose supportive nature and enduring friendship is revisited in her sympathetic depictions of such types in her novels, such as *Eleanor's Victory* (1863) and *A Lost Eden*. She does not descend into a mawkish tone, but portrays them as hardworking, sometimes intimidating in their expectations of those less experienced, but always determined and finally goodhearted and loyal.

To have sound, informed, well-read opinions is one admirable feature of such characters, in Braddon's view. They utilise their familiarity with literary and dramatic genres to express heartfelt sentiments, without abusing or misunderstanding the creative art of the writer. There is nothing more embarrassing to Braddon than the clumsy, fashionable attempts at composition and the misuse of poetic conventions by those who should know better.[22] The Zoophyte shows how literary allusion ought to be done, in style.

> 'I like Enid and Elaine best,' said he, 'Vivien is a Becky
> Sharp ... and Guinevere of course it is scarcely proper for a
> single man to mention, though I am ashamed to say I am
> rather interested in her. Arthur is a glorious fellow. Do you
> know what strikes me most in his character?'
> 'No?'
> 'His high breeding. He is one of the purest types ever created
> of an English gentleman. I don't think we have a dozen such
> creations in our language. Sir Roger de Coverley is one, Dr
> Primrose another, then there is Augustine Caxton of modern
> days, Sir Leicester Deadlock (but for a shade of the leaven of
> ultra exclusiveness) nearly perfect. Colonel Newcourt quite
> perfect, and Arthur, one entire and perfect chrysolite; the
> Saxon gentleman of that day when chivalry was not
> accounted Quixotism and high deeds and fair manners went
> hand in hand. How tenderly respectful he is to that fallen
> golden head, how sternly gentle, how gently stern, and not

one touch of the snivelling puerility of the gentleman in Hessian boots. How deeply every word he says strikes home to your heart and how much you feel and know that he does not say. The great poet creates, and leaves his creation to speak better than he can speak for him. How much more we know of Macbeth than was ever set up by mortal compositor. I can follow Arthur to those bowers of Camelot and note where one shadow *will* come, and one footfall *will* echo, and I account no man a great poet whose words do not suggest a world more of words that might have been written. Poetry for me should be suggestive and for unsuggestive poetry I would not give the opening line of the child's spelling book which tells us that "A was an archer and shot at a frog". A compendium of the life and adventures of A, in ten syllables.'[23]

Endnotes

[1] All quotations from *Circumambulatory* come from the unpublished MS contained in the Braddon Family collection, hereafter, BFC.

[2] *Circumambulatory*, MS BFC.

[3] Robert Lee Wolff, in *Sensational Victorian* (Garland 1979), 74-75, offers a brief overview of the story based upon a perusal of the MS, with a few quotations. He relates the work to Braddon's acting experience and her reputation for authorship amongst the companies she performed with.

[4] Wolff, *Sensational Victorian*, 74: '... no funnier to modern taste for the Dickensian polysyllables and circumlocutions that MEB so favored at the time...'.

[5] *Circumambulatory*, MS BFC.

[6] 'The three pence a liner' was later drawn as Sigismund Smythe in *The Doctor's Wife* 1864 and *The Lady's Mile* 1866.

[7] On the island of Jersey in the summer of 1876 she appeared in a special gala night for her old manager Wybert Rousby, at the Theatre Royal, where she played Pauline in Dance's comedy *Delicate Ground*.

[8] *Jersey Express* Aug. 1876, cited in Jennifer Carnell, *The Literary Lives of ME Braddon* (The Sensation Press, 2000), 12.

[9] *Circumambulatory*, MS BFC.

[10] Ibid.

[11] Ibid.

[12] Ibid.

[13] "'(M)oderately given to crinoline" means that she has only moderately adopted the fashion for wearing a crinoline cage under her skirts. Before the 1850s women wore copious amounts of petticoats to try and give the full, dome-shaped, silhouette that was in fashion. In about 1854, after various experiments and trials, the crinoline cage was invented, made of concentric circles of watchspring steel, either suspended on fabric or covered with cotton to give the correct shape. These crinoline cages liberated women from the layers of heavy petticoats they had had to wear before. They were

very flexible and relatively light. They did, however, cause accidents as it was easy to knock things over or worse, catch your skirts alight if you were too close to a fire'. This reference is via email from Lucy Pratt, Assistant Curator, Textiles and Dress Department, the Victoria and Albert Museum, London, November, 2000. The meaning she gives to Braddon's description of Hypatia's dress reinforces the possible date for the MS, and also shows the balance with concerns of fire safety in theatres and the ease of movement required for actresses in costume, underpinning Braddon's personal experience.

[14] *Circumambulatory* MS, BFC.

[15] Ibid.

[16] Ibid.

[17] Ibid.

[18] Ibid.

[19] Ibid.

[20] Ibid.

[21] Ibid.

[22] Braddon parodies this in much of her work, particularly in the character of the Duke's daughter, Violet's cousin, and her poem the *Tragedy of a Sceptic Soul* in *Vixen* (1879).

[23] *Circumambulatory* MS, BFC.

Drugs, Doubling, and Disguise: Sherlock Holmes and 'The Man with the Twisted Lip'

Nancy Anne Marck
Daemen College,
Amherst,
New York, NY14226
USA
nmarck@daemen.edu

Readers of Sherlock Holmes savour his facility with theatrical disguise, a skill that enables the detective to move in social circles he could not enter as a gentleman. In 'The Man with the Twisted Lip,' Holmes appears disguised as an old man in a London opium den, where he hopes to discover a clue to the disappearance of another gentleman, Mr. Neville St. Clair, of Kent. At the time of this encounter, dated by Watson as June of 1889, opium was still a legal substance, widely bought and used by the middle classes as a stimulant, a pain reliever, and a recreational drug, but Virginia Berridge and Griffith Edwards note in their history of opium use that 'the question of who used the drug was central; and the control of lower-class deviance was undoubtedly important'.[1] The crossing of class boundaries, through the physical space of London and Kent as well as the social space of dress and disguise, underlies the middle class appropriation of the opium den as the locus of transformation, signifying the possibility of escape from the restrictions of class-bound life.

The story opens with an appeal to Watson rather than to Holmes; as a personal friend and medical adviser, he is asked to locate one Isa Whitney, a gentleman whose opium addiction has kept him away from home for two days. Mrs. Whitney's gender and social class prevent her from retrieving her husband, although she knows he frequents the 'Bar of Gold' in Upper-Swandam-lane; Watson acknowledges the difficulty of crossing such barriers, observing that 'a young and timid woman' could hardly 'make her way to such a place and pluck her husband out from among the ruffians'.[2] Finding Whitney without difficulty, Watson meets Holmes and discovers they are on parallel courses; the detective is gathering evidence to locate another missing gentleman, Mr. Neville St. Clair, last seen by his wife in an upstairs window above the opium den.

In the course of the story, Doyle represents disguise as both work and play. St. Clair's career path – from actor to reporter to professional beggar – is particularly suggestive as a blurring of the distinction between professional work and creative play. As an actor, St. Clair plays various roles and learns the skill of make-up, which he uses to convert middle class guilt into cash as Hugh Boone. As a reporter, St. Clair first sets out to write authentically and authoritatively about the position of mendicants in the City, London's financial district, and concludes that 'it was only by trying begging as an amateur that I could get the facts upon which to base my articles'.[3] St. Clair's concern with providing an accurate description signals his lack of familiarity with this social class and suggests two middle class traits – both a fascination with social differences and a belief in the value of direct knowledge; St. Clair wants to experience begging himself rather than interviewing professional beggars, but he begins his career from an inauthentic position since his knowledge of make-up and the wit that makes him successful as a beggar are direct outcomes of his education and class position. His portrayal of Hugh Boone offers a middle-class interpretation of begging that romanticizes and exoticizes poverty and dependence, an interpretation that evades the reality of the beggar by treating it as a stage role. Accordingly, St. Clair's artistic conception of the beggarly character reveals that he associates beggars with deviance, as he creates a disfigured character with an actor's relish for a playing a challenging character: 'When an actor I had, of course, learned all the secrets of making up, and had been famous in the green-room for my skill. I took advantage now of my attainments. I painted my face, and to make myself as pitiable as possible I made a good scar and fixed one side of my lip in a twist by the aid of a small slip of flesh-coloured plaster'.[4] St. Clair proudly describes his knowledge of disguise as 'secret,' a special 'attainment' that distinguished his skill as 'famous,' and his description of the creation of Hugh Boone exposes the contradiction that is responsible for his success – his privileged educational background enables him to develop a reputation for the witty repartee that attracts the wealthy businessmen who patronize him in the City. St. Clair's financial success results directly from his connection to the class he evades through disguise, and his resumption each evening of a middle class identity further complicates his authenticity; few beggars could compete with the likes of Hugh Boone, who in the televised version of the story even quotes Shakespeare to passers-by. St. Clair in disguise exercises a middle-class mastery of the problems of class difference, minimizing the plight of the impoverished by role-playing an atypical beggar with ease and with relish, offering the public an experience that conflates charity with entertainment.

Donald Redmond traces the origins of the character of Hugh Boone to a story Doyle had read in Blackwood's Magazine, called 'Across Rannoch Moor', which included a description of a man with a twisted lip as well as a reference to Victor Hugo's *L'homme qui rit*, where a disfigured character is revealed to be a long-lost baron.[5] Like Hugo's character, Doyle's Hugh Boone is a gentleman in disguise, who not only infuses a lower class role with a solid middle class education but also uses disguise to advance middle class values. After the initial series of articles, St. Clair recreates the character of Boone in order to pay a debt of honour, having backed a friend's bill. As Boone, St. Clair is able to earn more than £700 per annum, and he demonstrates prudence by saving his money and purchasing a suburban home. St. Clair also fulfills traditional middle class domestic expectations by marrying and fathering two children in two years, and his marriage is characterized by his wife's irrational claim to an unusual degree of sympathy, such that she claims to be aware of his having cut himself upstairs even though she is downstairs. In one of the provoking inconsistencies of this story, Holmes uncharacteristically defends her claim, pronouncing that 'the impression of a woman may be more valuable than the conclusion of an analytical reasoner'.[6] Of course, this position proves false, as Holmes eventually penetrates Boone's disguise by spending a night in eastern-style meditation and smoking an ounce of shag tobacco, while Mrs. St. Clair was unable to see through her husband's hastily-applied disguise, even at close range. St. Clair also expresses a considerable fear of a blot on the family honour, preferring prison to his children's shame at the discovery.

As many critics have observed, money plays a crucial role in St. Clair's choice of disguise. Michael Atkinson notes the proximity of Boone's begging location in Threadneedle Street to the Bank of England, suggesting that 'St. Clair tries to convert the spare change of beggary and its sordid world into the solid fruitfulness of the middle-class domestic scene'.[7] At the end of the story, St. Clair is faced with a social and economic dilemma of some consequence: the police insist that he give up begging as Hugh Boone in exchange for privacy respecting his case, but this bargain jeopardizes the middle class stability of St. Clair's suburban life. As Hugh Boone, he earns more than two pounds per day, and on the day of his arrest, he has 556 pence, or £ 2.7.6, in his coat pockets, a daily rate that would provide him with an annual income of £717.6. If as a reporter he earned a scant two pounds per week, his annual income prior to assuming the disguise would have been £104, so he has realized a striking financial benefit from role-playing and by abandoning the role he accepts a significant financial and occupational loss. Even at the onset of his begging career, St. Clair identifies the relative merits of reporting and begging, telling Holmes, 'you can imagine how hard it was to settle down to arduous work at two pounds a week, when I knew that I could earn as much in a day by smearing my face with a little paint, laying my cap on the ground, and sitting still. It was a long fight between my pride and the money, but the dollars won at last'.[8] St. Clair must finally relinquish the role of Hugh Boone, but whether he will be able to resume his role as gentleman or whether he will seek acting as a profession remains uncertain at the end of the narrative, suggesting further complications of identity.

If disguise incorporates both work and play for Neville St. Clair, no less can be said for Sherlock Holmes himself, who employs his theatrical skills with great success in many cases, notably 'The Empty House,' where he fools even Watson. It is interesting to note that, in this case, Holmes apes disability, playing the role of 'an elderly deformed man', and causing Watson to faint by his histrionic revelation: 'I have given you a serious shock by my unnecessarily dramatic reappearance'.[9] In 'Charles Augustus Milverton', Holmes crosses class boundaries by becoming 'a rakish young workman with a goatee beard and a swagger', even going so far to become engaged to Milverton's housemaid in order to secure the information he needs.[10] 'A Scandal in Bohemia' offers two examples of Holmes' facility with disguise; he is at first 'a drunken groom, ill-kempt and side-whiskered', in which character he witnesses Irene Adler's marriage, and later he assumes the role of 'an amiable and simple-minded Nonconformist churchman', these diverse roles inspiring Watson to describe the quality of Holmes' dramatic skill:

> 'It was not merely that Holmes changed his costume. His expression, his manner, his very soul seemed to vary with every fresh part that he assumed. The stage lost a fine actor, even as science lost an acute reasoner, when he became a specialist in crime'.[11]

Speculating on Holmes' success in two disparate professions, Watson unwittingly points to his friend's unstable identity as he compares Holmes to John Hare, a well-known actor-manager of the St. James and Garrick Theatres during the 1880's, who himself crossed the class barrier when he was knighted in 1907.[12] Several critics and would-be biographers of Sherlock Holmes acknowledge the possibility that the detective had pursued a professional acting career that prepared him, like St. Clair, in the arts of disguise and furnished him with a store of characterizations, each with its own distinct language and vocabulary. D. Martin Dakin, in *A Sherlock Holmes Commentary*, attributes Holmes' solution of the mystery of Boone's identity to 'his recollection of St.

Clair's skill in the green-room', suggesting a professional awareness of the possibilities of costume and make-up.[13] In fact, the question of disguise as work and play assumes even greater significance in 'The Man with the Twisted Lip' as it redefines what is meant by a gentlemanly 'profession'. St. Clair and Holmes share the advantage of education and the desire to earn a living by employing intellect as well as creativity. Each has created a new profession – Holmes is the world's first consulting detective and St. Clair offers an early version of street theatre, not far removed from the performances of modern buskers – but their formulations critique the empty materialism of the rising Victorian middle class and its established professions even as their disguises rebel against dullness, which both men relieve through the exhilarating danger of exposure. St. Clair fears the loss of his reputation so much that he willingly endures imprisonment and separation from his family, while Holmes tells Watson that he is in danger of his life if the Lascar discovers his true identity. The risks that come with disguise suggest that its attractions lie in the psychological power of concealment, a concealment that resists the claims of an orderly society preoccupied with crime; imposture is an inherently subversive and potentially criminal tendency.

Holmes' range of disguises typically point to the need to cross class barriers in order to gather authentic information about the criminal world, which cannot be accessed except by direct observation and inference, but this methodology derives from an educated, rational perspective. To write articles on begging, St. Clair must become a beggar; to solve crimes affecting the upper and middle classes, Holmes must become a temporary member of the lower class. Rather than simply affirming the social order by solving crimes that threaten the privileged classes with the uncontrolled appetites and resentments of workers and criminals, Holmes critiques middle class values by creating his own profession and supporting that profession by moulding the signs of his own class identity (education, awareness of different psychological and lingual modes) into disguises that permit him to penetrate more authentic back-room sites like Irene Adler's stables, Milverton's kitchens, and the 'Bar of Gold'. Julian Symons' comment that the literature of crime and detection describes 'a reassuring world in which those who tried to disturb the social order were always discovered and punished' should be qualified by Holmes' discomfort with such markers of class stability as domesticity and public status; Holmes remains distant though courteous to women while he repeatedly refuses to defer to clients from the upper ranks of society, such as the King of Bohemia and the Duke of Holderness.[14] In the canon of Doyle's stories, Holmes is frequently guilty of disturbing the social order himself, not only by refusing to acknowledge class hierarchies, but more obviously by subverting class through disguise and supplanting the police by meting out his own brand of justice. Many critics have observed that Holmes occasionally lets a criminal escape, either through his sense of justice, as in 'The Abbey Grange' or, in cases where there is no real crime committed, by advocating the kind of self-policing that St. Clair assents to, an alternative justice Rosemary Jann observes in female characters like Lady Hilda Trelawny and Irene Adler.[15]

In 'The Man with the Twisted Lip', Holmes assumes the guise of an opium addict, an old man Watson describes at first glance as 'very thin, very wrinkled, bent with age, an opium pipe dangling down from between his knees, as though it had dropped in sheer lassitude from his fingers'.[16] The revelation of Holmes' true identity underlines the importance of self-control, as he metamorphoses before Watson's eyes:

> It took all my self-control to keep from breaking out into a cry of astonishment. He had turned his back so that none could see him but I. His form had filled out, his wrinkles were gone, the dull eyes had regained their fire, and there, sitting by the fire, and grinning at my surprise, was none other than Sherlock Holmes. He made a slight motion for me to approach him, and instantly, as he turned his face half round to the company once more, subsided into a doddering, loose-lipped senility.[17]

Not only is Holmes able to deceive Watson at close range, but he also demonstrates an unusual capacity for self-control by being able to slip back and forth between distinct class identities with relative ease. It is this slippage of the signifiers of class and age that evokes the power of the opium den as a site of transformation, and the association of opium with dreams and dream-like trances further emphasizes the insubstantiality of identity, and of reality itself. Throughout the story, there are repeated references to self-control and its absence. Watson manages to maintain his composure in the opium den, but in the opening request for help, Mrs. Whitney's identity is uncertain even to her friends: 'losing her self-control, she ran forward' toward Mrs. Watson, who only recognizes her intimate friend (they are on a first name basis) when she lifts her veil.[18] Gender and class confound her wish to intrude upon the opium den; as a middle class female, her identity is fixed, not malleable, and her role is limited to the domestic sphere. The same is true of Mrs. St. Clair, who is physically prevented from entering the room above the opium den until she secures male police assistance, and must await her husband's return at home. Unlike Irene Adler, these middle-class women cannot control their appearances at will and are therefore excluded from the male adventure of class-shifting; instead, their persistent identification with the tranquil refuge of the Victorian home underlines the dangerous instability of male scenes of transformation like the opium den.

That the opium den attracts men with money and time to spend on leisure is amply demonstrated by the otherwise unnecessary biography of Isa Whitney, whose claims to moral rectitude and privilege depend on his late brother, 'Principal of the Theological College of St. George', and whose addiction, labeled a 'foolish freak', results from his education, as he attempts to experience firsthand the 'dreams and sensations' recorded in DeQuincey's *Confessions of an English Opium Eater*.[19] Bettridge and Edwards link the popularity of DeQuincey's work, first published in 1821, to the anti-opium debate of the 1870's, as 'an established part of the domestic evidence with which the protagonists in the debate could buttress their arguments for and against the drug's consumption', noting that 'there were at least thirteen editions and reissues of the *Confessions* between 1880 and 1910'.[20] Although Doyle is a great pains to offer a negative portrayal of the consequences of addiction in his description of Whitney, who transforms from a respectable man into 'an object of mingled horror and pity' and 'the wreck and ruin of a noble man', evidence of Whitney's secure class identity take precedence in the opium den, where even after a two-day episode, he recognizes Watson without difficulty, asks for confirmation of the time and day, shows concern at having worried his wife, and expresses a desire to pay his bill.[21] These facts suggest that Whitney has not suffered many ill effects of his time in the 'Bar of Gold' and define the opium den as a recreational amusement for bored middle class gentlemen. Holmes also does not appear to suffer from his stay, although Martin Booth makes it clear that 'one does not have to be an addict, or an eater or smoker, to come under the effect of opium: passive consumption is possible'.[22] Although George F. McCleary defends the detective from charges of addiction, citing his rational faculties, his 'mental resources and initiative' as examples of behavior uncharacteristic of addiction, Holmes' staring into the fire may be evidence of opium's tendency to alter visual perception, and his silence during the long ride to St. Clair's home in Kent may suggest the residual effects of having spent several days in the opium den.[23] As opium was often credited with enhancing the creative faculties of its users, it may also have contributed to Holmes' solution of Boone's identity. Holmes himself asserts the comparison between opium and cocaine addictions, and Christopher Keep explains that 'as its addictive properties became better known, cocaine was increasingly associated with the degenerative effects of opium use The alkaloid effectively went from being a miracle of modern medicine to a vestigial horror of Europe's colonial enterprise'.[24] Holmes' habitual use of cocaine may increase his tolerance for the smoke, to which he seems impervious, while Watson holds his 'breath to keep out the vile, stupefying fumes of the drug'.[25]

Doyle's ambivalent treatment of the opium den is most evident in his description of the 'Bar of Gold', which shows respectable Victorians indulging in the private use of hallucinogenic drugs; in the darkness, the 'burning poison' glowing in metal pipes deprives users of rational thought as well as of intelligible speech, the failure of communication signalling the absence of social control:

> The most lay silent but some muttered to themselves, and others talked together in a strange, low, monotonous voice, their conversation coming in gushes, and then suddenly tailing off into silence, each mumbling out his own thoughts, and paying little heed to his neighbour.[26]

Language erodes into incoherence, a resistance to the claims of social intercourse that offers yet another escape from the demands of community; in this sense, the opium den serves as the occult, creative counterpart of the prosaic domestic setting, where language endorses the public ideology of marriage, family, and respectable occupations. Doyle further associates the opium den with transportation and escape, describing the 'long, low room, thick and heavy with the brown opium smoke, and terraced with wooden berths like the forecastle of an emigrant ship'.[27] Coming from his well-ordered home in Harley Street, Watson enters the den – the scene of uncertain identity – by passing down a staircase through a dark door that resembles the mouth of a cave, further implying the erosion of rational civilization into a primitive condition of sensations, verbal chaos, and transformational possibility.

The Victorians were divided about the social uses of opium; the medicinal properties of opium as a pain reliever were well-documented, and it was widely available for both medical and recreational use until reports of the working classes' abuse of the drug alarmed the middle class public. Morbidity and overdose were often explained as class-specific phenomena, and public awareness of Chinese users of opium in dock areas of London led to the 1868 Pharmacy Act, an attempt to regulate the sale and use of the drug. In practice, pharmacists and physicians continued to prescribe opium for medicinal as well as recreational use. In 1874, the anti-opium movement formed the Society for Suppression of the Opium Trade, founded less to distinguish between medical and non-medical uses of the drug than to agitate for controls on imports from both India and China. By the time Doyle wrote his story in the early 1890's, public opinion was starting to shift from widespread acceptance to call for increased regulation, in a sense registering an objection to the possibility of shifting class identity since in the minds of middle class citizens, opium dens 'were a sign of decadence and contact with Chinamen, as with other coloured races, was seen as socially polluting'.[28] Importantly, the 'rascally Lascar' who operates the 'Bar of Gold' has had previous dealings with Holmes, and as St. Clair's landlord, was paid to keep the secret of his identity, to provide him with a place to perform his transformation, and to prevent Mrs. St. Clair from unmasking her husband. Doyle also characterizes the opium den as a point of access to multiple cultures, as the Lascar has Malay and Swedish associates, and Watson observes the adjacent businesses are 'a slop shop and a gin shop'. Since Holmes locates the 'Bar of Gold' close to Paul's Wharf, the 'slop shop' is most likely an establishment that sells ready-made clothing, or 'slops', to sailors.[29] The gin shop normalizes opium by associating it with alcohol, an association that Doyle uses repeatedly; even though there is no evidence of alcohol in the 'Bar of Gold', the steps down to the opium den are 'worn hollow in the centre by the ceaseless tread of drunken feet', and Holmes refers to the 'sots' in the den and to Whitney as 'that sottish friend of yours'.[30] . Far from offering a pat, wholesale condemnation of drug and drink, Doyle aligns their use with the opium den to signal the critical need for transformation as experienced by both Holmes and St. Clair.

The two actors evade the restrictions of class and gender through the roles they construct, testing the experience of life in other social circumstances to satisfy their common curiosity about human life. The detective and the man who does something in the City serve as doubles, both gentlemen who find the limited occupations available to them inadequate, choosing rather to exercise their own extraordinary creative abilities by defining their respective professions apart from the typical avenues open to men of their class and education. If Holmes and St. Clair reproduce this position from different standpoints – detection and journalism – their conclusions about Victorian society are strikingly similar, making the theatrical scene of Holmes's unmasking even stranger. While some critics interpret Holmes's washing away of the Boone make-up as a baptism that restores St. Clair to his proper class identity, Audrey Jaffe argues that the scenes of revealed identity 'annihilate the idea of a stable or unified identity altogether', suggesting instead that 'the idea of respectability keeps identity in motion' throughout the story.[31] Through the similarities between the detective and his quarry, Doyle invites the reader to address the need for transformation as a sign of increasing class discomfort, blurring the distinction between work and play, avocation and occupation, to suggest the insubstantiality of social and individual identity.

116

Endnotes

[1] Virginia Berridge and Griffith Edwards, *Opium and the People: Opiate Use in Nineteenth-Century England* (London: St. Martin's, 1981), xxviii.

[2] Sir Arthur Conan Doyle, 'The Man with the Twisted Lip', *The Illustrated Sherlock Holmes* (New York: Crown, 1984), 70.

[3] Doyle, 'The Man with the Twisted Lip', 83.

[4] Doyle, 'The Man with the Twisted Lip', 83.

[5] Donald Redmond, *Sherlock Holmes: A Study in Sources* (Kingston: McGill-Queens University Press, 1982), 55.

[6] Doyle, 'The Man with the Twisted Lip', 80.

[7] Michael Atkinson, *The Secret Marriage of Sherlock Holmes and Other Eccentric Readings* (Ann Arbor: University of Michigan Press, 1996), 100-01.

[8] Doyle, 'The Man with the Twisted Lip', 84.

[9] Sir Arthur Conan Doyle, 'The Empty House', *The Illustrated Sherlock Holmes* (New York: Crown, 1984), 341-42.

[10] Sir Arthur Conan Doyle, 'The Adventure of Charles Augustus Milverton', *The Illustrated Sherlock Holmes* (New York: Crown, 1984), 433.

[11] Sir Arthur Conan Doyle, 'A Scandal in Bohemia', *The Illustrated Sherlock Holmes* (New York: Crown, 1984), 9-10.

[12] 'John Hare', *The Oxford Companion to the Theatre*, ed. Phyllis Hartnoll. 4th ed. (Oxford: Oxford University Press, 1983), 371.

[13] D. Martin Dakin, *A Sherlock Holmes Commentary* (Newton Abbot: David Charles, 1972), 67.

[14] Julian Symons, *Mortal Consequences* (New York: Schoken, 1973), 10.

[15] Rosemary Jann, 'Sherlock Holmes Codes the Social Body', *English Literary History* 57 (1990): 699.

[16] Doyle, 'The Man with the Twisted Lip', 72.

[17] Doyle, 'The Man with the Twisted Lip', 72.

[18] Doyle, 'The Man with the Twisted Lip', 70.

[19] Doyle, 'The Man with the Twisted Lip', 70.

[20] Berridge and Edwards, *Opium and the People*, 55.

[21] Doyle, 'The Man with the Twisted Lip', 70.

[22] Martin Booth, *Opium: A History* (New York: Simon & Schuster, 1996), 13.

[23] George F. McCleary, 'Was Sherlock Holmes a Drug Addict?' *The Baker Street Reader: Cornerstone Writings About Sherlock Holmes*, ed. Philip A. Schreffler (Westport, CT: Greenwood, 1984), 136.

[24] Christopher Keep and Don Randall, 'Addiction, Empire, and Narrative in Arthur Conan *Doyle's The Sign of the Four' Novel* 32.2 (Spring 1999), 209. Doyle, 'The Man with the Twisted Lip', 83.

[25] Doyle, 'The Man with the Twisted Lip', 72.

[26] Doyle, 'The Man with the Twisted Lip', 71.

[27] Doyle, 'The Man with the Twisted Lip', 71.

[28] Berridge and Edwards, *Opium and the People*, 215.

[29] *Oxford English Dictionary* (Oxford: Oxford University Press, 1989).

[30] Doyle, 'The Man with the Twisted Lip', 71-73.

[31] Audrey Jaffe, 'Detecting the Beggar: Arthur Conan Doyle, Henry Mayhew, and "The Man with the Twisted Lip"', *Representations* 31 (1990): 107, 110.

Gounod and The Gods: Audience Behaviour in Irish Theatres 1840-1900

Nuala McAllister
Department of History, Philosophy and Politics,
University of Ulster at Coleraine.
Cromore Road
Coleraine
County Londonderry
BT52 1SA
n.mcallister@ulst.ac.uk

'You have disgraced yourselves again'. Thus W.B. Yeats angrily admonished a Dublin audience in the early 1900s, referring to the riotous and disruptive behaviour within the theatre during a play performance.[1] Indeed, riot, disorder, the throwing of missiles and foul and abusive language had been an established part of theatrical life in Irish city and provincial theatres since the early 18th century. It had evolved as an essential aspect of audience participation, expected and sometimes eagerly awaited by theatre managers as a stimulus for 'full houses' in the near future. Such was the regularity of theatrical disturbances that In the 1830s, the *Belfast Newsletter* had commended a provincial audience in Newry for its restrained behaviour, intimating that audiences deserved praise and should be periodically rewarded with favourable comments in the press in return for allowing theatre performances to run without violent interruptions.[2] Disturbances in Irish theatres reached a peak during the mid-nineteenth century, subsiding in frequency towards the later 1880's, and declining in the decade before Yeats' comment was made. The major disturbances did, of course, occur in the theatre, where the tradition of disorder had been reinforced by successive generations of theatre-goers. But concert halls and opera houses in Ireland, regarded by contemporaries as the venues of the more elitist entertainments, were also subject to periodic exhibitions of riotous disruption alongside the more usual patterns of smoking, loud conversation and gross inattention. An exploration of the nature and sources of these disturbances highlights the

118

role of disorder as a dominant feature of Irish cultural life throughout the nineteenth century.

Provincial Theatre Audiences

Press advertisements, actors' memoirs and travellers' accounts indicate that Irish theatres between 1840 and 1880 had become the habitual resort of the lower orders, attracted by the cheaper admission prices, the spectacle and the excitement of a lengthy entertainment. Visiting Belfast in 1843, William Thackeray found the gallery of the local theatre 'quite full and exceedingly noisy and happy. They stamped, and stormed, and shouted, and clapped in a way that was pleasant to hear'. Thackeray was delighted by the impromptu performance of a song – albeit 'extremely ill-sung' – by a 'young god' between the acts, which was accompanied by foot-stamping 'in chorus' by his brethren. In contrast, Thackeray's somewhat respectable host in the city, had 'not only never been in the play-house, but ... [had] ... never heard of anyone going thither'.[3] And in keeping with this religious and moral tenor, which Thackeray had noted as being particularly strong in Belfast, the provincial press was reluctant to comment upon the behaviour of theatre audiences. The strong religious anti-theatre bias in Ulster, in particular, militated against theatre reviews becoming frequent features in the press. In Derry, for example, theatre performances failed to get press mention during the 1840s and 1850s, in contrast with the mid-1820s when the *Londonderry Journal* commented that the theatre had been 'filled to overflowing with all the rank and fashion of the city'.[4] In the intervening years between the 1830s and the later 1860s, the price of admission to the gallery had fallen from 2s to just 3d, allowing a relatively cheap night's entertainment for the local factory and shipyard worker. The practice of half price admission after 9 p.m., a practice which persisted in Irish provincial theatres until the early 1870s, further lowered the cost of admission.[5]

It is from carefully worded press advertisements that one derives an indication of the calibre of theatre performance during this period when the larger provincial theatres had closed and had been replaced by smaller, makeshift buildings in obscure locations. A series of advertisements placed by the theatre manager in the Derry press between 1844 and 1847, in the wake of the 1843 Theatre Repeal Act, illustrates that in spite of being freed from the restrictions on presenting drama, provincial theatre had lost its elitist appeal and was struggling to maintain its last vestiges of respectability. Drama was accompanied by 'other entertainments' – dancing, farces and 'burlesque extravanganzas and popular novelties' to appeal to 'the *vox populi*'. In 1854, the manager of the Derry theatre, Vivien Ryan, placed an advertisement in the local press assuring his patrons that 'all profane allusions would be carefully avoided' in his productions; in a bid to attract a higher level of patronage from within the city, he simultaneously emphasised that theatre elsewhere was patronised by 'the sovereign, nobility and body of the people'.[6] In contrast, the character of the theatre-goer in mid Victorian Derry was described by the local press, the 'Londonderry Sentinel', as the 'lower cream of the community', 'the rude gods whose boisterous manners are obnoxious' and 'the rough element'. The entertainment on offer comprised 'the lowest burlesques and farces by third and fourth-class actors'; the theatre itself was described as a 'miserable wooden structure'.[7]

Visiting actors also commented upon the mayhem from this 'rough element' within Irish provincial theatres. In 1851, the Dublin actor, Gustavus Vaughan Brooke, referred affectionately to the 'wild enthusiasm' of the Belfast audiences. This 'enthusiasm' also extended to the streets outside the theatre where Brooke's carriage was often surrounded by a 'retinue of ragged admirers' anxious to cheer on their 'hero'. Inside the theatre, Brooke had devised his own impromptu methods of dealing with disturbances. Faced with a contingent from the local garrison intent on maintaining a constant din throughout the opening piece, Brooke approached the offending party, brandishing his sword, and threatened to 'put this through one of you'. The resulting uproar from the largely supportive audience forced the soldiers to retreat, accompanied by threats, fighting and further displays of weaponry.[8]

In the years between 1840 and 1880, the reasons for disorder and riot within theatres derived from various sources, from tardiness in raising the curtain to dissatisfaction with performances by drunk and incapable actors. The presence of sizeable contingents from the local garrison was often a source of disaffection, their attendance being increasingly resented by politically minded audiences as tensions rose in Ireland from the later 1860s onwards. Heckling from 'pitties' – political jibes or more innocent asides – at inappropriate junctures in the dramatic action often resulted in ejections, whence the audience and the players combined to evict an unfortunate offender. Often disagreements arose between pit and gallery, as in the Belfast theatre in January 1864, when simultaneous hissing and applauding from both areas forced the theatre band to 'retire with precipitation'. These occurrences were further complicated by the ever-changing myriad of allegiances within the theatre: actors were hissed by sections of the audience, only to be immediately forgiven and recalled to the stage. Fights frequently broke out in the pit amongst those who had just previously been allied against those in the 'gods'. There was undoubtedly the 'humour' amongst the audience itself, the actors being often subservient to the ongoing entertainments between the acts. Often the target of jibes and insults was the theatre manager himself, against whom all members of the audience rebelled at some time, with claims of unfair management or sudden changes of programming.

The actor, Gustavus Brooke, also played in Derry in July 1843, where he fell victim to the local theatre manager who not only failed to pay him for the performance, but also borrowed money from the actor. Brooke was forced to borrow money to return to Carlisle for his next engagement.[9] Indeed, the theatre manager occupied an uncomfortable role in relation to his audience and the actors and companies whom he engaged. He was often the object of scorn, derisory comments and unbridled mirth, yet undoubtedly beloved by his audience and held as a 'notable' by the local theatre-going populace. In Belfast where protests against the theatre were vehemently led during the 1860s by the Presbyterian minister, Dr Henry Cooke, the English born theatre manager, J.F. Warden, attracted a popular local following, as much for his work in maintaining the theatre as a 'going concern' as for his reputation for developing a repartee and rapport with his unruly audience. In December 1881, his annual speech to the audience was greeted with 'the most enthusiastic cheers which were prolonged and renewed for several minutes', belying the criticisms of a Dublin newspaper which had recently described him as a 'game manager'.[10]

The role of theatre managers in the anticipation and control of theatre disturbances is worthy of comment. Ostensibly in favour of the retention of certain level of propriety within his theatre, one Dublin manager, writing in 1851 on 'Theatrical Riots, Their Causes and Consequences', viewed his circumstances as that of a 'tolerably potent monarch on a small scale ...in control of the internal economy of his own little dominion'. He acknowledged the threat and frequency of 'rows' as merely occasions on which 'he and the public happen to fall out'. The author acknowledged causes of riots for which he was responsible, such as the repetition of a play too frequently, the dismissal of a popular actor or an over-long interval which allowed trouble to 'foment'. Nonetheless, he did comment that 'A manager, like a general, should never be taken by surprise', suggesting that certain managers were negligent in not being aware of that 'rows', riots and disturbances were most often planned, executed and 'pre-concerted' by sections of the audience. The Dublin manager did concede, however, that contemporary riots, whilst of greater frequency, were not of such financial gravity as hitherto, as in 1754 when the Smock Alley Theatre was burnt down as a result of the 'Mahomet Row'.

The theatre manager did, however, provide concluding advice for his fellow-managers: 'the best of all preventative measures is to prohibit *sticks*'. He explained that sticks were not only used to incite and prolong a riot, but to break the panels of the boxes and galleries and to make a 'diabolical clatter' overall. Relating an incident in his Dublin theatre where he had confiscated in excess of three hundred and fifty sticks from his patrons on their arrival at the theatre, the manager revealed that on this occasion, he had a noisy – but comparatively trouble-free night – and enough sticks to make 'serviceable stage properties ... for the next twenty years'. Notwithstanding this precautionary advice, he did however, imply that a theatre riot was not always to be avoided: 'a row royal' between manager and patrons, carefully planned and executed, might, in fact prove beneficial, producing overflowing houses in the short term.[11] Although there is little direct evidence that theatre managers were in direct collusion with audiences to promote a spectacle within the theatre, there was at least one occasion when the manager himself provided the dramatic action. In 1898, the bankrupted proprietor/manager of the Alhambra Theatre, William John Ashcroft, attempted suicide on the Belfast stage. The audience, accustomed to spectacle and tragedy, was at first convinced that this was a new addition to the programme; only the intervention of members of the company averted the public suicide bid from proceeding further. Only one murder, allegedly 'perpetrated after a drunken night' by patrons of the Belfast theatre, had been previously recorded in 1844.[12]

The difficulties encountered by Irish theatre managers were given expression in the 1892 Report of the Parliamentary Select Committee which enquired into the licensing of theatres and 'other places of entertainment'. Michael Gunn, who had been a Dublin theatre proprietor for over twenty years, gave evidence of the situation prevailing in Ireland, where theatres were licensed by local corporations rather than coming under the aegis of the Lord Chamberlain. Gunn explained that he employed 'one serjeant and eight policemen', who were in attendance inside the theatre building to maintain order and eject unruly elements. These policemen were paid privately by the theatre for their evening work, as they were employed in normal police duties throughout the day. Gunn also referred to 'old rule' banning soldiers in uniform from his theatres, touching upon an area which had been fraught with potential conflict in the highly political atmosphere of later nineteenth century Dublin. The presence of soldiers from the garrison, albeit welcomed by theatre proprietors during previous decades, had become the source of several 'rows' and outbursts during the 1870s and 1880s.

In discussion of behaviour within his own two theatres, Michael Gunn mentioned the recent ban imposed on smoking and drinking in the auditoria, as such would 'lower the status of both actors and audiences'. Indeed, Gunn's evidence conveyed the impression of an overall improvement in audience behaviour, underpinned by better policing and the introduction of tighter rules on smoking and alcohol consumption during the performances. Instead, he insisted that it was the music-halls of Dublin, of which there were three in 1892, which now attracted the rougher and more unruly elements.[13]

In provincial terms, the hitherto unsubdued behaviour of theatre audiences had become more restrained by the later 1880s. The building of more grandiose playhouses, as in Derry in 1877 and Belfast in both 1881 and 1895, had attempted to lure a higher class of theatre-goer back to the drama. In common with the theatre-building boom in England, the plush surroundings of these new auditoria, complete with 'dress circle' and 'balcony stalls' had raised the tenor and status of theatre attendance.[14] However, these new approaches to the upper classes, particularly in Belfast where the Presbyterian ethos was strong, were not entirely successful. By April 1901, the Belfast theatre manager, Fred Warden, had written to the press, appealing to the 'artisans' of the city to return to patronise his new 'Grand Opera House' and 'Theatre Royale', which had been opulently designed by C.J. Phipps and Frank Matcham respectively, Attendances had fallen and both theatres were in severe financial difficulties. As inducements, admission prices had been lowered and the smoking ban had been reversed, in a bid to attract the former devotees – the 'pitties' and 'gods'. Critics replying to Warden's letter complained that he was reducing the two Belfast theatres to the level of music-hall. 'Anti-smoke' complained that the theatre would deteriorate into a 'low-class gaff' whilst 'Another Constant Theatre-goer' reminded the theatre manager that 'our friends in the Gods might straight away re-commence squirting tobacco juice at the "matinee hats" below'.[15]

These comments from theatre-goers, anticipating a return to the antics of the lively 'gods', confirm that theatre behaviour had improved considerably since the unbridled riotiousness of the 1850s and 1860s. Yet, in contrast with the more settled conditions in theatres elsewhere, examples of severe disorder did occur in Belfast theatres during the last two decades of the nineteenth century, albeit emanating mainly from political and religious rather than dramatic reasons. The increasingly heightened sectarian atmosphere in Ulster, following the highly-charged 1885 election and the first Home Rule crisis in 1886, found expression in the provincial theatres, where it was not uncommon for 'party cries' from opposing 'sides' of the audience to drown out the visiting companies. Plays by Irish dramatists, in particular, allowed sectarian tensions to find violent expression amongst the audience, with rivets and porter bottles being hurled from the Gods towards the stage of the 'Grand Opera House' in Belfast. Performances of Boucicault's play, 'The Shaughran', for example, which blends humour with sentimental patriotism, frequently aroused strong 'party' feelings amongst a mixed Belfast audience. By the early 1890s, a net had been installed at the edge of the stage to catch the missiles which rained down from the shipyard workers and factory workers, intent on making known their political objections to the dramas. By the close of the nineteenth century, this problem had been ameliorated with Catholics and Protestants establishing their own pattern of attending the city theatres on different nights.[16]

Politically motivated disturbances had also erupted in Derry in 1885. The visit of the Prince of Wales to the city on 25 April was the backdrop for a full scale riot in the 'New Royal Opera House', when large sections of the audience 'objected' to a particular scene in a pantomime which was considered a parody of Charles Stewart Parnell, the contemporary Catholic Nationalist leader. Given that political tensions were already raised in the city as a result of the Royal visit, the 'Opera House' incident was the climax of protests by the nationalist community against the reception and hospitality shown the Prince on his visit to Derry. The theatre riot lasted almost an hour, forcing the production to be abandoned in the hail of missiles, 'loud groans, hooting, vile language and cat-calls ... from the gallery'. After the initial taunts and jibes from above, the occupants of the 'pit' – who were mainly of the unionist persuasion – responded by singing the national anthem 'con amore' whilst the actors quickly vacated the stage and extinguished the footlights. A large wooden bench was then thrown from gallery to pit, followed by general panic as the lower reaches of the theatre were abandoned. The pro-Conservative *Londonderry Sentinel* described the incident as 'An Unrehearsed Scene' but implied that the riot had been carefully pre-planned 'with murderous intent' by the 'denizens of the Bogside'. In contrast, the *Derry Journal*, whilst condemning the riot, 'repeat[ed] emphatically ... there was cause'. This April 1885 riot had, in fact, been preceded by several theatre disturbances in Derry during the previous year, again mainly between pit and gallery and emanating from disputes over the playing of the National Anthem, during which nationalists had 'groaned and hooted'. Verbal and physical protests had also erupted a few months earlier when the occupants of the pit and upper circle (mainly Protestants) had 'hissed' during stage representations of 'Midnight Mass' and the 'Crypt of the Holy Sepulchre'.[17]

Disorder in Irish theatres deriving from politial circumstances was not a new phenomenon. The 'Bottle Row' incident in the Hawkins Street Theatre in 1822 was 'planned' as a protest against the presence of the Lord Lieutenant of Ireland at the Dublin theatre; the 1829 'Catholic Emancipation Theatre Riots' were amongst the more ferocious in Ireland's theatrical history.[18] But the spread and continuation of these disturbances into provincial theatres did mark a significant development in the raising of lower class political consciousness.

Concert Life and Audience Behaviour

The second half of the Victorian age was characterized by an expansion in concert life in Ireland and this brought in its wake changes in the patterns of audience attendance, participation and behaviour. Admission prices to concerts, which had been more than double the cost of theatre tickets during the 1830s, reduced suddenly during the mid 1850s, reaching 1s on average by the 1870s. This allowed a wider spectrum of the public to attend; the hitherto elitist nature of concert-going disintegrated with the advent of 'Popular' Saturday night concerts, 'ballad' concerts, 'at home' entertainments and operatic recitals by the numerous touring opera companies. The norm of 'evening dress' for provincial concerts had been all but abandoned by the later 1880s, with concerts attracting a wider spectrum of patrons, whose sometimes boisterous behaviour added a lively dimension to music-making. Irish audiences increasingly regarded concerts as an opportunity to express their delight, disgust or approbation with the musicians and the programmes presented. And, as in the theatre, there were precedents for this change in behaviour patterns, with concerts in Dublin during the mid 1820s having already attracted such disorderly behaviour that the upper gallery of a theatre was closed on concerts nights to exclude the rowdy 'inhabitants of the upper regions'.[19]

Provincial concerts had, however, remained largely sedate affairs until the later 1850s, with untempered enthusiasm rather than boisterousness attracting the notice of the press reviewers. At two concerts, for example, held in Derry in January 1855 in aid of the Crimean War 'Patriotic Fund', patrons stamped their feet, joined in choruses, demanded repeated encores and finally ended the evening's entertainment with a rendering of the national anthem, 'producing a loyal chorus of tremendous volume but questionable harmony'.[20] As in the theatre, the social aspect of concert-going was of significant importance, with members of the audience feeling free to smoke, chat and generally 'mingle' with one another whilst the performance was ongoing. Indeed, the unopposed use of tobacco remained a singular attraction of concert life, with 'smoking concerts' proving to be a popular attraction by 1900, whilst smoking was almost universally banned in Irish theatres. But a programme from a Belfast 'Anacreontic' concert in February1856, whilst tacitly acknowledging that ongoing conversation and social exchanges were acceptable at concert performances, requested that 'no gentlemen will stand up during the performance of the Music and that the Stewards be empowered to carry this request into effect'. Although this was a relatively minor offence in comparison with current theatre disorder, the concert stewards had been instructed by the committee members of the music society to enforce the ban vigorously.[21]

There were, however, certain stimuli which often provoked boisterous behaviour: the appearance of foreign musicians, the over-pricing of tickets and general dislike of the programmes on offer. And in contrast with their reticence regarding theatre behaviour, the press was forthright in condemning the 'young gods' who disrupted the opera performances and concerts in the provinces. Hissing, cat-calls and name-calling were a new phenomenon in concert life which the local press seemed anxious to eradicate, in contrast with their deliberate silence on the mayhem within the local provincial theatres. There were examples of unruly behaviour, for example, at a series of concerts organized and promoted by a German musician, Waldemar Malmene, in Derry between 1865 and 1868. Malmene was a prominent figure in the city's musical life throughout the 1860s, attracting frequent press mention by his concerts, teaching activities and his training of the local music society, 'The Londonderry Philharmonic Society'. But although the presence of German musicians was often a strong indicator of the growth of concert life in English cities, this was not the case in North-west Ulster where Malmene's concerts faced abusive language and jibes, missile throwing and overall mayhem from the occupants of the 'gods'.

At a concert in February 1865, in which Malmene was accompanied a young singer of German extraction, Miss Elizabeth Logier, the press reported that 'gods' en masse 'select[ed] Herr Malmene as an object for expressions of dislike ...We are not aware that he has done anything to warrant such a display'. Given that the disruptive jibes and comments halted the concert, the paper appealed for more 'courtesy towards this comparative stranger in our midst'. In the following years between 1863 and 1867, Malmene was subjected to criticism in letters to the press regarding his over-pricing of concert tickets and choice of programmes. Eventually, at a concert in February 1867, Malmene's rendition of a solo from Gounod's 'Faust' was greeted with 'mingled hissing and applause' whilst the local performers were applauded enthusiastically. Within ten months, he had announced that he was emigrating to America, leaving behind the prejudices and animosity of a provincial Irish concert audience.[22]

Conclusion

Malmene's concert experience in Derry may not have been wholly representative of provincial reception history during the second half of the nineteenth century. But it does serve to illustrate that relative disorder did impinge on the more elitist musical entertainments and was not wholly restricted to the theatre in the years between 1840 and 1900. The unruly behaviour of Irish theatre audiences did, of course, much in common with the contemporary experience in English theatres and music-halls at this time. As in England, the pattern of theatre design, in terms of the construction of theatres with 'deep pits and immense galleries', had increased the capacity of small city venues and increased the profitability levels for management.[23] The 'New Royal Opera House' in Derry, Ireland's second Opera House which was designed by C.J. Phipps, opened in August 1877, boasting a capacity of 1600 persons. The majority of these, however, were accommodated in the pit (twenty-two rows, holding 600-700) and the gallery (fourteen rows, holding 700) at the cheaper admission prices of 1s and 6d. This provincial theatre was modelled on the Gaiety Theatre in Dublin, which had an extra tier to accommodate yet more patrons.[24] Thus, although the character of theatre design was not a prime cause of disorder during the second half of the nineteenth century, it no doubt added considerably to the expression of the 'free and unbridled spirit of the inhabitants of the Gods'. Indeed, until the middle of the twentieth century, 'warm-up sessions' in the Gods prior to actual performances remained a perennial feature of entertainments in many theatres built during the Victorian age.[25]

Yet there were some differences between English and Irish audiences throughout the period. There was the increase in political expression and agitation in Irish theatres from the mid 1870s onwards, in addition to a marked 'Philistine tradition' towards theatre attendance in the northern Irish provincial towns. In 1900, for example, both 'sides' of the Belfast audience united to jeer Marie Lloyd off the stage of the 'Empire Theatre'. Miss Lloyd had already earned a reputation for a blend of 'innuendo and outraged innocence' in her stage representations, a trait not appreciated by the relatively 'puritan' Belfast audiences. Almost twenty years previously, in 1881, Sarah Bernhardt had suffered an identical fate when her appearance in a French play was considered offensive by Belfast playgoers. By the early 1890s, the combination of toughness and puritanism of Belfast audiences had earned the city theatres the reputation as difficult venues in which to 'play'. In common with her cross-channel shipbuilding neighbour, 'performers said if you could survive Belfast and Glasgow, you could survive anywhere'.[26]

Yet, by 1900, there were some theatre critics in Ireland who blamed England for the state of disorder and degradation within Irish theatres. Writing on English theatre audiences, Edward Martyn commented that 'It is here that decadence irrevocable and complete has set in', adding that ' the stage is degraded to a booth for the foolish exhibition of women'. In terms of Irish theatre audiences, he found 'an idealism founded on the ancient genius of the land', but nonetheless warned that there were those in England 'whose aim seems to be to create in Ireland a sort of shabby England'.[27] This portrait of a civilised theatre audience in Ireland at the close of the nineteenth century contrasts sharply with the ribald comments of an Irish theatre manager about his audience only fifty years previously:

> When Paddy feels his little sprig of shillelagh or blackthorn, affectionately enclosed within his fingers; at the first shout, he moves it mechanically a little, at the second he twirls it gracefully around his own head, and at the third it descends vigorously on the cranium of his neighbour. Take it from him, and he sinks into as peaceful and subdued individual as John Bull ...'[28]

Endnotes

[1] M. McLiammoir, *Theatre in Ireland* (Dublin: 1949), 44.

[2] Linenhall Library, Belfast. W.J. Lawrence, *'The Annals of the Old Belfast Stage'* (unpublished typescript: 1897), 393.

[3] W. Thackeray, *The Irish Sketchbook* (London: 1857), 310-11.

[4] *Londonderry Journal* 20 May 1823.

[5] *Londonderry Sentinel* 31 July 1830; *Londonderry Journal* 10 January 1866.

6 *Londonderry Sentinel* 13 November 1847; *Londonderry Journal* 7 and 28 June 1854.

[7] *Londonderry Sentinel* 2 August 1877.

[8] W.J. Lawrence, *The Life of Gustavus Vaughan Brooke* (Belfast: 1892), 98, 114, 138.

[9] Ibid., 245-249.

[10] *Belfast Newsletter* 23 December 1881; A.S. Moore, *Old Belfast* (Belfast: 1951), 16-17.

[11] 'Leaves From the Portfolio of a Manager- No.111: Of Theatrical Riots, Their Causes and Consequences', *Dublin University Magazine*, XXXVI (February 1851): 380-386.

[12] L. Gallagher, *The Grand Opera House Belfast* (Belfast: Blackstaff, 1995), 11.

[13] *Report from the Select Committee on Theatres and Places of Entertainment, together with Proceedings of Committee and Minutes of Evidence* (London: HMSO, 1892), IV, 232-237, 552.

[14] O. Byrne, *The Stage in Ulster From the Eighteenth Century* (Belfast: Linenhall Library, 1997), 17-19.

[15] *Belfast Newsletter* 26 and 27 April 1901.

[16] J. Gray, 'Culture and The Arts in Ulster Since 1891' in E. Phoenix, ed., *A Century of Irish Life: The Irish News and 100 Years of Ulster History 1890s-1990s* (Belfast: Blackstaff, 1995), 165.

128

[17] *Londonderry Sentinel* 28 April 1885, *Derry Journal* 29 April 1885.

[18] M.D. Condon, *The Dublin Theatre Riots of 1822 and Catholic Emancipation* (Ph.D. thesis, University of Southern California, 1950), 14-38.

[19] *Theatrical Observer* 28 June 1822. Ita M. Hogan, *Anglo-Irish Music 1780-1830* (Cork: 1966), 61-63.

[20] *Londonderry Journal* 31 January 1855; *Londonderry Standard* 1 February 1855

[21] The Linenhall Library, Belfast. *Programme of the Belfast Anacreontic Society Concert*, 21 February, 1856; *Derry Journal* 8 January 1900.

[22] *Londonderry Sentinel* 10 February 1865 and 22 February 1867; *Londonderry Journal* 25 January and 26 February 1868; C. Ehrlich, *The Music Profession in Britain since the Eighteenth Century* (Oxford: 1985), 62.

[23] V. Glasstone, *Victorian and Edwardian Theatres* (London: 1975), 78.

[24] *Irish Builder*, XIX no. 424 (15 August 1877): 245; *Londonderry Sentinel* 2 August 1877.

[25] L. Gallagher, *The Grand Opera House Belfast*, 17; *Londonderry Sentinel* 21 December 1894.

[26] C. Ehrlich and B. Walker, 'Entertainment and Entertainment: the Economic and Social Background' in B. Walker, ed., *Frank Matcham: Theatre Architect* (Belfast: Blackstaff, 1980), 28-29; L Gallagher, *The Grand Opera House Belfast*, 11.

[27] E. Martyn, 'A Comparison Between Irish and English Theatrical Audiences', *Beltaine*, No.2 (February, 1900): 12-13.

[28] 'Leaves from the Portfolio ...', *Dublin University Magazine*, XXXVII (February, 1851): 386.

The Pleasures of War: War and Popular Culture in Age of Victoria

Michael Paris
Department of History
University of Central Lancashire
Preston
Lancashire, PR1 2HE
m.paris@uclan.ac.uk

> With his rifle clubbed, Donald crushed the skull of one of
> [the Zulus], and was lifting it to repeat the stroke when the
> stock fell off, broken by the tremendous blow he had given.
> In an instant he snatched a stabbing assegai from the man he
> had just slain, and prepared to defend himself with it. Two
> Zulus rushed at him, but a bullet, fired by the man on his
> left, cut short the career of one of them. The other, with a
> spring, cleared the wall and lunged with his assegai. Donald
> had just time to spring aside, the weapon grazing his sleeve
> as it passed, and the next second he drove his assegai blade
> through his enemy's throat.[1]

This extract, from F.S. Brereton's tale of a young Briton at the Battle of
Rorke's Drift, written at the end of the nineteenth century, is typical of
the many war stories published in ever-increasing numbers from the
1880s for the enjoyment of boys and young men. *With Shield and
Assegai*, provides a useful example of the manner in which Victorian
authors transformed the brutality of battle into exciting and heroic
narratives for the pleasure of their readers. War stories such as these were
a major element in what can best be described as the 'pleasure culture of
war'; heroic representations of war, and which provided popular and
enthralling entertainment for many Victorians.[2]

The pleasures of war were disseminated through virtually every
channel of popular culture in formats that were appropriate for diverse
audiences. There was, for example, the verse of poets like Sir Francis
Doyle who proclaimed the gallant exploits of Britain's red-coated heroes
in the little wars of empire, and who's jingo rhymes almost certainly

inspired the young Rudyard Kipling to similarly focus attention on the common soldier. The poetry of war reached its climax in the anthologies glorifying the romance of past wars like W.E. Henley's *Lyra Heroica* (1897), or the imperial ideal of *The Imperial Reciter* by Sir Alfred Miles (1900). Readers could equally immerse themselves in the fantasy world of chivalric medieval warriors so powerfully evoked in the novels of Sir Walter Scott, particularly in *Ivanhoe* and *Quentin Durwood*; or in the adventures of Elizabethan heroes and their epic struggle against the tyranny of Spain, in Charles Kingsley's immensely popular *Westward Ho!* (1855). More serious-minded readers were catered for by the seemingly endless stream of soldiers' memoirs that were published throughout the century and which covered almost every one of the nation's conflicts, from the struggle against Napoleon to the war in South Africa. For the ever increasing numbers of new readers lower down the social scale, there were the anonymous war stories and garish images of battle published as penny- part novels, such as *For Valour: or, How I won the Victoria Cross* (1880) and *The King's Hussars* (1879); or the weekly story publications for boys and young men like *Boys of England* (1866) and the later Harmsworth Press papers like *Pluck* (1894) and *Boys' Friend* (1895).[3]

Throughout the century, military displays, parades and ceremonies held enormous fascination for a public anxious to be entertained by martial display. Even army manoeuvres were often conducted under the gaze of civilians looking for vicarious thrills from these 'war games'. As one commentator noted of the large scale manoeuvres at Cobham Camp in 1853, the spectacle proved, 'as popular [with the public] as the Great Exhibition'.[4] After 1859, British males were not just confined to watching these military spectacle but could actively take part and act out their martial fantasies as part-time soldiers in the Rifle Volunteers. Men from all social classes eagerly donned the often outlandishly flamboyant uniforms (usually purchased at the rifleman's own expense) of the Volunteers and basked in the reflected glory of Victoria's heroes with none of the discomfort or danger of the professional soldier. The Volunteers, of course, were initially created through fear of a French invasion, but while that crisis soon passed, the Volunteers, never mustering less than 200,000 men annually, remained active until the force was absorbed into the Territorial Army in 1908. Clearly, while few men were anxious to serve in the Regular Army, playing at war during evenings or at weekends was clearly a pleasurable pastime for a significant number of men throughout the remainder of the period.[5]

Theatrical managers, keen to exploit the public appetite for war-based entertainment, were quick to stage dramas reconstructing the latest wars or campaigns. In the 1850s, for example, productions based on the events of the Crimean War and the Indian Mutiny, such as *The Storming of the Malakoff and the Redan* (Manchester Belle Vue, 1855) or *The Capture of Delhi* (Astley's Theatre in Birmingham, 1858) proved highly successful with audiences, who cheered as plucky Britons defeated their Russian foes and ladies screamed in alarm, as barbarous sepoy mutineers were hurled from the battlements of a cardboard Delhi to meets their just deserts. Throughout the period, public entertainments, including dioramas and the spectacular open-air pyrodramas, taking war as their subject remained popular with the public. By the dawn of the new century, the cinema began to usurp the place of theatre as the main purveyor of the theatre of war, and by 1900, audiences were enthralled by short narrative films like *The Sneaky Boer* or *The Attack on the Red Cross Tent*, inspired by the contemporary drama of the Anglo-Boer War, and the brave deeds of British 'Tommies'.

From mid-century, newspapers and illustrated magazines featured a new style of reporting war, the work of a new breed of reporters, the war correspondents. The public, eager for war news, excitedly scanned the reports and battlefield illustrations of these 'specials' of the latest military adventures and deeds of daring. And while readers and correspondents alike appeared to agree that war was indeed a 'dreadful thing', in column after column, battles were described in the most romantic and inspiring terms for the reader. Bennet Burleigh's dispatch from the battlefield at Colenso was typical of such reports:

> It seemed impossible that anything could face and live in that fire ... Our indomitable soldiers walked erect and straight onward. Not Rome in her palmiest days ever possessed more devoted sons. As the gladiators marched proud and beaming to meet death, so the British soldiers doomed to die saluted, and then, and with alacrity, stepped forward to do their duty – glory or the grave.[6]

At home, such reports provided fascinating reading over the morning marmalade, and prompted the young and, at that time, cynical Rudyard Kipling to claim of the campaign to save General Gordon, that correspondents 'sweated and toiled' along with the soldiers for,

> it was above all things necessary that England at breakfast should be amused and thrilled and interested, whether Gordon lived or died, or half the British army went to pieces in the sand.[7]

The people 'have no arenas now', he later noted, but imperial wars provided a gory substitute, and war correspondent ministered to the 'blind, brutal, British public's bestial thirst for blood'.[8] Throughout the period, then, war and the exploits of the nation's warrior heroes provided exciting entertainment for the Victorian audience: a 'pleasure culture of war', which offered romantic escapist fictions through which ordinary citizens might temporarily forget the mundane routine of everyday life and indulge in heroic male fantasies.

That Victorians found war and the deeds of violent warrior heroes a source of pleasurable entertainment clearly needs explanation for it seems curiously at odds with the more common image of that rational, enlightened and civilized age. But, as Patricia Morton has pointed out, 'paradox was at the heart of Victorianism, both as a state of mind and a way of life in many ways rooted in sets of apparently contradictory attitudes'.[9] And no where is paradox more clearly visible than in the Victorian attitude to war. There was, on one hand, the pacifism of the liberal free traders, Cobden, Bright and the Manchester Movement, who opposed war and believed that commercial progress, international trade and common sense were sufficient to settle any dispute. On the other, there was the aggressive expansionism of Lord Palmerston or Charles Dilke, who appeared to believe that Britain had a divinely-sanctioned right to use unlimited violence in order to impress its rule on the lesser races of the world for the greater glory of the nation. While the enlightened attitudes of the former formed the rhetoric of official doctrine, it was in practice the latter that provided the basis for policy. And such policies were demonstrably reflected in the popular culture of the age, which justified and romanticised the act of war.

> The pleasure culture of war, however, was not a Victorian creation, but a legacy of the recent past. War, as Linda Colley has pointed out, was the midwife of national unity. The hundred years of warfare which ended with Waterloo was the period that witnessed the creation of the modern nation. Great Britain, was an invention forged above all by war. Time and time again, war with France brought Britons, whether they hailed from Wales or Scotland or England, into confrontation with an obviously hostile Other and encouraged them to define themselves collectively against it. They defined themselves as Protestants struggling for survival against the world's foremost Catholic power.[10]

A Protestant people under threat, then, was the bedrock on which national unity was founded, breaking down regional and sectarian barriers and creating a shared sense of destiny. And because for over a hundred years the 'Island Race' had successfully withstood the challenge of powerful Catholic enemies, there developed an almost mystic belief among many Britons that that in some way they had become the 'Chosen

People'; a shared belief that they had inherited the special relationship with God first experienced by Old Testament Israel.[11] The agent of this deliverance had been the sailor and the soldier who had not only saved the nation from alien domination but had also been responsible for enormous territorial gains, including Canada, the West Indies, Southern Africa and substantial parts of the Indian sub-continent, creating unrivalled opportunities for the commercial exploitation of this new empire. Yet, as Colley has noted, this was not the small and homogeneous empire that existed before the Seven Years War, but an empire no longer comprised of British emigrants, no longer predominantly Protestant or even Christian, but now including diverse 'heathen' races, most of whom had little liking for their new masters.[12] If commercial exploitation of this empire was the lifeblood of the British nation (and many contemporaries believed it to be so), then it was essential to hold that empire together and only military force could ensure its survival. The future would increasingly demand that what had been won by the sword would need to be held by the sword as well. The army now found its existence justified as the guardian of the nation's prestige and commercial prosperity and was feted as such.

It has often been suggested that the British public had little interest in war and the soldier until late in the nineteenth century. However, as Gillian Russell and others have shown, even the conflicts of the later eighteenth century were far from irrelevant to the common people but rather a focus of public interest.[13] The long-drawn out wars against Revolutionary and Napoleonic France were even more a source of national pride and victories were celebrated in songs, paintings, prints, poetry, statues and theatrical spectacle. This recurring imagery helped to sustain interest in war and created a more positive view of the army, as Geoffrey Best has noted, 'the common soldier and his trade were a bit better respected, not to mention better publicised, after the war than before it'.[14] Despite isolated incidents (Edward Spiers, for example, cites the cavalier treatment of the 30th. Regiment by the citizens of Ramsgate on its return from Waterloo), most soldier memoirs' record an enthusiastic welcome on their return from the wars, Sir George Bell was 'feted, feasted, and flattered' in Dublin and many of the rank and file testify to the same treatment.[15] While most praise was lavished on naval heroes, especially Nelson, attention was also paid to the exploits of the soldier particularly in the Peninsula campaign and at Waterloo. Waterloo Day was an annual celebration until mid-century and Wellington, Sir John Moore and others were acclaimed as national heroes, joining a succession of popular military icons that reached back to Marlborough, Clive and Wolfe. Memories of the war and of the soldier's role were maintained through a steady stream of veterans' diaries, memoirs, and autobiographies, many written by the rank and file, which found a ready market and which testify to a degree of public interest in the wars. Paintings commemorating the war and the military were, as Joan Hichberger has shown, never as popular in Britain as in France.[16] Nevertheless, there were numerous battle sketches, costume studies and cheap woodblock prints available from print sellers at the lower end of the art market and which indicate the popularity of heroic images glorifying the experience of battle. Plays, pageants and spectacles also reflected the public interest in battle and pride in the exploits of Wellington's Army. Even as late as 1824, Astley's Amphitheatre in Birmingham was playing J.H. Amherst's spectacular production 'The Battle of Waterloo', boasting a cast of over two hundred and elaborate and 'novel' effects. The century of warfare that ended with Waterloo thus created great interest in war and the exploits of military heroes. Even the rise of radicalism had little impact on the public appetite for the pleasures of war. As one officer noted in the early 1830s,

> The radical and leveling press ... has for years directed [its] fiercest attacks against the British army, but has not yet been able to destroy, or even weaken its popularity: the failure may seem strange to some but ... there is an honest manliness of feeling about the people of Britain that makes them delight in even the contemplation of deeds of hardihood and danger; and makes them proud of the unrivaled achievements of their sons, brothers and countrymen, as well as of the country that produced, and of the institutions that fostered such men....[17]

It was, however, in Victorian Britain that the pleasure culture of war became a major element in popular culture: in part a spontaneous celebration of the nation's military prowess but, more importantly, a reflection of the commitment to the expansion of empire, and widely disseminated by the new technical processes that made word and image easily accessible to all.

Following the development of the competitive international economic climate during the 1830s, war as an extension of foreign and imperial policy became far more acceptable. By 1860, for example, Palmerston was reflecting that 'trade ought not to be enforced by cannon balls, but on the other hand trade cannot flourish without security, and that security may often be unobtainable without the exhibition of physical force'.[18] But it was less a matter of a 'show of force', than a long-standing commitment to the use of military aggression to create trade 'opportunities' and enhance national prestige. A few examples will suffice to demonstrate how such policies operated. In India in 1838, the

Viceroy, Lord Auckland, fearful that upheavals in Afghanistan would unsettle the frontier regions, attempted to depose the legitimate ruler and install a puppet regime in Kabul backed by British troops. That the attempt misfired and resulted in the loss of a British army during the retreat from Kabul in 1842, does not detract from an inherently aggressive policy designed to secure northern India. Around the same time British policy towards China reveals even more clearly the willingness to resort to war to secure national advantage. China offered enormous potential for trade but the Chinese had little interest in what the British had to offer except perhaps opium. Relations with China eventually became so strained that in 1839 Palmerston ordered the blockade of the Chinese coast and the seizure of Hong Kong as a base for operations. When even this failed to achieve the desired result, the British resorted to war eventually forcing the Chinese to negotiate[19]. By the Treaty of Nanking (1842), the Chinese were forced to open their ports to British trade. While some Victorians expressed moral doubts about British policy in China, majority opinion, with quite staggering hypocrisy, saw the war as morally justified, fought not for sordid commercial gain, but to bring enlightenment to the heathen. A report in the *Illustrated London News* clearly expressed this view,

> The Chinese war was not a war of mighty prowess, it was not a war of trophy, vanity, and pride, but it was a great war for mankind. It opened the eyes of millions of human beings who were buried in the dark recesses of idolatry and unfurled the wings of commerce ... It shed the glorious gleam of Christianity upon an almost pagan world.[20]

While civilians might need to salve a tender conscience with such religious cant, soldiers were usually less circumspect. In 1843, before the conquest of the Sind, justified on the pretext of pacifying the region, the commander of the British forces, Sir Charles Napier, said: 'we have no right to seize Sind, yet we shall do so, and a very advantageous, humane, and useful piece of rascality it will be'. Napier believed, as did many others of his generation, that the 'great recipe for quieting a country is a good thrashing first and great kindness afterwards: the wildest chaps are thus tamed'.[21] Thrashing the Baluchis was ultimately for their own good, putting them under British rule and exposing them to the civilizing influence of Christian Britons! The Baluchis, incidentally were very soundly thrashed for Napier and his troops, in the General's own words, 'butchered over 6000' of them. Yet even Napier was unable to rid himself completely of contemporary hypocrisy for he was still able to consider his actions 'humane', when in reality, control of the Sind ensured that British interests in India were secured. Popular illustrations of these wars constantly emphasised the ferocious and 'outlandish' appearance of the enemy and reinforced ideas of their racial inferiority when compared with their 'civilized' conquerors, and the war became yet another glorious campaign to inspire the popular imagination. Nor was there any significant change in policy by the end of the period, and here we might cite the Zulu, Matabele or Anglo-Boer Wars. Clearly Victorian governments never really subscribed to their oft-repeated pacific policies; to believe that they did, as David French has pointed out, is to mistake the rhetoric of a handful of politicians like Cobden and the Manchester School for the reality of government, for most politicians 'were quite capable of pursuing simultaneously both what they conceived to be Britain's national interests and high moral principles'.[22] Thus for all their much vaunted humanitarian aims and peaceful commercial objectives, the Victorians inherited, accepted and considerably extended, an empire held together by force of arms. War, the legitimate use of state violence, was simply one means by which the British maintained their position in the world.[23] The pleasure culture of war did not simply reflect the realities of contemporary power politics, but made such policies acceptable to the nation at large, ensured future generations would be inculcated with the same attitudes and encouraged young men to emulate the martial deeds of their forefathers. As the popular novelist G.A. Henty noted in the preface to one of his many novels that promoted the 'romance' of war for young readers,

> The courage of our forefathers has created the greatest empire in the world around a small and in itself insignificant island; if this empire is ever lost, it will be by the cowardice of their descendents.[24]

The public's fascination with war and admiration for the warrior was, in large measure, made possible because after 1745 the nation's wars were fought on foreign fields; even the upheavals of the Revolutionary and Napoleonic wars were played out on a stage far removed from native shores. The population of Britain was thus spared the horrors visited upon the inhabitants of France, Spain and the other warring states, and this distancing from the reality of battle enabled them to enjoy the vicarious excitements of war without the hardship or danger. Real, but distant wars were thus little different from the exciting stories reconstructed on the stage or in the words of storytellers and ballad-mongers. For Victorians, war was simple 'theatre'. Yet the tendency of the nation to resort so easily to war, to employ state controlled violence for commercial gain, inevitably created a crisis of conscience for some Britons: how could these self-proclaimed champions of freedom, equate their role as imperial warlords with their professed claims of being peaceful traders? In part, this moral dilemma was never wholly resolved and was reflected in the pacifist movement – a diverse collection of individuals and associations that could unashamedly renounce war and aggression[25]. But such dissenters were always a minority, and subtle propaganda and appeals to patriotism could usually isolate them even more from the mainstream of political life. Most nineteenth century men (and women) could quote Evangelical nationalism and feelings of racial superiority and simply justify the increasing use of military force as 'necessary for the greater good'; as 'Heaven's Command' to spread Christianity and civilization. Bolstered during the later nineteenth century by a developing racist ideology and appeals to the biological necessity of war, it became increasingly easy to morally justify virtually any act of aggression on such grounds. And the acceptance of war had, undoubtedly, been made easier by the re-discovery of chivalry early in the century.

As Mark Girouard has explained, chivalry, the code of conduct evolved for medieval warriors, softened the barbarity of war by 'putting it into the hands of men committed to high standards of behaviour' and noble ideals,

> The ideal knight was brave, loyal, true to his word, courteous, generous and merciful. He defended the Church and wrongfully oppressed but respected and honoured his enemies in war, as long as they obeyed the same code he did.[26]

Chivalry, then, removed the most brutal elements of war by creating a strict moral code for the warrior – the generally accepted 'rules of war'. The nineteenth century interest in chivalry was, in large measure, due to the popular historical novels of Sir Walter Scott – particularly *Ivanhoe* (1820) and *Quentin Durwood* (1823), which helped shape the heroic chivalric stereotype. Scott himself was not blind to the less noble aspects of the middle ages, the fanaticism and superstition, for example; but while he saw chivalry as something of the past, other writers in their tales of the Crusades, translations of medieval romances and histories of chivalry, saw it as something vital and relevant for contemporary society. Chivalry gave women an honourable place in society (while of course defining them as weak and in need of protection), provided an education for young men calculated to imbue them with physical strength, bravery, grace, courtesy and respect for women but, above all, it dignified the conduct of war, essential for a 'civilized' society in an 'enlightened' age.[27] The most important of the didactic works on chivalry was Kenholm Digby's *The Broad Stone of Honour*, published in 1822. Digby's book, subtitled *Rules for the Gentlemen of England*, provided, through historical example, guidance for the conduct of gentlemen who, in accepting the privileges of such an estate incurs an obligation to both to self and nation.[28]

In the 1820s, interest in chivalry was limited to the social elites but was soon taken up by middle-class journalists and novelists and its values were disseminated throughout society. Indeed, at a time of rapid change and social instability it is not difficult to see the nostalgic appeal for a more ordered period, a time when kingship and the church were unquestioned and when all knew and accepted their place in the scheme of things. The chivalric code was later adopted by Charles Kingsley (a self-proclaimed 'joyous Knight-errant of God') and Thomas Hughes and would provide the underpinning for the cult of 'Muscular Christianity' – the cornerstone of reformed public school education.[29] Chivalry appealed to a diverse audience from Prince Albert to the radical William Morris and the pre-Raphaelite Brotherhood (whose paintings would disseminate an idealised and romantic reconstruction of the medieval world); and to churchmen, teachers and the aspiring middle classes. It was interpreted as the guide for behaviour of a 'true gentlemen' and was appropriate for civilian life. Scott and the other exponents of chivalry created, as Martin Green has perceptively argued, romantic day dreams and illusions, an alternative to the 'banks, counting houses and trading companies most readers saw as contemporary reality'.[30] But what is relevant here is that above all chivalry was the way of the warrior – a para-military code of conquest and inherently aggressive.[31] And Digby clearly stresses the connection. In the section of his book which explores honourable professions for those who wish to conduct themselves according to the chivalric code, the army, a 'noble calling', featured strongly.

> The great advantage of the profession of arms, is its practical influence, the effect which it produces upon the character; and this, you will remember, is the criterion by which we should judge of all professions and modes of employment. The soldier is religious and brave, humane and merciful, open-hearted and just, frank, sincere, faithful and firm ...The lamb and flag were borne by the knight templers, to signify the union of these qualities, of gentleness with the martial spirit.[32]

Who, then, better possessed these qualities than the new crusader for empire – the imperial warrior hero? As Jeffrey Richards has explained, the 'chivalric ideal was deliberately promoted by key figures of the age in order to produce a ruling elite for the nation and for the expanding empire who would be inspired by noble and selfless values',[33] including, we might add, the martial spirit. Most Victorian gentlemen, of course, saw little attraction in a military career but heroic images of chivalric warriors offered a pleasing and exciting fantasy, an antidote to the tedium of everyday life, an idealised image of masculinity and softened the barbarity of war.

The army itself was, as we have seen, suggested very much a 'theatrical' institution: uniforms, manoeuvres, flags and stirring music were all part of a spectacle designed to arouse the soldier to courageous acts and intimidate the enemy,[34] but at home, such activities were regarded by the people as entertainment and were enormously popular. It was but a short step, then, from the public enjoyment of this kind of military spectacle to that of enjoying the entertainment of war – it was, after all, just another military spectacle and vitally important to the continued prosperity of the nation! In 1845, the radical journalist Douglas Jerrold pointed to the dangers of portraying the brutality of war as theatre,

> When nations ... cut each others throats ... we must have red
> coats and muskets and sabres; but seeing how that the duty
> of their bearers squares neither with our innate good sense,
> nor our notions of what ought to be – we are fain to gild the
> matter over- to try to conceal, from ourselves, the butchering
> nature of the business we are sometimes forced to undertake,
> and so spring up military spectacle-military finery-military
> music ... Clothe war therefore in gayer colours than peace ...
> let the steel which cuts glitter like valued gems; the
> evolutions which destroy, be graceful as the motions of
> dancing girls.[35]

The pleasure culture of war reflected the national interest in war but, by representing it as exciting and romantic spectacle, distanced the public from its brutality and provided a forum through which the moral uncertainties over the use of violence could be partially resolved: battles were fought far away; were never unjust but fought for high moral purpose by chivalric volunteers who performed their killing function according to the well-defined rules of war, and of course most casualties were always to be found among the Other – the uncivilized and outlandish foreigner.

However, wars of empire were not the only inspiration for the pleasure culture of war, for starting in the 1870s authors began to speculate on the horrors of future warfare, especially the great European war which many believed to be inevitable given the increasing tension between the Great Powers. Beginning with George Chesney's story, *The Battle of Dorking*,[36] dealing with an imaginary invasion of Britain by the Prussians, the nation's appetite for such dire fictions continually expanded, and by the 1890s had even invaded boys' story papers like

Pluck and *Boy's Friend*.[37] Young Britons, constantly exposed to such to such tales, could hardly fail to absorb the idea that the nation was poised on the brink of disaster; that a major war was inevitable. Such a belief, combined with constant exposure to a pleasure culture that taught them that war was little more than a romantic escapade, proved a lethal combination in August 1914. As Robert Roberts has explained,

> For nearly half a century before 1914 the newly literate millions were provided with an increasing flow of fiction based on war and the idea of its imminence ... Popular fiction and mass journalism now combined to condition the minds of the nation's new readers to a degree never possible before the advent of general literacy. In France and Germany, too, writings in the genre were equally successful in stimulating romantic conceptions about the carnage to come. When the final cataclysm did arrive, response to such ideas set the masses cheering wildly through the capitals of Europe. 'Der Tag'! – 'The Day – was hear at last'! They could hardly wait.[38]

August 1914 was simply the fufilment of the expectation of war; it was what young men had been prepared for, and they rejoiced in the opportunity to take part in the 'great adventure'.

Endnotes

[1] Captain F.S. Brereton, *With Shield and Assegai: A Tale of the Zulu War* (London: Blackie, 1900), 151-52.
[2] The idea of the 'pleasure culture of war' was suggested by the work of Graham Dawson, see, *Soldier Heroes: British Adventure, Empire and the Imagining of Masculinity* (London: Routledge, 1994).
[3] On the development of the literature of war see, Michael Paris, *Warrior Nation: Images of War in British Popular Culture, 1850-2000* (London: Reaktion, 2000).
[4] General Sir Henry Hardinge to Lord Seaton, 16 June 1853, quoted in, Scott Hughes Myerly, *British Military Spectacle*, Cambridge, Mass: Harvard University Press, 1996), 151.
[5] On the Volunteers see, Hugh Cunningham, *The Volunteer Force* (Hamden, Conn: Archon, 1975); Ian F.W. Beckett, *Riflemen Form: A Study of the Rifle Volunteer Movement, 1859-1908* (Aldershot: Ogilby Trusts, 1980).
[6] Quoted in Roger T. Stearn, 'War Correspondents and Colonial War, c.1870-1900', in John Mackenzie, ed., *Popular Imperialism and the Military, 1850-1950* (Manchester: Manchester University Press, 1992), 148.
[7] Rudyard Kipling, *The Light that Failed* (London: Macmillan, 1891), 19.
[8] Ibid, 48.
[9] Patricia Morton, 'Another Victorian Paradox: Anti-Militarism in a Jingoistic Society', *Historical Reflections*, V: 8 (1981): 169.

[10] Linda Colley, *Britons: Forging the Nation, 1707-1837* (London: Vintage, 1996), 5.

[11] John Wolffe, 'Evangelicalism in Mid-Nineteenth Century England', in Raphael Samuel, ed., *Patriotism: The Making and Unmaking of British National Identity*, Vol. 1, (London: Routledge, 1989), 189.

[12] Colley, *Britons*, 109.

[13] See Gillian Russell, *Theatres of War: Performance, Politics and Society, 1793-1815* (Oxford: Oxford University Press, 1995); Myerly, *British Military Spectacle*.

[14] Geoffrey Best, *War and Society in Revolutionary Europe, 1770-1870* (Leicester: Leicester University Press, 1982), 199.

[15] Edward M. Spiers, *The Army and Society, 1815-1914* (London: Longman, 1980), 73. See also, B.H. Liddell Hart, ed., *The Letters of Private Wheeler, 1809-1828* (London: Michael Joseph, 1951); John Greene, *Vicissitudes of a Soldier's Life* (Louth: Morton, 1827) and William Surtees, *Twenty Five Years in the Rifle Brigade* (Edinburgh: R. Martin, 1833).

[16] J.M.W. Hichberger, *Images of the Army: The Military in British Art, 1815-1914* (Manchester: Manchester University Press, 1988), 13.

[17] 'JM', *Fragments from the Portfolio of a Field Officer* (1831), quoted in, Myerly, *British Military Spectacle*, 151.

[18] Quoted in Bernard Porter, *The Lion's Share: A Short History of British Imperialism, 185 -1983* (London: Longman, 1984), 11.

[19] For a short account of the conflict see, Byron Farwell, *Queen Victoria's Little Wars* (New York: Norton, 1985), 12-22; David French, *The British Way in Warfare, 1688-2000* (London: Unwin Hyman, 1990), 126-128.

[20] *Illustrated London News*, 18 February 1843.

[21] Quoted in Farwell, *Queen Victoria's Little Wars*, 27.

[22] French, *British Way in Warfare*, 121.

[23] Interestingly, the British use of war as an extension of diplomacy existed long before Karl von Clausewitz's famous treatise, *On War*, was translated into English. See, Michael Howard, *Clausewitz* (Oxford: Oxford University Press, 1983).

[24] G.A. Henty, *St. George for England*, 5. Quoted in Jeffrey Richards, 'Popular Imperialism and the Image of the Army in Juvenile Literature', in Mackenzie, *Popular Imperialism and the Military*, 89.

[25] For Cobden's views on war see, Daniel Pick, *War Machine: The Rationalisation of Slaughter in the Modern Age* (London: Harvard University Press, 1993).

[26] Mark Girouard, *Return to Camelot: Chivalry and the English Gentleman* (London: Yale University Press, 1981), 16.

[27] Ibid, 33.

[28] Kenholm Digby, *The Broad Stone of Honour* (London: C. & J. Rivington, 1822), 2-3.

[29] On the public schools and chivalry see, Jeffrey Richards, *Happiest Days: The Public Schools in English Fiction* (Manchester: Manchester University Press, 1988).

[30] Martin Green, *Dreams of Adventure, Deeds of Empire* (London: Routledge, Kegan & Paul, 1979), 98.

[31] Harold Perkin, *The Origins .of Modern English Society* (London: Routledge & Kegan Paul, 1972), 274.

[32] Digby, *Broad Stone of Honour*, 487.

[33] Jeffrey Richards, 'Popular Imperialism', 87.

[34] Myerly, *British Military Spectacle*, 8-9.

[35] Douglas Jerrold, *The Shilling Magazine* (1845), quoted in ibid, 151

[36] On the fictions of future war see, I.F. Clarke, *Voices Prophesying War: Future Wars, 1763-3749* (Oxford: Oxford University Press, 1992).

[37] See, Paris, *Warrior Nation,* chapter four.

[38] Robert Roberts, *The Classic Slum: Salford Life in the First Quarter of the Century* (London: Penguin, 1990), 179-180.

Dandy rats at play: the Liverpudlian middle classes and horse racing in the nineteenth century

John Pinfold
Rhodes House Library
South Parks Road
Oxford, OX1 3RG
john.pinfold@rhodes-house-library.oxford.ac.uk

In his pioneering history of horse racing Wray Vamplew stated that 'There is no hard evidence that the middle class attended race meetings. Certainly the respectable middle class would not go racing'.[1] More recent work by Mike Huggins has challenged this view,[2] and this paper seeks to throw further light on this question by looking at the involvement in racing and betting of the Victorian middle classes in Liverpool. It will also consider whether the ostensibly 'respectable' middle classes may in reality have been indulging in some decidedly unrespectable activities in their leisure time.

'Salford lads, Manchester men, Liverpool gentlemen'. This sardonic phrase, more often employed outside Liverpool than within it, nevertheless expresses an important truth, that Liverpool, although containing many industries within its boundaries, was not primarily an industrial, but rather a commercial centre, where trade rather than manufacturing was king, and merchants formed the local elite. B.G. Orchard, who compiled an extensive biographical dictionary of Liverpool's merchants, wrote that he regarded a merchant 'as a benefactor to humanity', and added that 'creators of wealth, unrefined though they often are, deserve more honour than do those who, inheriting what others amassed, become their superiors in general knowledge, refinement and grace'.[3]

This unrefinement, characteristically ascribed to newly rich, self-made men, was what struck many observers of Liverpool's wealthy middle classes. In his novel *Perversion*, the Rev. William John Conybeare drew a deliberately crude picture of one merchant family: the women are vulgar snobs, whilst the men were 'thoroughly well-informed on all that concerned their business, but indifferent to more general topics: evidently absorbed heart and soul in the one great object of making money'.[4] The Liverpool merchants were also known as heavy drinkers. As Samuel Smith, himself a cotton merchant (and temperance reformer), memorably commented 'As Ephesus was said to be a worshipper of the great goddess Diana, it might be said that Liverpool was a worshipper of the great goddess Beer'.[5]

The nature of the trades in which the Liverpool merchants were engaged involved a good deal of speculation, and the connection between the cotton trade in particular and gambling was one that was often made at the time. The Liverpool journal *Porcupine* regularly ran articles on 'Cotton gambling'; in one of these, a satirical piece entitled 'Mr. Porcupine Abolishes Betting', it was reported that on the Exchange floor could be found 'betting, booking and gambling of all descriptions', and that there were busloads of merchants princes 'who had been discovered in the act of arranging bets'.[6]

The merchant princes constituted Liverpool's elite, but the middle classes were much more broadly based. In particular, the commercial nature of Liverpool's businesses meant that the city provided employment for as many as 17,400 clerks.[7] Some of these were well-off and lived in substantial houses in the affluent suburbs of Aigburth or New Brighton, others were barely able to scrape a living, but there appears to have been a feeling in Liverpool that 'a clerk is a gentleman and an artisan is not', and it was reported that 'commercial clerkship is to the middle classes what the Church is to the aristocracy, a refuge for sons who are capable of nothing else'.[8] Nevertheless, the merchants tended not to recognise their clerks as gentlemen, even though, such was the self-made nature of Liverpool society, many of them had started out as clerks themselves.[9]

The consequence was that the term 'gentleman', as used in Liverpool, meant something different to what it may have meant elsewhere. The Liverpool crusading journalist Hugh Shimmin answered the question 'What is a gentleman?' thus: 'all one can be sure of is this, that a man who is called so occupies a certain social position, and has done nothing glaringly opposed to the rules that govern society, his moral qualifications are not necessarily known anything of'.[10]

The newly rich merchants of Liverpool were keen to enhance their social standing and one way in which they could do this was through involvement in hunting and other equestrian sports, which might bring them more into contact with County society. This form of social climbing is expressed most clearly in a series of verses called *The Lays of Cotton Broking*, which were written by Edward Bradyll, himself a cotton broker, and published in 1865:

> And many a man who first began
> With scarce a coat to his back,

Now thought it the thing, that Cotton was king,
To become a sporting crack.

There was many a one in the hunting field
Who didn't know how to ride,
And was told by the plough-boy urchins there
He had better get inside!

To don a scarlet coat, and go
To the meet, became him well;
He loved to be seen in the collar green,
Like a Cheshire County Swell!

And a man who hadn't a seat at all,
Now thought it a matter of pride
To ride full tilt at a six foot wall,
With a ditch on either side.[11]

This view was echoed later in the century by Orchard, who noted that the Liverpudlian middle classes, unlike their contemporaries in Manchester, had 'a widespread fondness for field sports which has led them ... to keep horses in the country'. The upward social mobility that this brought them, he thought, made them 'less influential in giving a high tone to local sentiment'. Moreover, even amongst the Liverpool merchant classes, there were 'some very black sheep in the flock', who included 'gamblers, profligates [and] infatuated lovers of sport'. There were, for example 'many young fellows, men of means, who ... devote themselves to the lower forms of sport – wild riding, rat-killing, hard-drinking, fisticuffs between others for pay, or amongst themselves for amusement, every distraction which may seem not unnatural and is excused among sporting miners, prosperous grooms, and others of the lower class which lives by gambling or the turf'.[12] Nor was this interest in the turf confined to those at the top or bottom of society, for even amongst the clerks, most of whom aspired towards respectability, there were those who 'while at the desk talk of the Star Music Hall or the coming race'.[13]

Although Liverpool races can be traced back to the late 16th century, they had fallen into abeyance after 1786, and the 19th century interest in racing in the city can be dated from the late 1820s, when the traditional summer meeting was revived first by John Formby on a course at Maghull, and then by William Lynn at Aintree.[14] Immediately popular, within ten years it was reported that racing had 'decidedly hit the taste of a vast number of Liverpudlians'.[15] Crowds as big as 40,000 were reported, and by this time Lynn was staging four meetings a year, including the July Summer meeting, which had rapidly developed into one of the premier fixtures in the Racing Calendar, and the Liverpool Grand Steeplechase which, as the Grand National, became the most important steeplechase of the year. And although Aintree has understandably attracted the most attention from turf historians, it should also be remembered that in the nineteenth century there were many other meetings within a twenty mile radius of the city centre: these included not just the long-established and prestigious meeting at Chester, but also now long-forgotten meetings at such places as Old Roan, Ormskirk, Croston and Southport to the north, and at Rock Ferry, Storeton, Parkgate and Hoylake over the water on the Wirral.[16] As early as the 1820s Liverpool had its own sporting paper, *Bethell's Life in London and Liverpool Sporting Register*, which covered pugilism as well as racing, and later in the century the city supported a twice-daily racing paper, the *City Racing Record*.[17]

It is clear from the newspaper reports of the time that the middle classes attended the races at Aintree in large numbers. In 1836, for example, at the first running of the Grand Steeplechase, it was noted that 'the assemblage was composed principally of the middle classes',[18] and three years later, amongst the great crowd which witnessed Lottery's victory and the christening of Becher's Brook, were 'merchants and wealthy manufacturers'.[19] F.C. Turner's picture of this event shows that many of the crowd had travelled out to the races in their own carriages, a long line of which can be seen stretching all the way from the grand stand to the Sefton Arms, and this suggests that many of the crowd were wealthy enough to be have their own transport, and also perhaps that many of them had gone as groups of family or friends.

Later, in the mid-1850s, Hugh Shimmin gave a graphic description of the crowd at the Summer meeting:

> Here are earls, viscounts, noble lords, honourable captains, gallant admirals, members of Parliament, magistrates, aldermen, town councillors, merchants, brokers, publicans, business men of every grade, and many men of questionable character ... Many of the men have, as magistrates, presided at county sessions lately; others have spoken at public meetings on the duty of making earnest efforts to purify and regenerate society. Several have been found on platforms, supporting, either by their presence, purse, or advocacy, missions to the benighted heathen, the Additional Curates', the Pastoral Aid, or Home Church Building Societies; and some of them will no doubt, if they succeed today, stand an

extra dozen of champagne in the evening, or make a very handsome donation to some religious or benevolent association.[20]

This comment is interesting in suggesting that the race course was a place where normally respectable people could let off steam and behave quite differently to how they might have done at home or at work. Going to the races was a day out, and, like the seaside, it was a place where different rules applied. Nor was this necessarily a bad thing, for even Shimmin, who was no friend of horse racing, had to admit that out in the centre of the course one could see 'what a neat style of pic-nic can be done. How speedily bottles can be opened and emptied, and how pleasant and affable even Liverpool merchant princes may become under the influence of good air and healthy appetite'.[21]

If this was true of Aintree, it was even more so at the smaller meetings which took place in the environs of the city. The Croxteth Hunt meeting which took place in April 1870 at Halewood was attended by 'the elite of Liverpool', many of whom had travelled out in family carriages or omnibuses hired for the occasion. On arrival at the course 'Pic-nic fashion the carriage people drew forth from safe recesses portly hampers containing all the delicacies of the period'. In between races they were entertained by music provided by a German band, and there were also shooting and archery stands, height and weight machines and a photographic tent to tempt the racegoers. Yet even at small meeting such as this, which seems more akin to a modern day point-to-point meeting, there were other less respectable temptations on offer in the form of thimble riggers and card swindlers.[22]

At Aintree there was all this and more, much of it of a decidedly unrespectable nature. First of all there was alcohol. This of course was true of all race meetings, but there is some evidence to show that there was more drinking at Aintree than elsewhere. One journalist who attended the 1870 Grand National, for example, thought that the crowd differed from that at all other sporting gatherings, and that one of its distinguishing features was the openly expressed desire for 'a big drink afterwards'.[23] That this was something that was common to all classes is clear from Shimmin's account where he reports that after racing 'In the booths dancing is general, and men half and wholly drunk stagger about in all directions', and that the police had their work cut out 'in keeping the respectable people within bounds for drink is now telling on all'.[24]

Secondly, there was sex. On race days the roads out to Aintree were crowded with 'coaches filled with harlots'. Shimmin gave a graphic description of the scene as follows:

At every coach you see well dressed men dancing attendance on these women ... Cards have been distributed amongst the fashionable and sporting gentlemen during the morning, and in imitation of the cards of the horses these ladies' cards have written on them the colours in which their owners will appear, and are in this style – 'Matilda, primrose and pale blue', 'Fanny, pink and French white', 'Sarah, white and green', 'Jemima, pink and blue', &c., &c., the colours corresponding with the bonnets and dresses. The great event being over, lazy-looking and fashionably attired men cross the course and enter the ploughed gallop, drawing from their pockets the cards they have received in order that they more easily distinguish their favourites. The girls, flushed with wine, waited on by bullies and pimps, watched keenly by their keepers, who are hovering about, are thus decorated to captivate the turfites.

Nearer the grand stand was a tent with 'a very aristocratic title' over the entrance, which was specifically intended for 'respectable people', yet here too the behaviour was less than respectable:

> Young girls and women are here – their faces daubed with paint, their persons profusely adorned with highly coloured dresses. They pass the time in drinking, laughing and giggling with men – with merchants who on the Exchange and at home pass for gentlemen.

This tent was run by a 'notorious brothel-keeper'. Shimmin watched a young man sip wine with this 'bloated and brazen-faced hussey' and commented:

> And active as this young man may be on the Exchange in the morning, when cotton is on the carpet, leering and simpering as he is now, he will in all probability meet his mother and sisters in the evening without a blush.[25]

Thirdly, of course, there was betting, which to many people was an even greater sin than drink or prostitution. It was, however, one of the principal reasons for going racing: 'it cannot be anything else for the throng is so great that the racing cannot be seen by one in twenty of those upon the course, and thousands do not take the trouble to clear out the tents to witness the running'. At Aintree the main betting ring was situated in front of the grand stand, and one needed stand tickets to gain entry to it. Here were situated the 'professional betting men of the higher class',[26] who serviced the 'crowd of well-dressed men in the ring'.[27]

Lower class bookmakers who served the poorer sections of the crowd were situated in a double row outside this privileged enclosure.

Nor was horse racing the only medium for betting at Aintree. There was cock fighting, pugilism, archery and a whole host of sideshows offering gambling games of all descriptions. Many of these survived on the racecourse long after they had been made illegal. Cock fighting, for instance, although outlawed in 1849, continued to take place at Aintree for many years afterwards. In 1875 the police raided a building on the course where they found 'a large number of dead fowls', about thirty live ones, and sets of weights and scales. In all about one hundred people were thought to have been present, including some who occupied 'high positions in society', and the fact that the owners were said to have bet as much as £3,000 on the match suggests that it was supported from a wider cross-section of society than the list of defendants implies.[28]

Women, and especially middle class women, are even less visible in the sources than middle class men, and to read some accounts one might think that the only women to attend the races were loose women or prostitutes. At the Summer meeting in 1862 it was even reported that 'the will to be riotous displayed itself more on the part of the women than the men'.[29] This comment was probably directed at young working class women, who, like their male counterparts, were well-known for their uninhibited behaviour at the fair which accompanied the race meeting.[30] Yet there is much evidence to show that at Aintree many middle class women did attend the races, and were encouraged to do so by the racecourse management. When Aintree opened in 1829, for example, the new grand stand included a spacious withdrawing room specifically designed 'for the accommodation of ladies',[31] and at the inaugural meeting that July it was noted that the balcony was crowded with 'ladies, attired in all the dazzling variety of the present fashions'.[32] Similarly, when the first steeplechase was run at Aintree seven years later it was again reported that 'ladies and gentlemen appeared in great numbers from various parts of the country', with the lower part of the grand stand filled with 'elegantly dressed females';[33] and later in the century, when 'Wizard' Topham controlled the course he expressed a desire to attract more 'Liverpool ladies' to attend the races.[34]

What proportion of the crowd was composed of women is virtually impossible to say, although there are some clues to be found in the various engravings that were published of early Grand Nationals. Some of these depict sections of the crowd in quite considerable detail and from these a few tentative conclusions can be drawn. F.C. Turner's view of the grand stand at the 1839 Grand National, for example, shows 14 women and 56 men standing at the front of the balcony. This can be compared to a similar view by G.H. Laporte done at the 1853 Grand National which shows 11 women and 138 men on the same balcony. A rather different view taken at the 1845 Grand National and published in the *Sportsman's Magazine* shows a section of the crowd in the centre of the course opposite the winning post; here there are two women in a coach who from their dress can clearly be identified as prostitutes, but there are also eight soberly dressed women in plain bonnets and seventeen men. This picture is also interesting in showing two well-dressed and clearly middle class children. Another view of the same race shows 16 women in a crowd of rather more than 100 men. Clearly it would be unwise to be too dogmatic in the conclusions one draws from so small a sample as this, but I think it is not unreasonable to state that these pictures reinforce the view that middle class women did attend Aintree, and that they may have formed something between 10% and 20% of the crowd; or, as the *Daily Post* reporter at the Croxteth Hunt meeting put it, there was 'always ... a sociable representation of the fair sex'.[35] Unsurprisingly, many of the ladies used the races as an opportunity for flirtation. And sometimes much more than flirtation took place. A little-known ballad, entitled *The Liverpool Races*, and written at the time of the first meeting at Maghull in 1827 ends as follows:

> And a thousand or more I could name,
> Who are all in the like kind of cases.
> They've started and think it no shame,
> To catch sweethearts at Liverpool Races.
> And when next April comes round,
> What lots of sweet innocent faces
> Will then come to light and be found
> Three months old at next Liverpool Races.[36]

Did women bet at the races? In 1872 Topham planned to move the betting ring so that the 'Liverpool ladies' he planned to attract to the course would be less offended by the 'noisy Welchers', as he privately termed the bookmakers.[37] Of course, this would not have prevented women from asking their husbands or chaperones to put on their bets for them, but there is also some evidence that they did bet directly. They were certainly known to speculate on the Cotton Exchange on their own account, as a further extract from *The Lays of Cotton Broking* shows:

> That lady there, so neatly dressed,
> To em-bon-point inclined,-
> Let us follow her in, she has lots of tin,
> And hear a bit of her mind.
>
> Having seated herself by the Broker,
> At the subject she went with a dash,-

> I have come for a fresh spec in Cotton,
> I'm expecting a little spare cash:
>
> ...
>
> The Broker was sadly distressed,
> What was the poor beggar to do?
> It must be confessed she was charmingly dressed,-
> So he booked her a hundred or two!'[38]

The Maybrick case, discussed below, presents convincing evidence of middle class women betting on horses as well as cotton. Occasionally, there is also evidence from the courts of women betting, as in this instance from the Liverpool County Sessions House, which occurred after the 1897 Grand National, when:

> a very determined looking female charged a stylishly dressed young man with swindling her out of 1s 6d, to which extent she had backed Manifesto in the Grand National. After apologising for the insignificance of the bet, the lady went on to relate that how, after Manifesto came in, the prisoner gave strong indications of a desire to 'go out'. 'Then', said the witness, 'he ran away. I went with him he asked me to mind the board. 'No', says I, 'I'll mind you, where you go I go'. The prisoner stoutly denied the charge, and accused the witness of a want of veracity, but this nineteenth century Ruth only smiled, and winked a knowing wink at the policeman standing by. The prisoner was sent to gaol for a month.[39]

Given the connection between the cotton trade and gambling, it should not come as a surprise to learn that on the Exchange Floor 'the odds on sporting events are quoted quite as often as the prices of produce',[40] or that there was a considerable amount of off-course betting in Liverpool. Hugh Shimmin wrote in 1857 that 'Betting houses in Liverpool are more numerous than is generally supposed, and less respectable than the proprietors would wish the public to believe'.[41] Shimmin's writings provide a vivid description of some of these establishments and make it clear that people from 'every class in life' could be found in them, including, on a typical day, 'broken-down merchants, clerks, foundrymen, one convicted dog-stealer, a 'gent' said to be worth a 'plum, in the shape of £20,000, cartowners, brewers and their draymen, counter-skippers, billiard players [and] the fellow who 'does the music on his cheeks' for coppers in the low houses about the docks'.[42]

Betting off-course was illegal after the passing of the Act for the Suppression of Betting Houses in 1853, but despite this there is ample evidence that in Liverpool the magistrates and the Watch Committee were reluctant to use their new powers, and that betting houses continued to exist for many years afterwards, tobacconists and stationery shops often acting as fronts for the bookmakers.[43] At least one music hall (a 'free and easy') was also used as a 'betting meet', which was frequented by gentlemen 'of education and intelligence'.[44] By the 1870s, however, most off-course betting, at least during the daytime, was taking place on the streets. The centre for this activity was Williamson Square, which was 'crowded daily with the betting rabble of the town'. These included 'several young men, sons of highly-respected parents', and middle class involvement in off-course betting was shown even more clearly by the fact that 'regular messengers are despatched almost daily during the season from select coteries around "the Flags" to "put the money on" in and around "the Square"'. So important was this trade to the bookmakers that some of them even set up stall on the Exchange Flags themselves, without fear of being molested by the police or the magistrates, who seem to have turned a blind eye to their activities in the city's commercial heartland;[45] at the Watch Committee 'if any ugly subjects, such as this, occasionally crop up, they are quietly and speedily smothered or ushered out by certain eminently respectable officials' and 'strangled with red-tape'.[46]

Nevertheless, in November 1877 a number of the bookmakers were prosecuted for obstructing the streets around Williamson Square. The case was heard before Liverpool's Stipendiary Magistrate, Thomas Stamford Raffles, who, whilst finding against the bookmakers, made the helpful suggestion that 'If they took a club belonging to themselves it would be all right enough'.[47] The bookmakers took the hint and by 1887 over twenty sporting clubs had been established in the city.[48] The first of these was the Top Club which was opened by a bookmaker called Ben Hughes, but by 1879 this had been forced out of business by the Waterloo. The Waterloo's premises were in Brooks Alley, off Church Street, and it seems always to have been the busiest of the clubs, as well as appealing to sporting gentlemen of all classes. It had a 'congenial and aristocratic' atmosphere, and it was said that if a raid was made on it by the police 'the extent and variety of the capture would considerably astound the public; and many men well known in Liverpool society would certainly be in the haul'.[49] By 1893 it was regarded as 'a well-managed Liverpool racing centre',[50] and it seems to have survived up until the First World War.[51]

Of the other clubs, some, such as the Camden, were mainly for 'mechanics and working men' but others aimed at a higher class of member. St. Thomas's Club, which was situated in the business district, was frequented by men who had a 'character for respectability to maintain'. It was 'better furnished than the ordinary betting clubs' and food as well as drink was provided. This club had about 300 members, who paid a subscription of 5/- a year. They included ship brokers, corn merchants and 'people in business for themselves' as well as clerks, and it was noted that 'the members keep going coming in and going out, evidently devoting to the club all the precious moments they can steal from the absorbing cares of business'. The Grosvenor Club in Williamson Square was also regarded as respectable and exclusive, with a membership of between 200 and 300. Here bets could be made with any one of three resident bookmakers, and in the evening there was gambling on cards.[52]

The clubs were clearly successful and were generally left alone by the police and the magistrates. By 1884 the *Liverpool Review*, which had run a longstanding campaign against them, felt obliged to report that 'betting seems rapidly to be increasing, and from the immunity, and, we might say, protection that the clubs are receiving from the police authorities, it is beginning to be thought a trifle respectable to belong to a betting club'. In the same article, the *Review* noted that it was 'from the respectable class of backers that the bookmakers extract their money'.[53]

There were occasional attempts in the courts to close down some of the clubs, but these tended to be dismissed on technicalities, and the sympathies of Mr. Raffles, the Stipendiary Magistrate, towards the bookmakers were commented on on more than one occasion.[54]

Nor was it just on matters connected with betting that the magistrates showed their partiality towards racing. In 1870 there was a very close finish to the Grand National, and subsequently the R.S.P.C.A. took George Holman, the jockey on The Doctor who was second, to court on grounds of cruelty. This was one of the first cases of its kind and attracted considerable press attention. The evidence for the prosecution was convincing: the *Daily Telegraph*'s racing correspondent had written that 'The Doctor's sides were fairly ripped up with the spurs', and a policeman who was present said that 'he had never before seen a horse with so much blood on his side after a race'; perhaps most tellingly, a cab driver said that if one of his horses had been in a similar condition he would certainly have been summonsed. Yet, after hearing the evidence from the defence, which consisted largely of people who had bet on The Doctor saying that if he had been punished a little more he would have won the race, the magistrates dismissed the case, with costs awarded against the R.S.P.C.A. This verdict was greeted by a 'wild cheer' from the public gallery. *Porcupine*'s rather sour comment on these proceedings was that 'the gentlemen on the bench had a great deal more sympathy with sporting institutions than with the attempt to reduce cruelty on the race-course to an endurable limit. It is no wonder that the Houghton Street patrons of the turf were quite unable to confine their demonstrations of satisfaction within decent bounds. It is not every day that they are gratified with such proof of magisterial feeling'.[55]

Many of these themes come together in the lives of James Maybrick, a Liverpool cotton merchant born in 1838, who had offices in Tithebarn Street, and his American-born wife Florence. This couple were to achieve notoriety in 1889 when James Maybrick died of arsenic poisoning in suspicious circumstances and, after a manifestly unfair trial, Florence Maybrick was convicted of his murder and sentenced to death. After a considerable public outcry, the Home Secretary commuted the sentence to penal servitude for life, on the grounds that Mrs Maybrick had administered and attempted to administer arsenic to her husband 'with intent to murder', a crime with which she had not been charged. In the event she spent fifteen years in gaol, before being released in 1904, after which she returned to the United States where she died in 1941. This remarkable case hit the headlines again in 1993 when a document came to light which, it has been claimed, is a journal of James Maybrick, in which he admits to being Jack the Ripper. Unsurprisingly, this claim has been hotly contested, and the genuineness of the journal remains unproven.[56]

The sensational nature of this case has led to considerable research being carried out into the Maybricks, with the result that we now know a good deal about their lifestyle. Fortunately, one does not need to pronounce on whether or not Mrs. Maybrick was guilty of murder, or whether James Maybrick was or was not Jack the Ripper, or even whether the so-called 'Ripper diary' is genuine, to accept that in many respects they can be taken as representative of at least a segment of Liverpool middle class society of the time. The picture which emerges confirms the view that respectability was often only a surface veneer, behind which lay a pleasure-seeking involvement in a range of unrespectable activities, amongst which racing and betting were prominent.

John Aunspaugh, another member of Liverpool's business community, once said of James Maybrick that he was 'one of the straightest, most upright and honourable men in a business transaction I have ever known'.[57] Despite this, he was a womaniser and a drug addict, whose life as it was revealed at the inquest into his death and at Mrs. Maybrick's trial pulled back the veil on 'a form of existence in the social sphere to which he belonged that is distressing to contemplate',[58] a comment that suggests that his lifestyle was not uncommon amongst the Liverpool business class. Like many merchants he was a gambler: John Aunspaugh's daughter Florence recalled that 'He bet on the races and played stud-poker';[59] and this is echoed by a comment in the 'Ripper diary' where he states on one occasion 'tomorrow I will make a substantial wager'.[60] He was a regular racegoer, not just locally at Aintree and on the Wirral, but at the fashionable southern meetings such as Ascot and Goodwood, and was also fond of hunting; after his marriage he kept six horses, two of them saddle horses for riding.[61]

His love of horses and racing was something he shared with his wife. Indeed this shared interest may even have contributed to their whirlwind romance on board the *S.S. Baltic* in March 1880, for Florence had already attended the Grand National at least once, and she recalled later that her special pastime during her childhood was riding.[62] Certainly after their marriage they 'both played whist and danced the polka, but most of all they followed the horses on whatever track they were running'.[63] Although Florence was regarded as 'good natured and pretty',[64] she was far from innocent, and like her husband, led a far from respectable life. Recent research has revealed that she almost certainly had an illegitimate child when still a teenager, and after her marriage she is known to have had at least three affairs, with a man called Williams, about whom nothing is known, with her brother in law Edwin Maybrick, and finally, with fatal consequences, with Alfred Brierley, another cotton merchant.

This affair came out into the open at the 1889 Grand National. James Maybrick had invited a number of his friends and business associates, including Brierley and Charles and Christina Samuelson to join him on a hired omnibus to go to Aintree, but Mrs Maybrick travelled to the course separately, accompanied by another woman friend. No-one appears to have thought this unusual, nor that Maybrick's party included 'both ladies and gentlemen'. But during the afternoon, Maybrick observed his wife flirting with Brierley; husband and wife quarrelled and Mrs. Maybrick was overheard to say 'I will give it him hot and heavy for speaking to me like that in public', a remark that was to count against her at the subsequent inquest and at her trial.[65]

It was Mrs. Maybrick's affair with Brierley which provided the prosecution with a motive for murder and which destroyed her reputation in Liverpool, but her love of the turf was also held against her by respectable society. As the *Liverpool Courier* somewhat disingenuously put it:

> It has been a matter of some surprise that Mrs. Maybrick should have been so desirous of attending race meetings. She was present not only at those in Cheshire and at Aintree, but at others, and some of those acquainted with the family say that it came to her husband's knowledge that, like many

other ladies who take an interest in matters of sport, she sometimes risked a little on the result of races.[66]

Mrs. Maybrick's love of racing clearly survived her fifteen years in prison. Although her later years in America were spent in impoverished obscurity, in 1927 she managed to find the money for one last visit to England during which she revisited some of her old haunts, 'not forgetting the Grand National', which had played so important a part in her tragedy.[67]

The lives of other members of the Maybricks' party at the 1889 Grand National are also instructive. Alfred Brierley was 38 years old at the time of the Maybrick affair. Described as having 'an irreproachable commercial standing',[68] he was the senior partner of Brierley & Wood, cotton merchants, whose office was in Old Hall Street, and lived at 60, Huskisson Street. Somewhat 'dashing', like the Maybricks he too was a keen racegoer and went to many meetings with them before the fateful encounter at Aintree.[69] The exposure of this outwardly respectable merchant as being far from respectable was devastating, as was recognised at the time, the *Liverpool Echo* commenting that 'to a Liverpool merchant placed his his unenviable position, the expos9 must have been peculiarly painful'.[70] Although he was never called to give evidence at the trial, his business was dissolved and he emigrated to America.[71]

Two other members of the party at the Grand National, Charles and Christina Samuelson, got off more lightly. Although Mrs. Samuelson gave evidence at the inquest, thereafter she and her husband coveniently disappeared and neither of them was called to give evidence at the trial. No doubt they realised that they had to protect their own reputations, for Charles Samuelson was a partner in the firm of Edward Samuelson & Co., tobacco brokers, and his father, the head of the firm, was Alderman Edward Samuelson who had been mayor of Liverpool in 1872/73.[72]

There is one final, rather gruesome, connection between the Maybrick case and the racing world. The day the verdict was announced some racegoers at Brighton races wanted to bet on the outcome, but, rather to their credit, the bookmakers refused to bet on 'such a terrible subject'; even so, after the result came in 'there was a general offer to lay long odds that the sentence was never carried out'.[73]

This paper has set out to show that significant numbers of the middle classes in Liverpool took an active interest in horse racing and the many unrespectable activities associated with it, but it should never be forgotten that many other members of the community – Nonconformists, Evangelicals, social and moral reformers and a significant portion of the local press – were passionately opposed to racing throughout the

Victorian period. Perhaps the last word should be left to Asquith's Chief Secretary for Ireland, Augustine Birrell. The son of a Baptist minister in Liverpool who was born in 1850, he remembered that in his youth there had been a marked distinction between the inhabitants of Liverpool who were not allowed to go to the Grand National and those, 'the large majority' who were; rather wistfully, he recorded that he was 'as usual' in the minority.[74]

Endnotes

[1] W. Vamplew, *The turf* (Harmondsworth: Allen Lane, 1976), 133.

[2] See for example M. Huggins, *Flat racing and British society 1790-1914* (London: Cass, 2000), chapter 3.

[3] B.G. Orchard, *Liverpool's legion of honour* (Birkenhead: the author, 1893), ix, xi.

[4] W.J. Conybeare, *Perversion* (London: Smith, Elder, 1856), chapter 14.

[5] S. Smith, *My life work* (London, 1903), 108.

[6] *Porcupine*, 17 May 1862, 49.

[7] B.G. Orchard, *The Clerks of Liverpool* (Liverpool, 1871), 10.

[8] *The Clerks' Journal*, Vol. 3, no. 30, 1 August 1890.

[9] B.G. Orchard, *The Clerks of Liverpool* (Liverpool, 1871), 42.

[10] *Porcupine*, 5 October 1867, 265.

[11] E. Bradyll, *The Lays of cotton broking* (Liverpool: Harris, 1865), 4. This was published anonymously; Bradyll's authorship is revealed in Orchard. *Liverpool's legion of honour*, 196.

[12] Orchard, *Liverpool's legion of honour*, 32, 65-66.

[13] Orchard, *The clerks of Liverpool*, 16.

[14] For a general account of racing at Liverpool see J.R. Pinfold, *Gallant sport* (Halifax: Portway Press, 1999).

[15] *Liverpool Chronicle*, 19 May 1838.

[16] See the list in C. Pitt, *A long time gone* (Halifax: Portway Press, 1996). A general history of racing in the area is given in P. Thompson, *On the turf* (Bebington: Quarry Publications, 1991).

[17] *Bethell's Life in London and Liverpool Sporting Register* appears to have lasted only from 1824 to 1827. The set of the *City Racing Record* in the British Library Newspaper Library covers 1887-1897.

[18] *Liverpool Courier*, 2 March 1836.

[19] *Liverpool Standard*, 1 March 1839.

[20] J.K. Walton and A. Wilcox, *Low life and moral improvement in mid-Victorian England: Liverpool through the journalism of Hugh Shimmin* (Leicester: Leicester University Press, 1991), 79.

[21] *Porcupine*, 15 March 1862, 283.

[22] *Liverpool Daily Post*, 25 April 1870.

[23] *The Field Quarterly Magazine and Review*, Vol. 1, 1870, 138.

[24] Walton and Wilcox, *Low life and moral improvement*, 85.

[25] Walton and Wilcox, *Low life and moral improvement*, 75-76, 84-85.

[26] *Porcupine*, 25 March 1871, 651-652.

[27] Walton and Wilcox, *Low life and moral improvement*, 79.

[28] *The Times*, 17 April, 19 April, 5 May 1875.

158

[29] *Porcupine*, 19 July 1862, 125.

[30] H. Shimmin, *Liverpool life*, 2nd series (Liverpool: Egerton Smith, 1857), 13-19.

[31] *Liverpool Chronicle*, 11 July 1829.

[32] Ibid.

[33] *Liverpool Courier*, 2 March 1836.

[34] Letter from Topham to Halifax Wyatt, 24 February 1872, Molyneux Muniments (Croxteth Hall, Merseyside) DDM 55.

[35] *Liverpool Daily Post*, 25 April 1870.

[36] *Bethell's Life in London and Liverpool Sporting Register*, 28 July 1827.

[37] Letter from Topham to Halifax Wyatt, 24 February 1872, Molyneux Muniments (Croxteth Hall, Merseyside) DDM 55.

[38] E. Bradyll, *The Lays of cotton broking* (Liverpool: Harris, 1865), 8-9.

[39] *Liverpool Echo*, 27 March 1897.

[40] *Porcupine*, 7 January 1865, 327.

[41] H. Shimmin, *Liverpool life* (Liverpool: Egerton Smith, 1857), 98.

[42] Shimmin, *Liverpool life*, 100, 102.

[43] *Liverpool Review*, 2 November 1889.

[44] H. Shimmin, *Town life* (London, 1858), 152-153.

[45] *Porcupine*, 17 March 1877, 810.

[46] *Porcupine*, 10 March 1877, 790, and 24 March 1877, 823.

[47] *Liverpool Review*, 8 December 1883.

[48] This figure has been arrived at by comparing the clubs mentioned in a series of articles in the *Liverpool Review*, 1883-84, with the list of Liverpool clubs in *Kelly's Directory of Lancashire, Liverpool and Manchester*, 1887, 639-640. Most, but by no means all, of the clubs were situated in the streets surrounding Williamson Square.

[49] *Liverpool Review*, 8 September, 13 October 1883.

[50] Orchard, *Liverpool's legion of honour*, 62.

[51] The Club appears in the annual volumes of *Gore's directory of Liverpool*, 1879-1913, but does not appear in the 1917 issue. The Waterloo was the longest-lived of the Liverpool betting clubs, the majority of the others having disappeared by the mid-1890s.

[52] *Liverpool Review*, 13 October, 24 November, 8 December 1883.

[53] *Liverpool Review*, 26 July 1884.

[54] See for example the case against the Caxton Club, *Liverpool Review*, 1 December 1883; for Raffles' views see *Liverpool Review*, 15 December 1883, 26 July 1884.

[55] *Liverpool Daily* Post, 26 April 1870, *Porcupine*, 30 April 1870, 50.

[56] There is a considerable literature on the Maybrick case. See, for example, T. Christie, *Etched in arsenic* (London: Harrap, 1969) and B. Ryan, *The poisoned life of Mrs. Maybrick* (London: Penguin, 1977). The most recent life of Mrs. Maybrick is A.E. Graham and C. Emmas, *The last victim* (London: Headline, 1999). The 'Ripper diary' has been published in full in S. Harrison, *The diary of Jack the Ripper* (London: Smith Gryphon, 1993). For a spirited defence of the diary which uncovers much new information about the Maybricks see P. Feldman, *Jack the Ripper: the final chapter* (London: Virgin, 1998).

[57] Quoted in A.E. Graham and C. Emmas, *The last victim* (London: Headline, 1999), 28.

[58] *Liverpool Echo*, 8 August 1889.

[59] Quoted in P.H. Feldman, *Jack the Ripper: the final chapter* (London: Virgin, 1998), 304.

159

[60] Quoted in S. Harrison, *The diary of Jack the Ripper* (London: Smith Gryphon, 1993), 275. All the entries in the 'diary' are undated.

[61] S. Harrison, *The diary of Jack the Ripper* (London: Smith Gryphon, 1993), 36.

[62] Christie, *Etched in arsenic*, 32.

[63] Christie, *Etched in arsenic*, 43.

[64] *Liverpool Review*, 6 July 1889.

[65] *Liverpool Courier*, 29 May 1889, *Liverpool Echo*, 29 May 1889.

[66] *Liverpool Courier*, 1 June 1889.

[67] *Liverpool Post and Mercury*, 2 May 1927.

[68] *Liverpool Echo*, 13 August 1889.

[69] *Liverpool Courier*, 6 June 1889.

[70] *Liverpool Echo*, 8 June 1889.

[71] *Liverpool Echo*, 14 August 1889, 23 August 1889.

[72] Orchard, *Liverpool's legion of honour*, 619-20.

[73] *Liverpool Echo*, 12 August 1889.

[74] A. Birrell, *Some early recollections of Liverpool* (Liverpool: Henry Young & Sons, 1924), 10.

'The Mysteries of Midnight': Low-Life London 'Penny Dreadfuls' as unrespectable reading from the 1860s

John Springhall
School of History and International Affairs
University of Ulster at Coleraine
Coleraine
County Londonderry
BT52 1SA
jo.springhall@ulst.ac.uk

'Respectability' was a virtue much sought after by a large majority of Victorians, if we exclude those at the highest and lowest levels of the social hierarchy. Even so, from a cultural standpoint it was periodically under threat from the popular British taste for sensational gothic melodrama in theatrical and literary entertainment. Great literary gothic horrors, from Matthew Lewis' *The Monk* and Ann Radcliffe's *Mysteries of Udolpho* in the 1790s, through Mary Shelley's post-Napoleonic *Frankenstein*, to the late-Victorian climax of R.L. Stevenson's *Dr Jekyll and Mr Hyde* and Bram Stoker's *Dracula*, 'have proved the most resounding and pervasive British literary influences on global culture and mass entertainment'. Yet sanctimonious early-Victorian critics argued that the popularisation by cheap publisher Edward Lloyd and others of gothic's sado-masochistic and horrific elements, combined with the criminality of Newgate fiction, in mass-produced serials such as James Malcolm Rymer's *Varney the Vampire, or the Feast of Blood* (1846-7), could well corrupt the innocent young or infect the 'dangerous' lower orders.[1]

The mass market for cheap reading matter, created in the 1830s through weekly serial publication, had been accelerated by the new rotary printing presses, cheap manufactured paper, improved transport and rising literacy. By the 1860s, penny-a-line authors seeking work in London publishing offices in and around Fleet Street had learnt that macabre and exciting fare could be cast just as successfully in contemporary as in historical dress, thus providing an accessible version of gothic for the English common reader. Hence a fascinating source for the historian anxious to explore the less respectable and private side of Victorian recreation is the category of low-life London 'penny dreadful' serial, read undoubtedly as it was by those young men and women in the upper-working and lower-middle-classes who might well have adopted, in less relaxed circumstances, the conventional earnest, improving and puritanical Victorian positions.[2]

Middle-Class Moral Panic

The enduring appeal of the highly stylised 'sex and violence' in popular Victorian writing that appealed to the young was a particular target of those evangelical and high-minded critics of penny fiction who abhorred its sensationalism, bad taste and general unrespectability. Such a one was Charles Knight, former editor of the self-improving but didactic *Penny Magazine* (1832-45), who was admonished in 1854 by a self-righteous but kind-hearted Charles Dickens:

> The English are, so far as I know, the hardest-worked people on whom the sun shines. Be content, if, in their wretched intervals of pleasure, they read for amusement and do no worse. They are born at the oar, and they live and die at it. Good God, what would we have of them!

Much of the middle-class moral panic directed at 'penny dreadfuls', or cheap post-1860 instalment and periodical fiction intended primarily for juveniles, derived from anxiety that their own sons and daughters were as much at risk from contamination by 'pernicious' reading as the children of the urban poor. 'It [penny fiction] is creeping not only into the houses of the poor, neglected, and untaught, but into the largest mansions; penetrating into religious families and astounding careful parents by its frightful issues', warned the Seventh Earl of Shaftesbury in 1878, addressing the Religious Tract Society in the year before they launched the eminently respectable and manly *Boy's Own Paper* (1879-1967). Earlier, crusading journalist James Greenwood startled his middle-class magazine readers in 1869 by depicting the voracious 'penny dreadful', like the 'fabled vampire', having already 'bitten your little rosy-cheeked son Jack. He may be lurking at this very moment in that young gentleman's private chamber, little as you suspect it, polluting his mind and smoothing the way that leads to swift destruction'.[3]

Significantly, among melodramatic low-life tales directed at juveniles, such as *The Wild Boys of London: or, The Children of Night. A Story of the Present Day* (1864-66), the same publisher also put out more titillating fare presumably aimed at adults, such as *The Young Ladies of London; or, The Mysteries of Midnight* (1867-68). The errand boys, junior clerks and schoolboys who enjoyed *The Wild Boys* may also, of course, have avidly read *The Young Ladies of London*. Evidence for the precise readership of individual 'penny dreadfuls' from this period is imprecise and difficult to assess; we are reliant on generalised speculation by contemporaries in order to gauge the potential audience. Dreadfuls were read, as a rule, claimed a hostile 1872 report from the Society for the Diffusion of Useful Knowledge, 'by ignorant shop and office-boys, young apprentices and factory hands, and by, perhaps, a small number of school lads'.[4]

Low-Life Dreadfuls

Low-life 'penny dreadfuls' were simply one category among various other serialised forms of cheap fiction sold to juveniles, among them: highwaymen, historical-adventure, and boarding-school stories, plus Robinsonnades, women-in-peril, rags-to-riches, and pirate stories. The fashion for stories set in non-respectable parts of a present-day London emerged out of a literary formula pioneered by Pierce Egan's serialized *Life in London* (1820-1), with its colourful account of the exploits of innocent rustic Jerry Hawthorn, who is taken on a guided tour of the capital's sporting low life by urban sophisticates Corinthian Tom and Bob Logic, their wanderings suitably engraved by the meticulous George Cruikshank. The flood of English serial publications which took the urban low-life theme and adapted it extensively for a largely juvenile audience were chiefly inspired, however, by the extraordinary success of an anglicised version of Eugène Sue's exciting *feuilleton* bestseller *Les Mystères de Paris* (1842-3). The most successful penny-issue work of its time, long-running serial *The Mysteries of London* (1845-50) was written in a commercial style that juxtaposed the radical with the thrilling and was soon selling nearly 40,000 weekly copies. This was followed by the even lengthier *The Mysteries of the Court of London* (1848-56) which made late-Chartist activist, serial-novelist and newspaper editor George William MacArthur Reynolds (1814-79) arguably the most widely-read English author of the nineteenth century. He updated the Gothic novel by casting it in modern dress and setting it with great precision in familiar, everyday London locales that highlighted his shock effects, unveiling lurid criminal conspiracies which took place just behind the scenes, exchanging city houses for Gothic castles, slum cellars for dungeons, and financial extortioners for the evil count or mad monk.[5]

Authors of London low-life tales and mysteries suffused the commonplace with dramatic encounters, conveying extremes of emotion and fortune through concrete detail of daily life. The mostly anonymous authors of the Newsagents' Publishing Company's (NPC) widely-distributed London serials of the 1860s hence placed their youthful heroes in highly dramatic and often incongruous situations which often took place among sordid and criminal milieux in the lower reaches of metropolitan society. Hence *The Wild Boys of London* (1864-6), whose

WILD BOYS OF LONDON;

OR,

THE CHILDREN OF NIGHT.

THE DISCOVERY IN THE SEWER. (See next Number.)

"Speak lower; his wife is dangerously ill, and if you accelerate her death you will be liable to an action for manslaughter."

The policeman looked considerably taken down.

"I must do my duty," he said.

"So must we all," was the doctor's curt rejoinder; "but the quieter you are doing yours the better it will be for you."

"Joseph Lane is my prisoner."

"And his wife is my patient; so stay where you are, and wait till I come down."

The policeman descended grumbling; he did not like to have his authority disputed, but he knew

No. 21.

that parish doctors are awkward customers to deal with.

"Now, Joseph," said the doctor, briskly, "just tell me the truth. How did you come by that parcel?"

"As there's a Lord above, I don't know."

"You were drunk when you came in."

Lane hung his head in shame.

"This fellow, your companion, stole the parcel; I suppose you both got drunk together, and you carried it home. It's a bad case."

Lane went cold to his heart with fear.

To him the thought of being taken before a magis-

NOTICE! With this Number is given away a Sheet of the New Pantomime.

popularity and notoriety exceeded that of any other NPC 'dreadful', depicts in serialized form, and with some grasp of urban vernacular, the often violent and lurid adventures of a gang of Cockney street urchins who run the gamut of delinquencies from piracy to lynching. The first edition in the mid-1860s was published in 103 weekly parts of eight double-columned pages each, making a combined total of about 800,000 words, or ten times the length of the average modern thriller. The street-arab gang of the title hatch their mischief 'round a fire in their haunt beneath the sewers of London', somewhere near London bridge pier, from whence they fight off ruffians, salvage corpses, and traffic in stolen goods. Above ground, they come to grips with thieves, murderers, kidnappers, incompetent policemen and grave-robbers, not to mention child-stealers. 'At times', wittily reported E.S. Turner in 1948, 'the scene shifted to a mutinous convict ship, or to the Australian bush, but sooner or later the writer would return, nostalgically, to the sewers of London'.[6]

Subverting the melodramatic plot elements and occasional Reynolds-like radical sentiment in *The Wild Boys* is the reader-identification figure of Dick Lane, the fastidious boy-hero. Better educated than his scavenging companions, Dick is driven to make a living on the streets because his father, a previously sober and industrious Lambeth bricklayer, has taken to drink after being led astray when his corrupt union calls an unnecessary strike. Meanwhile, Dick's *alter ego*, Arthur Grattan, has been brought up by a poor schoolmaster but is, in reality, the kidnapped son of Lord Wintermerle, heir to a vast fortune. The anonymous author could not conceal ultimate reliance upon the hackneyed *Oliver Twist*-plot device of the stolen child, reared in obscurity, fallen among young street thieves and beggars, while in the background a mysterious stranger plots his downfall. Consumption of such penny serials probably reached adolescents closer to Dick Lane, the well-spoken protagonist of *The Wild Boys*, than to the homeless orphans of the title. Thus sons and daughters of skilled working men and clerks, seeking a romantic escape from uneventful daily lives, could vicariously enjoy the adventures of boy thieves, actresses and heroes not unlike themselves from the comfort of outwardly respectable, semi-suburban homes. Whether in the school, the office, the warehouse, or the workshop, youngsters could participate in the criminal yet exciting escapades of vagrant ragamuffins without having their own life-styles radically altered in the process.[7]

In contrast to the focus on Dick Lane at the outset of *The Wild Boys*, the opening chapters of *The Young Ladies of London* introduce the sinister Count Lewiski, man about town, who entraps rich gentlemen visitors to the wicked metropolis, using as bait the beautiful Emma Langton, his mistress, once a happy farmer's daughter. This serial's engraved frontispiece depicts women importuning fashionably-dressed and stovepipe-hatted male clients in the Haymarket district of central London, notorious for its prostitution. Once near Petticoat Lane, Lewiski is transformed into Edward Lewis, 'the keeper of several lodging-houses and brothels in the east-end of London; a shrewd fellow, who had amassed a considerable sum of money by his dishonest and filthy calling'. Great play is made with the vulnerability of exploited seamstresses in the area as a means of sketching in local colour: poor, pale, weak girls with half a dozen shirts to finish, paid only ninepence for 18 hours of toil to support children or a dying mother. By the late 1860s vicitimised East End seamstresses had become part of a sentimental and safe iconology, their usage evident since the radical journalism of the 1830s. The real conditions of East London's huge casualised labour force, characterised by low wages, irregular employment, and foreign immigration, are never directly confronted in penny fiction. Any radical sentiment is both subordinated to and subverted by the melodramatic plot. In *The Young Ladies of London*, the Count employs one Ghastly Gaskill to drug then kidnap unsuspecting girls who are then put to work in his Haymarket *serraglio* – '"another poor wretch doomed to fall a victim to your accursed toils"' cries Emma unavailingly.[8]

Women-in-Peril Dreadfuls

The NPC responsible for the above and other Fleet Street area serial publishers sought to appeal not only to boys, their primary audience, but also to factory girls, shop assistants, milliners, and domestic servants. The latter were reached through the seemingly inexhaustible appeal of the cheap literature of aristocratic seduction, possibly a metaphor for the exploitation of the poor by the upper classes. '"No, no! a long and glorious career of profligacy and dissipation is still in store for me!"' Count Lerno reassures himself, following a threat to his reputation, in the NPC or London Romance Company's *Rose Mortimer, or, The Ballet-Girl's Revenge* (1865?). This was judged by one literary trade paper 'a sensational tale of love and intrigue, illustrated with suggestive woodcuts, representing the abduction of the heroine at the stage-door of the theatre, and similarly exciting subjects'. Hence, after Rose's successful performance as the Queen of Beauty in a Boxing Day pantomime, the Count carries her resisting, and still in ballet costume, to his carriage. The kidnapped girl is taken to a large house in that part of London's Fulham, lying west of Walham Green, supposedly known as 'Dead Man's Land'. Lerno confesses that he is master of the house and seeks to make Rose its mistress. '"Count Lerno", said Rose drawing herself up to her full height – "Count Lerno, sooner than agree to your degrading proposals I would kill myself"'.[9]

The wicked and lecherous aristocratic villain like Count Lerno was a stereotype from early-Victorian 'penny bloods' resuscitated in the 1860s by the authors of women-in-peril stories. '"Tut," was the cruel answer', of Lord Dundreary in *The Work Girls of London, Their Trials and Temptations* (1865), '"do you think I have nothing to do but to marry every girl who wishes to father a child on me? I tell you all I will do for you is to give you some money, but I never want to see you again: as for the brat, never let me hear of it!"'. The over-heated and hyperbolic opening chapters of *The Outsiders of Society; or, The Wild Beauties of London* (1866) are devoted to the unscrupulous and licentious Lord Vineyard – 'a proud name in "Burke's Peerage" sounded well in the eyes of the world; but if people only knew the infamy attached to it!' This stage villain adopts the tragically orphaned but 'well-proportioned' Lydia Wilson and lavishes money upon her in order to satisfy his evil designs, leading the ruined girl to attempt suicide by throwing herself off Westminster Bridge. In Harry Hazleton's *Fanny White and Her Friend Jack Rawlings: A Romance of a Young Lady Thief and a Boy Burglar* (1865?), published by George Vickers, great play is made with the attempted seduction of the sedated heroine, Fanny White, a music-hall dancer, by an old Palmerston-like roué, Lord Crokerton, in yet another isolated house somewhere in Fulham. Miss Fanny is 'a spanking, bouncing young wench – beautiful enough, in all conscience, to excite the desires of the most cold-blooded' yet also, 'as strong as a young bull. Voluptuous, graceful, pliant, and muscular. She could love and languish; but, when her blood was up, she could scratch and bite'. Thus the redoubtable yet erotic heroine, recovering from the effects of a drug, makes short work of the 'horrible old rascal' who had set out to seduce her. 'Then, as he strove once more to seize her, she doubled up that pretty fist of hers ... and dealt my Lord Crokerton such a terrific right-hander on the nose, that it spread him out flat upon the floor, where he lay, bleeding and gasping, a sight pitiful to behold'.[10]

Women-in-peril and low-life stories appear to have inherited an earlier London-based radical-populist demonology, exemplified by G.W.M. Reynolds, which cast titled landlords living off their rents and property, rather than the new entrepreneurial middle-class, as the chief exploiters of the labouring poor. Given the current emphasis on the continuing hegemonic importance of the aristocracy throughout the nineteenth century, Reynolds should perhaps be reclaimed as someone who was trying to define the real nature of the Victorian state. In serialised popular fiction it was usually the rich aristocrat, hardly ever the grasping capitalist, who set out to assail the virtue of the modest heroine. 'As though temptation and immorality were only to be found in wealthy neighbourhoods', commented *The Bookseller* astutely in 1867, 'and lewd thoughts were the special and particular property of noblemen and "swells", with rent rolls of ten thousand a year'.[11]

Assumptions like this were, of course, as much part of the ideological baggage of the thrusting, upwardly-mobile, middle-class businessman, with his Manchester-bred intolerance for aristocratic privilege and unearned wealth, as of the downwardly-mobile penny novelist. The popular literature of seduction none the less evaded the reality of sexual assault within the working class in mid-Victorian times, for very few unmarried mothers or victims of rape fell prey to genuine aristocratic villains. Perhaps the theft of poor men's daughters by profligate aristocrats symbolised the betrayal of the working class by their elite rulers, investing the public rhetoric of class struggle with personal and emotive images of women's sexual oppression. This kind of writing also contributed to a wider rhetoric of the poor as weak and passive victims who needed to be protected by kindly middle-class paternalists.[12]

London's Literary Subculture

London was crowded with penny-a-line writers, underpaid journalists, eccentric well-bred scribblers, improvident artists and despised plagiarists who made up a kind of sub-literary, bohemian subculture. Cheap fiction writers commonly lived in the many courts or squares off Fleet Street itself, or in lodgings around the Gray's Inn Road, or further out in unfashionable London suburbs. One of the most prolific and popular of all boys' story authors for 'low-class' weekly periodicals in the late-Victorian and Edwardian years was Norwich-born hack author Edwin Harcourt Burrage (1839-1916), who churned out countless serials and millions of words in a writing career of over 35 years. Burrage merited the accolade of the boys' Charles Dickens for quantity, if not quality, of output (the British Library catalogue lists 56 items but this overlooks many unattributed titles).

As a young man Burrage lived in Wine Office Court, off Fleet Street, and recalled years later that, after his first story was published in the Emmett brothers' *Young Ladies of Great Britain* (1869-71), rather than pay the single-room rent owed to his landlady, he spent the 35 shillings earned on celebratory drinking among his fellow scribes. Burrage's most famous creation was the wily Oriental hero Ching-Ching, a sort of juvenile Charlie Chan, whose breezy ingenuity in the face of incredible dangers in far-flung climes generated so much reader enthusiasm that the young Chinaman was featured in *Ching-Ching's Own* (1888-93), for which Burrage wrote practically all the major stories. Ching-Ching became the only serious rival to Jack Harkaway, the most popular schoolboy hero of the age (see below). Burrage had, by this stage, forsworn his bibulous past and was no longer a Grub Street habitué, even writing a pseudononymous total abstinence tract, *The Ruin of Fleet Street* (1885), exposing the pitfalls of drink and the literary life. He eventually became a valued bourgeois resident of Redhill in Surrey, where he was elected to the local council. Burrage outlived his Fleet Street drinking companions and died in his 70s of natural causes during the First World War.[13]

The unrespectable career of old Etonian and Oxford-educated but unemployed barrister Samuel Bracebridge Hemyng (1841-1901) perhaps best exemplifies the bohemian subculture of this lower stratum of the literary life in mid-to-late-Victorian London. By the age of thirty, this versatile and prolific author had already attempted tortuous three-volume novels like *The Curate of Inveresk* (1860) and *Gasper Trenchard* (1864); 'edited' first-person narratives exposing various criminal practices, such as *Secrets of the Turf, or How I Won the Derby* (1868); authored reputedly licentious stories about London's 'fast' women, such as *Skittles* (1864) in the 'Anonyma series' for George Vickers; and two-shilling 'yellowback' novels sold at railway bookstalls, such as *Eton School Days* (1864) and *Called to the Bar* (1867); as well as writing the section on 'Prostitution in London' for the fourth volume of Henry Mayhew's *London Labour and the London Poor* (1864). Yet Hemyng, like many another decayed gentleman-scribbler, only discovered his true vocation in 1871 when he created his most commercially-successful character, adventurous schoolboy Jack Harkaway, for Edwin Brett's long-running *Boys of England* (1866-99) and turned at last to popular juvenile literature. In 1874 when he arived in New York to provide Harkaway serials at the invitation of expatriate English publisher Frank Leslie, Hemyng was rapturously received as he came down the gang-plank by a brass band and thousands of cheering boys lining the pier. This was fame indeed and at a much higher rate per word than he was paid in London. Into the 1890s, by then returned to London once more seeking briefs, Hemyng continued to write novels, serials and magazine articles until he died at 60, practically penniless, in a dreary flat in London's then unfashionable Fulham.[14]

The first of the long-running Harkaway series, 'Jack Harkaway's Schooldays' (1871-72) serialized in *Boys of England*, takes over what had already become the traditional stock figures of the 'penny dreadful' boarding-school story: the stupid and hypocritical headmaster, the ridiculous French master, the school bully, the devoted friend, the schoolboy sweetheart, the snobbish young aristocrat, and so on. All of these stereotyped characters, with the exception of the headmaster, were to be transported overseas to exotic destinations, as Jack's companions, in the countless sequels. There is a curious sado-erotic episode in this first serial, a reminder of Hemyng's apprenticeship writing quasi-pornogra-

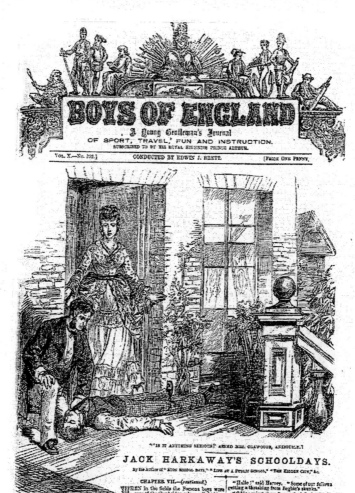

"'IS IT ANYTHING SERIOUS?' ASKED MRS. CRAWOOUR, ANXIOUSLY.'

JACK HARKAWAY'S SCHOOLDAYS.

By the Author of "ETON SCHOOL DAYS," "LIFE AT A PUBLIC SCHOOL," "THE HIDDEN CITY," &c.

CHAPTER VII.—(continued)

WHEN in the fields the Foxcon boys wore caps of the Cambridge colour, a light blue, while the boys of Dr. Beghie had always the dark blue of Oxford.

It was easy to count four dark caps and two light.

"Hullo!" said Harvey. "Some of our fellows getting a thrashing from Beghie's skunks."

"Odds against them," remarked Jack; "only two to one; that's nothing; we're used to that. Jog along; we must have a cut in."

The fight, for such it was, between the rival factions was an unequal one, and the lively phic novels for George Vickers, such as the 'Anonyma' series purporting to tell the life stories of the most notorious women about London. In chapter nine Mrs Crawcour, the headmaster's mysterious, 'beautiful pythoness' wife, has Jack severely whipped, while he is standing upright in his shirt-sleeves arms drawn up over his head, for flinging stones in the direction of her carriage: 'Cane the little wretch as severely as you can, and go on until I tell you to leave off. It will be some satisfaction to me to see him suffer what he so well deserves'. She then abjectly apologizes for this flagellation by offering to have her maid rub Jack's back with liniment: 'I have come to ask your forgiveness for my passionate and cruel conduct to you this afternoon. Oh! If you only knew what a dreadful curse my temper has been to me all my life. Had it not been for my temper, I should not now be the wife of a schoolmaster in a country town'. Not surprisingly, Jack maintained an ambivalent relationship with the headmaster's vivacious and 'strangely contradictory' wife until, perhaps at the editor's behest, she was abruptly dropped from the serial.[15]

Similarly, the NPC's *Red Ralph; or, The Daughter of Night: A Romance of the Road in the Days of Dick Turpin* (1866?) by 'Percival Wolfe' is not the conventional highwayman 'dreadful' it might on first glance appear but a sensational, if crudely expressed, work of Gothic imagination. It opens with Red Ralph, prince of thieves, seeking refuge from Bow Street Runners in a lonely house upon the banks of the Thames, near to old Westminster Bridge, and then discovering two grisly corpses inside, from the female one of which he removes costly pearls, rubies and emeralds, until 'a cold clammy hand clutched the robber's wrist, and a death-like embrace encircled him!' An engraved illustration by Robert Prowse, 'Torturing A Witch', decorates the third issue of this serial, depicting a semi-naked and nubile young woman in the process of being burnt alive by hard-faced ruffians. 'Like fiends from hell the rabble danced and screamed around her, stirred up the fire, and fanned the flames. Their savage cries drowned her agonizing shrieks of terror'. Rescue is at hand, however, since gallant Red Ralph gallops up with the famous Yellow Band and catches the 'half-naked palpitating form in his arms', then springs back through 'the roaring flames'. The witch turns out to be a mysterious 18-year old, 'with golden hair which fell in silken tresses upon a neck and bosom white, polished, and beautifully moulded as the bust of the Medicean statue', who in a previous instalment had become his bride but only as part of a sinister conspiracy while he was in a half-drugged state. 'But before proceeding further with his adventures upon this occasion', the author intrudes, 'it is necessary to return to the point where we left our hero in a considerable fix. Some startling

THE FIVE CENT
WIDE AWAKE
LIBRARY

No. 1225. {COMPLETE.} NEW YORK, PUBLISHER, 34 & 36 NORTH MOORE St., N. Y. NEW YORK, May 30, 1896. {PRICE 5 CENTS.} ISSUED WEEKLY. Vol. II.

Entered according to the Act of Congress, in the year 1896, by FRANK TOUSEY, in the office of the Librarian of Congress, at Washington, D. C.

JACK HARKAWAY'S SCHOOLDAYS.

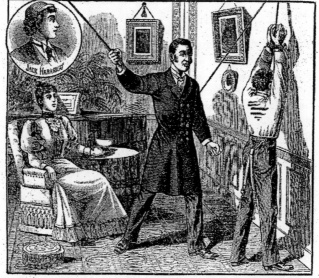

Mr. Mole redoubled his exertions. A low sob, and then another, which he could not repress, broke from Jack. It seemed as if the tension of the ropes was dragging his arms out of their sockets.

CHAPTER I.

After an animated discussion between Mr. and Mrs. Scratchley upon some method of reforming their unruly adopted son, whose many pranks had become unbearable, they were in despair. Mrs. Scratchley recommended a long list of his terrible doings about the house, and suggested various remedies, among them thrashing, all of which failed to meet the approval of Mr. Scratchley.

"There he must go to school. He shall not stop his pranks here any longer with impunity," Mrs.

adventures had occurred to him in the interval, and some more startling still are to follow all in good time'.[16]

Clearly, the vast undergrowth of non-respectable Victorian literature is not limited to such well-known pornographic fare as Walter's *My Secret Life*, given the suggestive if melodramatic serials put out by publishers like the NPC who specialized in youth-oriented 'penny dreadfuls'. Even a serialized NPC novel with an innocuous-sounding, juvenile title like *The Boy Rover; or, The Smuggler of the South Seas* (1866), by the mysterious 'Lieutenant Parker USS', unexpectedly turns out on closer examination to be a narrative of imminent female seduction narrowly averted. Hence the murderous Boy Rover robs shipwrecked sailors in an underground smuggler's cavern but rescues the attractive Ellen because 'there was a demon in his heart, urging on his base passions to more unholy deeds'. The rest of this 'soul-stirring nautical romance' is really an extended tale of attempted rape, if nowhere as explicit as genuinely erotic Victorian writing. *The Boy Rover* is none the less puzzling and possibly unique among such daring 'penny dreadfuls' in that it masquerades as an adventure tale. Authors of popular fiction for the urban masses were normally convinced of their own rectitude, because their story lines usually saw vice punished and virtue rewarded. They did not corrupt their readers with 'the foul sexual problems that disgrace so many of the society novels of today', according to a letter-writer to the *Daily News* in 1895. 'The masses, partially educated, vulgar perhaps, but certainly clean-minded, read the "penny dreadful" for its fare is strong, satisfying and healthy. The people love melodrama, but society prefers the immoral play' as well as 'detective stories, dealing with gruesome crimes, unlawful love, the triumph of evil over good'.[17]

Conclusions

'"I wish I know'd as much as you, Dick. How did you manage to pick it up?"' asks one of the eponymous Wild Boys of London of the well-mannered young hero in the first chapter. '"Mother taught me most, and I read all the books I can get"', he replies. '"So do I; sich rattling tales, too – 'The Black Phantom; or, The White Spectre of the Pink Rock'. It's fine it is; somebody's killed every week, and it's only a penny". "That is not the sort of book I mean", said Dick. "Mother does not like me to read them". "Why?'. "She says they have a bad influence". "Who's he?". "That means a bad effect". "Don't know him, neither". "You would, if you read proper books"'. Many among the aspiring lower-middle and educated middle classes believed, as this self-parodying dialogue suggests, that 'penny dreadfuls' were dangerous and corrupting because they did not lead the newly- literate working classes towards the high ideal of self-improvement but were merely entertaining. Middle-class reformers came to exaggerate or distort the nature of popular reading so as to nurture due chagrin at the disappointingly escapist fruits of a working-class literacy that they had themselves helped to nourish.[18]

What the more hostile commentators generally chose to overlook was that 'penny dreadfuls' were probably read equally by the sons of the middle, lower-middle and skilled working classes, especially in periodical form, as well as by a less discriminating and poorer, semi-literate market. Generally harmless, if stodgy and melodramatic, this widely read and genuinely popular fiction for the young was, by the early 1870s, labelled as non-respectable or 'dreadful' to incite middle-class 'moral panic'. Yet the consequences of discrimination in taste, by which certain tastes, values and hierarchies are established as culturally adult, 'respectable' or preferential and others not, are that aesthetic distinctions become a symbolic weapon in the struggle between classes and generations for ideological domination. Labelling thus represents a way for cultural authorities to construct taste hierarchies and to amplify anxiety or rejection over products of the mass culture, such as cheap fiction, which threaten established adult taste. Hence the invention of labels like 'horror comic' or 'penny dreadful' signify the continuous modern struggle between middle-class moralism, commercial provision and juvenile market demand.[19]

Endnotes

[1] Richard Davenport-Hines, *Gothic: 400 Years of Excess, Horror, Evil and Ruin* (London: Fourth Estate, 1999), 11, 248. Much the same outraged critical response greeted Hammer Films' initial Dracula and Frankenstein movies in the late 1950s: Jonathan Rigby, *English Gothic: A Century of Horror Cinema* (London: Reynolds & Hearn, 2000).

[2] Louis James, *Fiction for the Working Man, 1830-50: A Study of the Literature Produced for the Working Classes in Early Victorian England* (Harmondsworth: Penguin, 1974 edn.); John Springhall, *Youth, Popular Culture and Moral Panics: Penny Gaffs to Gangsta-Rap, 1830-1996* (Basingstoke: Macmillan, 1998), 57-66.

[3] Walter Dexter, ed., *The Letters of Charles Dickens*, vol. 2 (London: Nonesuch Press, 1938), 548; Edwin Hodder, *The Life and Work of the Seventh Earl of Shaftesbury*, vol. 3 (London: Cassell & Co., 1886), 469; James Greenwood, 'Penny Packets of Poison' [1874] in: Peter Haining, ed., *The Penny Dreadful, Or Strange, Horrid & Sensational Tales!* (London: Gollancz, 1975), 367.

[4] J.P. Harrison, 'Cheap Literature–Past and Present', *Companion to the Almanac of the Society for the Diffusion of Useful Knowledge or Year Book of General Information for 1873* (London: SDUK, 1872), 70.

[5] J.C. Reid, *Bucks and Bruisers: Pierce Egan and Regency England* (London: Routledge, 1971), 52-69; Rohan McWilliam, 'The Mysteries of G.W.M. Reynolds: Radicalism and Melodrama in Victorian Britain', in Malcolm Chase and Ian Dyck, eds, *Living and Learning: Essays in Honour of J.F.C. Harrison* (Aldershot: Scolar, 1996), 182-98.

[6] Anon., *The Wild Boys of London, or The Children of Night. A Story of the Present Day* (London: NPC, 1864-6), 2; E.S. Turner, *Boys Will Be Boys: The Story of Sweeney Todd, Deadwood Dick, Sexton Blake, Billy Bunter, Dick Barton, et. al.* (London: Michael Joseph, 1948), 66.

[7] Anon., *The Wild Boys of London, op cit.*, 2-18; Paul Schlicke, ed., *Oxford Reader's Companion to Dickens* (Oxford: University Press, 1999), 437-41; 450.

[8] Lieut. Parker, S.U.S. [pseud.], *The Young Ladies of London; or, The Mysteries of Midnight* (London: NPC, 1867-8), 3, 6-7, 10; Gareth Stedman-Jones, *Outcast London: A Study in the Relationship Betrween Classes in Victorian Society* (Harmondsworth: Penguin, 1984), 67-126.

[9] Anon., *Rose Mortimer; or, The Ballet-Girl's Revenge* (London: NPC, 1865?), 12, 15; 'Michievous Literature', *The Bookseller*, CXXVI, 1 July 1868: 446.

[10] Anon., *The Work Girls of London: Their Trials and Temptations, A Novel* (London: NPC, 1865), 38; Anon., *The Outsiders of Society; or, The Wild Beauties of London* (London: Henry Lea, 1866), 6; Anon. [Harry Hazleton], *Fanny White and Her Friend Jack Rawlings: A Romance of a Young Lady Thief and a Boy Burglar* (London: George Vickers, 1865?), 54-5.

[11] McWilliam, 'The Mysteries of G.W.M. Reynolds', 192; 'The Literature of Vice', *The Bookseller*, CX, 28 Februray 1867: 122.

[12] Anna Clark, 'The Politics of Seduction in English Popular Culture, 1748-1848', in Jean Radford, ed., *The Progress of Romance: The Politics of Popular Fiction* (London: Routledge, 1986), 47-70.

[13] 'A Latter-Day Pilgrim' [E. H. Burrage], *The Ruin of Fleet Street* (London: E.W. Allen, 1885), 22-3; 'Death of E.H. Burrage', *The Surrey Mirror and County Post*, 10 March 1916: 5; Frank Jay, 'Peeps into the Past', supp. to *Spare Moments*, 17, 15 February 1919: 65; Tom Hopperton, 'Digging Round the Roots, Pt. 4', *Story Paper Collector*, IV (1963): 115.

[14] 'Ralph Rollington' [John Allingham], *A Brief History of Boys' Journals, with interesting facts about the writers of boys' stories* (Leicester: H. Simpson, 1913), 7-8; 'Our New Story', *The Young Englishman*, II, 7 February 1874: 264; Albert Johannsen, *The House of Beadle and Adams and its Dime and Nickel Novels: The Story of a Vanished Literature*, II (Norman: Univ. of Oklahoma Press, 1950), 138-9.

[15] John Springhall, '"Boys of Bircham School": The Penny Dreadful Origins of the Popular English School Story, 1867-1900', *History of Education*, XX (1991): 77-94; Bracebridge Hemyng, 'Jack Harkaway's Schooldays', *Boys*

of England, X, 9 September 1871: 241-44; Graham Greene, 'Harkaway's Oxford', *Collected Essays* (Harmondsworth: Penguin, 1970 edn.), 180-83.

[16] Percival Wolfe, *Red Ralph, or The Daughter of Night. A Romance of the Road in the Days of Dick Turpin* (London: NPC, 1866?), 2-8, 13-17.

[17] Lieut. Parker [pseud.], *The Boy Rover; or, The Smuggler of the South Seas* (London: Henry Lea, 1866), 4-6; 'The Penny Dreadful', *The Daily News*, 28 September 1895, 7.

[18] Anon., *The Wild Boys of London*, 6-7, 18.

[19] Springhall, *Youth, Popular Culture and Moral Panics*; Pierre Bourdieu, trans. Richard Nice, *Distinction: A Social Critique of the Judgement of Taste* (London: Routledge, 1984); Lawrence W. Levine, *Highbrow/Lowbrow: The Emergence of Cultural Hierarchy in America* (Cambridge, Mass: Harvard University Press, 1988).

Respectability takes a holiday: disreputable behaviour at the Victorian seaside

John K. Walton
Department of History
University of Central Lancashire
Preston
Lancashire, PR1 2HE
j.k.walton@uclan.ac.uk

On certain assumptions the seaside resort might seem to be the classic place to look for disreputable Victorians: or at least for Victorians who chose this setting to cast aside the constraints of respectability, to wear their hedonistic hats and defy the conventions which normally constrained them. The disreputable acts which seemed to connote disreputable identities actually marked out a recurring phase of existence and experience for individuals or groups, a moment of escape and freedom, in which a usually-hidden identity or facet of personality could come forth, express and display itself, being donned along with holiday clothing which might itself acquire an extravagant showiness which would not 'do' at home.[1] Moreover, notions of the liminality of the seaside, as gateway between the elements and open, ambiguous setting where nature reasserts its dominance over culture and constraints of legality, property and propriety are suspended, have almost arrived at the status of cliche, at least in those academic circles where social history meets cultural studies.[2] On similar criteria the seaside qualifies as a potential site of carnival, where release from workaday disciplines and responsibilities and the pursuit of untrammelled pleasure as safety-valve, on sites set aside for such escape, enables the temporary upending of the social order, the transgression of mundane boundaries, the display of what is conventionally hidden and the inauguration of an ephemeral regime of festive excess.[3] And in most cases the seaside offered a relatively anonymous environment, in which excessive behaviour, disguise (in, for example, flamboyant garb which laid claim to enhanced status and pretensions (see Figure 1)) and defiance of convention could be indulged in without serious danger of embarrassing or otherwise painful recognition or exposure, although the fear of such exposure, or of humiliating responses to excessively loud or pretentious clothing or outrageously affected mannerisms, nevertheless became the staple fare of Victorian cartoonists.[4]

It should be emphasized at the outset, however, that this is only part of the story. The post-Victorian plot of *Hindle Wakes*, which depended on Victorian assumptions about sexual propriety and struck such a significant chord with playgoers and then with the cinema public of the inter-war years, depends (at least in the stage version) on a cross-class flirtation in Blackpool between millowner's son and 'mill lass', which has to move to Llandudno to be consummated because of the multitude of observant eyes in the Lancashire resort. Such an outcome could not have been so publicly articulated a generation earlier, but its premises would have been completely recognisable. Where whole towns went on holiday to the same place (or so it seemed), the suspension of everyday constraints on behaviour was limited by recognition of the consensual limits beyond which high spirits and enjoyment could not go without adverse consequences for reputation; and where, as at Blackpool, masters and workpeople, Sunday School teachers and scholars, spinners and piecers crossed paths in the same or overlapping recreational spaces (most famously the Tower Ballroom), the authority systems of home reinforced the sanctions of teasing or disapproval to form an effective set of safety-valves to contain and regulate the exuberant letting off of steam.[5] This incarnation of the popular seaside holiday came into full bloom in the last quarter of the nineteenth century, as the cotton town holidays of the Lancashire Wakes (and their analogues elsewhere in the North and Midlands) invented and reinvented themselves at the seaside; and in the early railway age, as the first cheap trips puffed and clanked their way to the coast, the excursions that brought their own internal controls (the works or Sunday School outings which brought local authority-figures with them with a view to channeling enjoyment in approved directions) showed up in stark contrast with the purely profit-seeking open promotions of railway companies and private speculators, which brought hedonistic minorities, often careless of reputation, to drink, belabour donkeys and cavort promiscuously in the waves: or at least, so the censorious commentaries of alarmed local tradesmen in the resorts would have it.[6] Where resorts drew on more diffuse catchment areas and attracted minorities of working-class holidaymakers at the crest of the poverty cycle (especially young people as yet unencumbered by family responsibilities), such moral panics about drunkenness and unseemly behaviour were still in evidence in the 1890s and beyond, especially along the extensive arc of resorts from Great Yarmouth to Margate and Brighton that drew on the working classes of London's East End and southern inner suburbs, but also (for example) when well-paid (or temporarily affluent) but unconstrained Liverpudlians found their way

178

THE RAREY ZEBRA PATTERN—A SWEET THING FOR THE SEASIDE.

Figure 1.

CLARA. Why, dear me! What do you wear your hat in the water for?
MRS. WALRUS. Oh, I always wear it when I bathe; for then you see, dear, no one can recognise me from the beach!

Figure 2.

by steamer to the more sedate resorts of North Wales. Not that behaviour that was deemed to be problematic was solely a working-class prerogative, of course: the seaside also offered scope for public misbehaviour to men of the lower and comfortable middle classes, especially, again, the young and unattached; and it took two to make a seaside flirtation, when (as in the marriage market of eighteenth-century Bath) neither of the parties could be certain of the status of the other. For these purposes, the seaside was a theatre of dreams and, potentially, disasters.[7]

So were other places, of course, and despite its vaunted status as a 'place on the margin', the epitome of liminality, the seaside shared the promises – and threats – of the anonymous and irresponsible spree with (most obviously) central London and the emergent entertainment districts of all the larger towns of the later nineteenth century. Simon Gunn convincingly emphasizes the importance of Manchester's middle-class rituals of public performance, like the Saturday morning promenade in St Ann's Square: but in such settings (as in certain seaside resorts which recruited their visitors from rarefied or concentrated high-status groups with high levels of mutual recognition) the aim was to display and sustain a solid identity validated by other means, rather than to aspire to it through a bravura and perhaps deceptive performance before an audience which itself had imperfect information and uncertain social standing.[8] But a provincial capital (in cultural and economic if not in overtly political terms) like Manchester also had popular entertainment areas (around Deansgate or Oldham Road, for example, or at Belle Vue on the outskirts) which brought people of all classes (though exclusively men from the higher ones) together on pleasure bent from the surrounding industrial towns as well as from Manchester's more immediate environs, boosted by the early spread of railways and the mid-century invention of the week-end in the cotton industry. This was a more anonymous crowd, as the reminiscences of Manchester policemen suggest, and the scope for shedding the constraining demands of consensual respectability was enhanced accordingly.[9] Among the (invariably male) middle-class seekers after disreputable pleasures in the dangerous but alluring central entertainment districts anonymity, or at least discretion, was a shared priority. The Liverpool journalist Hugh Shimmin, trawling the 'low' music-halls, singing-saloons, dance-halls and places of assignation in the city centre and at the Aintree racecourse, claimed to recognise several members of well-known middle-class families sloughing the shackles of respectability; but he named no names, and the frequent commentaries on these nether worlds in the local periodicals that flourished through the mid-Victorian years (Shimmin's own *Porcupine*, Manchester's *Free Lance*, Birmingham's *Owl*) provided their picaresque details of dubious activities through generalised conventions of journalistic caricature and a vocabulary of social 'types', without identifying individual actors or spectators.[10] London offered such opportunities for escape on the grand scale, of course, and those who wished to replace the public garb of respectability with the cloak of invisibility which descent towards the 'underworld' (that loaded label for an imagined space) entailed were able to gravitate towards the music-hall, pleasure ground, gathering-place for street bookmakers or pornographers, rat-pit, dogfighting beerhouse or back-street sexual encounter of their choice. The removal of some of the seedier activities that gave spice and danger to London's West End, as more of it became sanitised through the rise of the shopping and theatre districts and the need to protect newly-visible 'respectable' women from harassment, was an important late Victorian theme; but it changed the map of London's disreputable places and pleasures rather than excising them.[11]

However liminal it might be regarded as being, the seaside as 'place on the margin' could not match the metropolis itself for disreputable and dangerous pleasures, which were so readily accessible practically on the doorstep of London's bohemian, bachelor, clubman and even suburban paterfamilias, with plentiful provincial analogues. Switching into disreputable guise did not require a distancing journey to a separate pleasure periphery: it could be integrated into the everyday life of the apparently upstanding male Victorian citizen.

Complaints about disreputable seaside behaviour, indeed, owed much to the enhanced susceptibilities of traders and residents in what were, after all, generally quite small towns, despite the rapid Victorian growth of the most dynamic in percentage terms whose magnitude was inflated by the prevailing low base figures.[12] The dominant market in most Victorian seaside resorts was that ultimate bastion of ostensible respectability, the middle-class family, whose subordinate members were increasingly screened through suburban residence, sanitised city centres and private schooling from day-to-day encounters with boisterous and indecorous pleasures, and did not care to be confronted by them in obtrusive and threatening form on what was supposed to be a healthy and improving holiday. The boarding-house, as the predominant form of holiday accommodation, imposed temporary constraints of respectability on the guests within its expanded household, who could only escape this stranglehold by renting cottages or seeking out the more impersonal atmosphere of the large hotel, which, like Scarborough's Grand, imposed dress, dining and deportment codes but left much greater scope for coming and going unobserved by anyone who mattered.[13]

Even in late Victorian Blackpool, which pioneered working-class entertainment at the seaside on both the grand and 'penny capitalist' scale, from pleasure palaces run by public companies to peep-shows and fortune-telling on the beach and from converted front gardens, the concern not to compromise respectability led to regular, and controversial, local authority purges on street music, or beach traders, or hawkers and touts, or public-house singing-saloons. In more mainstream resorts the reinforcement of respectability, to protect the dominant market in competition with rivals displaying similar priorities, was much more sustained; and here respectability was expected to take a holiday in the sense of transplanting its values to the decorous, controlled environment of the middle-class resort, rather than in the more obvious and tempting sense of being displaced and giving free rein to pleasures and practices which were normally hidden.[14]

So most Victorian seaside resorts became protected environments, assiduously and ostentatiously guarded against unseemliness by the by-laws and inspectorates which were quickly installed to counteract the relaxed mores which the transplanting of pleasure-seekers to this new setting soon invited, as was apparent from the earliest days of Brighton and Margate. Nothing could be done about the less obtrusive sins of omission which could be indulged, most obviously neglect of Sunday worship in the absence of neighbours and regular co-worshippers to notice this dereliction of respectable duty (although, for those who valued display, the subsequent church parade, which often began before the services had finished, was observed punctiliously). A plausible excuse came from the inability of church buildings to accommodate the seasonal influx. The hiring of carriages or cabs on Sundays for frivolous purposes could be discouraged, however, and Sunday restrictions on commercial entertainment continued to prevail in Victorian resorts, with even the concerts of sacred music which enlivened piers, bandstands and Winter Gardens becoming contentious whenever their programmes deviated from a narrow range of acceptable pieties. When Blackpool went so far down the road to secularity as to allow Sunday tram services in 1896, a local Methodist minister denounced the Corporation, presciently complaining that compared with such excesses 'Paris is sweet, and Sodom was a paradise'.[15] Most resorts, and Blackpool some of the time, sought to err on the side of restriction: the Home Office files, and minutes of evidence on by-law proposals in the House of Lords Record Office, are full of efforts by central government officialdom to protect free trade and the liberty of the subject against proposals for the stringent regulation or prohibition of activities deemed undesirable, which went beyond the dominant culture of the developing civil service.[16] Resorts with a strong residential component, like Hove, or a preferred market based on the staid, affluent elderly, like Sidmouth, were particularly restrictive, and their controls (which extended to strict limitation of the range of permitted entertainment and a preference for word-of-mouth rather than public advertising) were still a by-word among external commentators in the inter-war years and well beyond, by which time Frinton, which had been in its infancy at the turn of the century, had emerged to provide the ultimate example of frigid defensiveness, with its stern exclusion of picnic parties, its rigorously precise policing of bathing and bathing-hut occupancy, and its pathological horror of anything resembling a 'tripper'. It had direct Victorian ancestors, most obviously Westgate-on-Sea, whose dangerous proximity to rollicking Margate helped to heighten the moral barricades, just as did Frinton's own juxtaposition with plebeian Walton-on-the-Naze and Clacton; but its career (and notoriety) offers a reminder that 'Victorian' restrictiveness (and subversive challenges to it, through music-hall, cartoon and popular journalistic sketch) had a long post-Victorian career, although the tide began to ebb during the inter-war years and to go out in earnest from the 1960s onwards. Ideas of seaside liminality and carnivalesque cut more ice in the popular parts of Blackpool and Brighton, Southend and Great Yarmouth, than in the medium-sized havens for family parties and the elderly that dominated the Victorian resort panorama.[17] These were particularly vulnerable in the late Victorian years to external invasion by working-class day-trippers, predominantly young couples, who had not yet learned (or chose not to accept) the sedate conventions of seaside behaviour that ruled in such places, suffocating the liminal under a grid of imposed regulation and internalized convention. Thus the South Wales miners and tinplate workers, who came across the Bristol Channel to Ilfracombe in the 'floating beershops' of the late nineteenth century to escape restrictions on Sunday drinking, scandalised the predominant elderly spinsters, quiet families and devotees of scenery and natural history who made up the regular visiting public, until the local authority succeeded in excluding them; and they had their noisy, uninhibited counterparts in many other places, especially on the Kent and Essex coasts, and in North Wales wherever the Liverpool excursion steamers penetrated.[18] How far this was a matter of exporting the usual high jinks of a week-end's pleasure to a different setting, and how far the seaside venue added extra spice and even a desire to shock, is another question.

Perhaps the most genuinely and distinctively liminal incarnation of the Victorian middle-class seaside holiday was to be found in the most marginal (in the sense of remote and physically isolated) of settings: the little fishing and farming villages, the 'resorts beyond railways', that took in devotees of the 'simple life', of relaxed bohemianism and of an appreciation of the quaint, the picturesque (in a broad sense) and the historical (or archaic). Here John Urry's 'romantic gaze', and its 'anthropological' variant, could be indulged, directed at the 'otherness' of fisherfolk and rustics; the outward and visible trappings of a despised fashionable civilisation could be set aside; and bathing could be enjoyed without the restrictions of bathing-machines and segregation of the sexes that prevailed in the more formal and established places, with their artificial promenades and conventional landscaping.[19] Within some of the larger resorts, as at Scarborough and Hastings, the old fishing quarters offered similar attractions; but the other, overlapping incarnation of the liminal that stands out in behavioural terms is the 'plotland Arcadias' so brilliantly analysed by Ward and Hardy: the congeries of shacks and converted railway carriages and tramcars that mushroomed on cheap, marginal and especially seaside land, on shingle spits and estuaries, to provide a cheap, unsupervised, unconstrained escape for determined bohemians who were prepared to forego conventional comforts, and to express an alternative aesthetic of sprawling, untidy abundance which was to anger and disturb the emergent planning profession of the first half of the twentieth century beyond all measure. These haunts of writers, actors and actresses, unorthodox professionals and defiers of convention drawn from all but the most impoverished social strata offered an alternative form of Victorian disreputability that challenged aesthetics and moralities of geometry and tidiness, and subverted technologies of control more dangerously by rejecting them (at least for the period of the holiday or week-end), rather than suspending or defying them in more conventional (and self-consciously illicit) pleasure-seeking beyond respectable bounds.[20]

These little resorts tended to have only the most rudimentary forms of local government, and their small scale, together with the like-minded and relaxed attitudes of their visitors, enabled them to manage without the usual restraints on everything from building to bathing. Nor was commercial entertainment an issue: this minority of 'simple life' visitors had chosen to avoid it. And the patrons of the coves and inlets of Cornwall or Cardiganshire, or the habitues of the 'bungalow towns' of Sussex or Essex, were indeed a small minority, limited by problems of access and disposable time as well as by cultural preferences and resistance to mainstream versions of fashion and fun. In larger resorts where the more mainstream conventions of Victorian England carried clout, there was more likely to be controversy over what was prescribed and acceptable, especially where larger visiting publics were less united in their tastes and expectations. A particularly telling example is the regulation of bathing, which was particularly closely entwined with notions of liminality, carnival and more mundane challenges to respectability, and carried a more powerful charge because (in all but the largest resorts with the most elaborate and alluring entertainment industries) sea-bathing retained its place at the core of the seaside holiday experience, although the nature of that place changed considerably during Victoria's reign.

Bathing was an obvious potential flashpoint of controversy because it challenged taboos about undress and bodily exposure at exactly the site that constituted the centrepiece of the 'respectable' seaside visit: the place where the sea conferred health on her votaries, but (initially, at least) under a medical regime that prescribed frequency of immersion, length of exposure, and elaborate rituals of preparation for and recovery from the shocking encounter with the raw elements. Bathing was supposed to be as controlled and free from undue excitement as the circumstances could allow. But the practice was never so simple, and expectations about proper behaviour in this ultimate 'place on the margin' (in some senses rather than others: Brighton was also 'London-by-sea) followed a moving frontier of debate between the 1830s and the 1890s.[21]

John Travis has argued convincingly against the established belief that a clampdown on nude and mixed-sex bathing at the resorts in the 1850s and 1860s imposed a regime of propriety and prudery on the shoreline, consigning bathing to the wheeled wooden horse-drawn bathing-machines that squatted on the beach in segregated rows, and that a tentative return to mixed bathing, in suitably decorous costume, was inaugurated at Bexhill in 1901 and spread steadily to other resorts thereafter before becoming the norm in the more liberated (and sun-seeking) inter-war years. He points to a sustained attachment to nude bathing among middle- and upper-class men, and a much more widespread willingness among both sexes to shed inhibitions about bodily exposure in what was recognised to be the distinctive environment of the beach. The resorts of the mid-Victorian years faced a dilemma. Evangelical campaigners for the strict regulation of bathing were in tune with the dominant value-system to which most people paid lip-service, and resorts felt the need to introduce bathing by-laws (sometimes adopting the whole paraphernalia of urban local government for this initial purpose) to avoid losing the patronage of the self-consciously respectable. On the other hand, too precise an actual enforcement of the by-laws would deter lucrative visitors who wanted the freedom to bathe unencumbered, and argued that the full benefits to health were lost by wearing bathing dress. Such people included clergymen, although it would perhaps be dangerous to generalise too readily from the example of the Rev. Francis Kilvert.[22] So bathing regulations tended to be honoured more in the breach than the observance, to the gratification of the large numbers of people of both sexes (Kilvert again included) who enjoyed watching the carnivalesque spectacle: Brighton's bathing beach was a haven for voyeurs with opera-glasses from the later eighteenth century onwards, and the practice was common, and attracted censorious comment, at (for example) Scarborough and Margate. The by-laws were most likely to be invoked when large numbers of boisterous working-class trippers challenged the proprieties by a combination of nudity and horseplay in a prominent situation: thus Blackpool was well to the fore in adopting and using bathing by-laws from 1853 onwards.[23] Those twin (and intertwined) Victorian bogeys, class and hypocrisy, thus make their appearance in this setting; and the issue was also complicated by the development of the beach as children's territory, with the cult of the sandcastle and of innocent, supervised play already in the ascendant by the 1840s. Margate was prominent among the resorts that failed to enforce by-laws, leading to complaints like the one in the 1870s about the woman who sported in the waves 'with her nude and whiskered friend upon her back';[24] and Scarborough resolved the issue by requiring men to wear drawers only between 7 a.m. and 9 p.m. in the most public part of the beach: elsewhere freedom ruled, and the democratic imperative to provide reasonable access to those who could afford neither bathing-machines nor drawers was part of the expressed justification for the policy in this socially-mixed resort. Mixed bathing, too, remained quite common in English resorts throughout the later nineteenth century, as informed press comment showed in 1895; and the steady switch from health to pleasure as the predominant motive for sea-bathing during a slightly longer period helped to liberate the practice from medical as well as moral constraint. This in turn contributed to the notion that mixed bathing allowed families to enjoy themselves together, thereby providing a powerful moral counterweight against the segregation of the sexes, though the price of this relaxation was the covering of potentially controversial areas of the body.

Travis thus draws attention to a fault-line running through the Victorian middle classes, in a setting whose combination of the liberating and the threatening juxtaposed therapy and hedonistic display and was bound, in context, to generate conflict. Here, disreputability was very much (and very literally) in the eye, or the gaze, of the beholder. The role of the beach as a place for displaying the body and flirting was clearly understood by the cartoonists who plied their trade in *Punch*, *Fun* and the other Victorian comic weeklies (see Figure 3); and exchanges like this show a more general awareness of the devouring gaze that might be directed from the shore, and the widespread equation of respectability with anonymity:

CLARA. Why, dear me! What do you wear your hat in the water for?

MRS. WALRUS. Oh, I always wear it when I bathe; for then you see, dear, no one can recognise me from the beach.[25]

Some, like the pairs of trippers photographed cuddling recumbent on the Great Yarmouth beach by photographer Paul Martin at the turn of the century, were less worried about either of these things; and here worries about display in the sea passed over into censorious comment about behaviour on land.[26] This went a stage beyond the 'parasexuality' and glamour with which the bathing belle, like Peter Bailey's barmaid, might be invested: she might be an object of desire, or at least interest; her fashionable bathing wear and flowing locks might be assiduously and eagerly illustrated in the public prints; but she was out of her element, beyond the bathing machine, as untouchable as the mermaids to which she was often wistfully compared.[27] On land, even (or especially) the liminal land of beach and promenade, matters might be different.

Cartoon representations (and postcards, when the time came) of the Victorian seaside laid great emphasis on flirting as a holiday pastime (or more serious activity) (see figures 3-7). Young men cruised the beaches and promenades in pursuit of young women, who deployed wit and subterfuge as weapons in the resulting battle of the sexes; fashionably-clad older women were the objects of attention until the faces beneath the protective hats became visible; unflattering remarks were overheard by the victims, as were apparent compliments which turned out to be directed elsewhere; and legs, male and female, became the focus of appraising looks, especially when a boisterous seaside wind sportingly lifted petticoats or made skirts (or trousers) cling to bodies.[28] As a contributor to *Once-a-Week* remarked of Brighton in 1861, 'The universal occupation of every living soul seems to be staring and being stared at; so much so, that if an inhabitant of some of the spheres were to witness for the first time a fashionable promenade, he would think that everybody had something inside them that everyone else was desirous of getting at'.[29] Quite how innocent this was, as with a great deal of Victorian seaside humour, is difficult to reconstruct at this distance; but all this calls to mind Steven Marcus' decoding of the undercurrent of pornography that flowed alongside and sometimes mingled unobtrusively with mainstream Victorian fiction. Whether the presence of prostitutes alongside the 'respectable', and difficult to distinguish from them in their seaside finery, added spice to these games (as opposed to merely encouraging men to be a predatory nuisance) would need teasing out from sources which are usually reticent on the surface. Brighton, where they were most obviously in evidence, was also home not only to the generic figure of the flirtatious 'summer girl', but also to what *Once-a-Week* labelled 'the Fastlies', young middle-class sisters who wore rouge, rode hard along the cliffs in the morning, smoked cheroots and talked loosely, exhibiting a 'bearing of insouciance, and ... unfeminine independence of style, and the

WE SHOULD THINK SO.

AUNT. Now, Clara, you should do as I do. Whenever any man follows me, I turn round, and give him one of *my* looks, and he is off immediately.

Figure 3.

THE GALE. (1862.)

" Don't be alarmed, darlings—the Captain has got quite enough to do to look after himself."—*Punch.*

Figure 4.

WIND, S.W. FRESH.
Tomkins, who is not grand in the leg department, says, "It's a very disagreeable day." The young ladies, however for obvious reasons, enjoy it amazingly.

Figure 5.

"Now, Charley! here's that pretty round hat again—we *will* have a look at her this time."

Figure 6

HEARTLESS PRACTICAL JOKE. (*Period* 1858.)

CHARLOTTE. Here they come, Blanche. Let us pretend we don't recollect them.

Figure 7.

PERCY AT BRIGHTON.

That awful swell Percy de Gosling finds himself by accident at Brighton on Whit-Monday. His nerves have been terribly shocked. Already he has been asked if he wanted any tea-accommodation ; and now a boatman requests him to " jine this party, and make up the 'arf dozen for a row." (1862.)

Figure 8.

total absence of quiet, modest bearing in every movement and gesture'.[30] Whether such presentations of self were accentuated by seaside freedom is left unclear; but this blurring of the respectable and the disreputable was another way in which the seaside defied the rigid moral categories with which the Victorians sought to reassure themselves, and with which historians seek to make sense of them.

As this shift from beach to urban dry land might suggest, the leisured and increasingly pleasure-orientated atmosphere of the seaside resort prompted a more general air of release which carried a pervasive sexual charge. Celebrations of the arrival of the 'husband boat' (a great Margate institution) or the 'husband train', bringing working husbands to join their holidaymaking families for the week-end, carried sub-texts not only of the renewal of domestic affections but also of the opportunities for dalliance that might arise during the week.[31] A caricature of 'that awful swell Percy de Gosling' (Figure 8), making the mistake of visiting Brighton among the plebeian festivities of Whit Monday (a reminder of the mutability of resort life by day and week as well as season), presents one of the shocks to his system as being 'asked if he wanted any tea accommodation', which looks like an allusion to the practice of prostitutes touting for custom by offering tea (or in the case of New Brighton 'ham and eggs', on the infamous Parade which acquired the nickname) which was expected to be continued upstairs, behind drawn curtains, as Jerome K. Jerome made (almost) explicit in *Today* in 1895.[32] The pervasiveness of seaside sexuality might be encountered even among the younger boatmen, a seaside genre normally presented in terms of knowing but safe 'old salts' whose main concern was to exploit the visitors commercially. Stephen Reynolds, the middle-class writer with Bloomsbury connections who lived and worked with the Sidmouth fishermen in the early twentieth century, offered suggestive commentary on one of his colleagues who allegedly took out 'ladies' for a row and offered sexual as well as general maritime services to them.[33] To all this could be added (for example) the ambiguities in the coquettish poses of the young fisherwomen who were captured by Frank Meadow Sutcliffe at Whitby and by other photographers elsewhere; the sexual and otherwise titillating and sensational content of waxworks and sideshows, and not only at Blackpool; and the possibilities for the signalling of alternative meanings which might be looked for in the output of minstrel shows and pierrots, to say nothing of Punch and Judy.[34] If inter-war Blackpool 'seethed with sex', as Anthony Burgess had it (although we must set this against the ambivalence of Mass-Observation as well as endorsing it through the oral evidence collected by Steve Humphries), the Victorian antecedents of such seaside preoccupations may not be far to seek.[35]

The Victorian seaside was not necessarily, or perhaps even usually, a cosily boring place, although that aspect of the smaller watering-places is acknowledged ironically in contemporary humorous writing, which also deals sympathetically with the loneliness of the solitary holidaymaker.[36] At the other extreme, excursionists were capable of rioting, on one Southend occasion having to be suppressed by the military; and a pattern of occasional disturbances over attempts to privatise open spaces and move fishing activities out of resort areas can be identified. However smooth the surface of resort life might be, there was always conflict and a struggle for survival just below it: unemployment, a high throughput of casual workers, seasonal itinerants, and the potential for disruption and depredation by local children. Cartoons and humorous sketches reveal an endemic expectation that visitors will be fiddled and cheated, whether by donkey drivers, boatmen, waiters or landladies.[37] Not only might the seaside offer an atmosphere conducive to sexual disrepute: it might become positively crimogenic, to borrow a word from Gerald Mars, as so many petty traders and providers of services, living from hand to mouth, had neither need nor scope for building up relationships of mutual trust with transient visitors, and strove to reap their seasonal harvest as best they could.[38] Unease about being cheated went hand in hand, among the visiting public, with their own concern with role-play and the uncertain status and antecedents of those they met. The Victorian seaside systematically compromised both respectability and personal security, which is why most mainstream resorts had to set such overt store by providing and maintaining it. The situation varied resort by resort, and fluctuated over time, but the seaside holiday put respectability on trial, as visitors might live in perpetual hope of temporary escape from its confines, and in perpetual fear of being compromised and found wanting. Disreputability, as subtext and accessible other side of the coin or even alternative reading, was always waiting in the wings.

Endnotes

[1] Peter Bailey, *Popular culture and performance in the Victorian city* (Cambridge, 1998), especially Chapters 2-3.
[2] Rob Shields, *Places on the margin* (Cambridge, 1991).
[3] J.K. Walton, *The British seaside: holidays and resorts in the twentieth century* (Manchester, 2000), 3-5, 18-19; Gary Cross, *Worktowners at Blackpool* (London, 1990).
[4] Bailey, *Popular culture*, Chapter 3; J.A. Hammerton, *Holidays and travel* (London, n.d.), 22, 27, 34, 36, 47, 52.
[5] J.K. Walton, *The British seaside: holidays and resorts in the twentieth*

century (Manchester, 2000), 8; idem., *Blackpool* (Edinburgh, 1998), 47-59.

[6] Walton, *Blackpool*, 25-6 and Chapter 4; idem., *The English seaside resort: a social history 1750-1914* (Leicester, 1983), Chapter 7.

[7] Walton, *Seaside resort*, Chapter 7; and (for example) the novels of Jerome K. Jerome.

[8] Simon Gunn, *The public culture of the Victorian middle class* (Manchester, 2000), 75-6.

[9] J. Bent, *Criminal life* (Manchester, 1891).

[10] J.K. Walton and A. Wilcox, eds, *Low life and moral improvement in mid-Victorian England: Liverpool through the journalism of Hugh Shimmin* (Leicester, 1991); Gunn, *Public culture*, 61-71.

[11] Judith Walkowitz, *City of dreadful delight* (London, 1992), Chapters 1-2; Lynda Nead, *Victorian Babylon* (New Haven and London, 2000).

[12] Walton, *English seaside resort*, Chapter 2.

[13] J.K. Walton, *The Blackpool landlady: a social history* (Manchester, 1978), 11; Scarborough Public Library, Scarborough Room, Grand Hotel pamphlets.

[14] Walton, *English seaside resort*, Chapter 8.

[15] J.S. Balmer, *Blackpool, Paris and Sodom* (Blackpool, 1896).

[16] See especially minuted comments and marginalia on by-law proposals in Public Record Office HO.45.

[17] Laura Chase, 'The creation of place image in inter-war Clacton and Frinton', Ph.D. thesis, University of Essex, 1999; D. Crouch, 'Westgate-on-Sea 1865-1940', Ph.D. thesis, University of Kent, 1999.

[18] F.B. May, 'Victorian and Edwardian Ilfracombe', in J.K. Walton and J. Walvin, eds, *Leisure in Britain 1780-1939* (Manchester, 1983), 199.

[19] John Urry, *Consuming places* (London, 1995).

[20] C. Ward and D. Hardy, *Arcadia for all* (London, 1984).

[21] For what follows see especially J. Travis, 'Continuity and change in English sea-bathing 1730-1900', in S. Fisher, ed., *Recreation and the sea* (Exeter, 1997), 8-35.

[22] W. Plomer, ed., *Kilvert's Diary* (Harmondsworth: 1972 edn.).

[23] Walton, *Blackpool*, 25-6; and for the case of Dawlish, Travis, 'English sea-bathing', 17.

[24] *Keble's Gazette*, 8 August 1872.

[25] Hammerton, *Holidays and travel*, 127.

[26] Steve Humphries, *A secret world of sex* (London, 1988), Chapter 7, especially 172.

[27] Bailey, *Popular culture*, Chapter 7; F. Stafford and N. Yates, *The later Kentish seaside* (Gloucester, 1985), 129.

[28] Hammerton, *Holidays and travel*, 4, 14, 18-19, 28, 44-5, 50, 52.

[29] Ibid., 30 ('Sketches at Brighton').

[30] Ibid., 39-43; S. Marcus, *The other Victorians* (London, 1975).

[31] Hammerton, *Holidays and travel*, 224; Stafford and Yates, *Later Kentish seaside*, 28, 32.

[32] Hammerton, *Holidays and travel*, 29; Maurice G. Hope, *Castles in the sand* (Ormskirk, 1982), 15-16.

[33] Stephen Reynolds, *A poor man's house* (London, 1908).

[34] Walton, *English seaside resort*, Chapter 8 offers an introduction to these possibilities, which might be taken much further.

[35] Walton, *British seaside*, 5; Humphries, *Secret world*, Chapter 7.

[36] Hammerton, *Holidays and travel*, 135.

[37] Ibid., 30, 206, 217, 221, and Walton, *Blackpool Landlady*, Chapters 1 and 6.

[38] J.K. Walton, M. Blinkhorn, C. Pooley, D. Tidswell and M. Winstanley, 'Crime, migration and social change in north-west England and the Basque Country, *c.* 1870-1930', *British Journal of Criminology* 39 (1999): 98.

Wanton Women and Malignant Murderesses: the female criminal and the Victorian reader

Chris Willis
Department of English
Birkbeck College
Malet Street
London, WC1E 7HX
chris@chriswillis.freeserve.co.uk

The female criminal was a figure of endless fascination to the Victorian reader. According to the *Medical Critic and Psychological Journal* of 1863, 'A heroine who was not an adulteress and a poisoner would disgust a modern novel-reader, and would prevent him [sic] from following, even as far as the second volume, the fortunes of a person so uninteresting'.[1] Penny Dreadfuls such as Mary Elizabeth Braddon's *The Black Band* and Edward Ellis' *Ruth the Betrayer* featured female criminal masterminds whose sexual and homicidal misdemeanours give the lie to any assumption that the Victorians were invariably prudish and proper. Sensation novels elevated such stories to middle-class reading-matter, with respectable readers eagerly lapping up the adventures of Braddon's Lady Audley, Wilkie Collins' Lydia Gwilt and a host of other murderous, bigamous women. By the turn of the century, even family magazines such as the *Strand* featured the serialised exploits of female super-criminals such as L.T. Meade's Madame Sara.

The very shortage of terms available to define such women is significant: there is no female equivalent of the terms 'mastermind' or 'master-criminal'. Victorian convention expected criminal masterminds to be male. However, some of these women were presented as being far more dangerous than their male counterparts: Ellery Queen commented that L.T. Meade's Madame Sara 'made rogues like Colonel Clay and Raffles look like sissies'.[2] Most of them are highly successful, becoming rich as a result of their crimes. All are young, beautiful and murderous, and all escape the gallows, meeting their end by extra-legal processes rather than in the courts. Each of the texts discussed in this paper ends with the anti-heroine being defeated, but her final fate is suicide or madness. Their punishments are dealt out by private individuals (often their own husbands, lovers or fathers), not by the law. In sensation novels, the scandal of the female villain is kept firmly within the family, maintaining the public facade of middle-class respectability. Penny dreadful villainesses meet a less private but equally extra-legal end. None of the women I discuss in this paper is convicted of murder in a criminal court. If brought to court they are acquitted or let off lightly, and go on to commit further crimes until Nemesis overtakes them at the hands of those they have wronged. Writing in 1868, the renowned anti-feminist Eliza Lynn Linton shrewdly commented that:

> British chivalry objects to the public laying-on of hands in
> the case of a woman, even when most recalcitrant and
> disobedient; more particularly if a small and fragile-looking
> woman.[3]

The intelligent fictional female criminal can exploit this misplaced chivalry to her advantage: Edward Ellis' Ruth Trail[4] and Wilkie Collins' Lydia Gwilt[5] use their fragile feminine beauty to persuade the courts to acquit them or give them lenient sentences. This echoes some well-publicised criminal trials of the era. A Scots jury found the murder charge against attractive young Madeline Smith 'not proven' and there was great hostility against police attempts to accuse fragile teenager Constance Kent of the murder of her baby brother, despite the strong evidence in both cases.

Murderous women presented an additional threat to Victorian values through their sexuality. The strongly sexualised visual iconography of the mid- and late-nineteenth century *femme fatale* owes a great deal to the seductive sorceresses of Pre-Raphaelite paintings. Many Pre-Raphaelite portraits show murderous or predatory women who are beautiful and strongly sexualised: Frederick Sandys' *Morgan le Fay* (1862-1863) and *Medea* (1868), Edward Burne-Jones' *The Beguiling of Merlin* (1874), Dante Gabriel Rossetti's *Astarte Syriaca* (1877), Frank Cadogan Cooper's *La Belle Dame Sans Merci* (1877-1958) and John William Waterhouse's *The Magic Circle* (1886), *Circe Offering the Cup to Ulysses* (1891) and *Circe Invidiosa* (1892). The figure of Circe is particularly significant, offering a paradigm for figures such as Ruth Trail and Lydia Gwilt, who deliberately use their sexuality to bring out the worst in the men they use as tools.

Mid-century villainesses created for working-class consumption tend to commit more varied and spectacular crimes than their sensation novel equivalents. It is probable that penny dreadfuls provided for working-class women the kind of enjoyment that middle-class women readers found in the more expensive Gothic and sensation novels. Some of the serials in Edward Lloyd's penny magazines of the 1850s were aimed specifically at female readers.[6] Mary Elizabeth Braddon, who began her career by writing for penny and halfpenny papers, summed up her readers' requirements:

> This work is most piratical stuff & would make your hair stand on end, if you were to see it. The amount of crime, treachery, murder, slow poisoning & general infamy required by the Halfpenny reader is something terrible. I am just going to do a little paracide [sic] for this week's supply.[7]

'[C]rime, treachery, murder, slow poisoning and general infamy' would certainly be a fair description of the criminal career of Braddon's murderous bigamist Lady Edith Vandeleur, anti-heroine of *The Black Band, or the Mysteries of Midnight*. Lady Edith is a dissolute aristocrat whose criminal career makes Lady Audley look demure and restrained in comparison. It is possible to see Lady Edith and Lady Audley as basically the same character: one packaged for a middle-class readership and one packaged for the halfpenny press readers who, as Braddon was to put it in *The Doctor's Wife*, 'want ... plot, and plenty of it; surprises and plenty of 'em; mystery, as thick as a November fog'.[8] Middle-class reviewers were scandalised by sensation heroines but, as Jennifer Carnell comments, characters such as Lady Edith 'would have sent a reviewer apoplectic if he had come across [them] in a three decker'.[9] Authors of moral tales for children were certainly 'sent ... apoplectic' by such tales. Ascott R. Hope's 1900 children's novel *Sandy's Secret* recounts the adventures of two young boys who are led into mischief by reading penny and halfpenny fiction, including:

> the gory adventures of the 'Black Band,' and the dark thread of the 'Midnight Mysteries' always snapped off so provokingly 'to be continued in our next.'[10]

Unlike Lady Audley, Lady Edith cannot offer poverty as an extenuating circumstance for her entry into a criminal career. A latter-day Vittoria Corombona, Edith plots to poison her rich husband in order to be free to marry her murderous lover. The plot fails, and her husband and father conspire to have her declared mad and imprisoned in her husband's castle in Scotland. There are strong echoes of *Jane Eyre*. Her fate is similar to that of Rochester's wife, but unlike Bertha Rochester she is perfectly sane, and escapes to continue a spectacular criminal career. The first murder, Lady Edith's murder attempt and her subsequent incarceration all take place within *The Black Band*'s first hundred pages. The plot meanders on for another 506 pages, through a variety of complicated sub-plots involving kidnap, rape, murder, fraud, illegitimacy and prostitution. The action frequently returns to the career of Lady Edith, who escapes from her husband's castle, re-marries bigamously, becomes involved with an Italian secret society and plots further murders as a member of an English secret society known as 'the Black Band'. Her eventual fate is gruesome. After betraying her husband and his confederates, she is captured by members of the Italian secret society and buried alive, being walled into a niche to die a slow and painful death from thirst. She is eventually rescued, but dies of shock shortly afterwards. Burial alive is a frequent fate for the transgressive woman in the penny dreadful, and could perhaps be taken as symbolic of patriarchal society's attempts to confine women to the tight restrictions of the domestic sphere. The sensation fiction equivalent is internment in a lunatic asylum: a figurative rather than literal form of burial alive. As Jennifer Carnell comments, the similarity between the two punishments is evident from Braddon's own chapter headings: Lady Audley is confined to the asylum in a chapter headed 'Buried Alive', and Lady Edith is immured during a chapter called 'The Burial of the Living'.[11]

Braddon's portrayal of Lady Edith is crude and unsympathetic. She is portrayed as evil incarnate with no redeeming features, and is 'utterly incapable of love'.[12] The sensation villainess is a less crude creation. She may be partially reformed by love (like Lydia Gwilt) or may transgress because of love (like Isabel Vane). The motives of the penny dreadful villainess are purely financial, but the sensation villainess is often driven by her emotions. In an era when virtuous women were meant to subdue their emotions, they could indulge in them vicariously through their reading matter. Critics were deeply concerned by the sensations novel's supposed bad influence on the passions of its female readers.[13] The penny dreadful shows villainesses who are immune from the 'womanly' passions: sensation fiction shows anti-heroines who indulge too freely in them. In *East Lynne*, Mrs Henry Wood famously warns her readers against letting their passions run away with them:

> The very hour of [Lady Isabel's adulterous elopement] she awoke to what she had done; the guilt, whose aspect had been shunned in prospective assumed at once its true, frightful colour, the blackness of darkness; and a lively remorse, a never-dying anguish, took possession of her soul for ever. O reader, believe me! Lady – wife – mother! should you ever be tempted to abandon your home, so will you awaken! Whatever trials may be the lot of your married life, though they may magnify themselves to your crushed spirit as beyond the endurance of woman to bear, *resolve* to bear

them, fall down upon your knees and pray to be enabled to
bear them ...[14]

Transgressive sensation heroines such as Wood's Isabel Vane feel love:
penny dreadful villainesses feel sexual passion without any associated
tenderness. Lady Edith is incapable of love (although she has an active
sex life), and Ruth Trail, whom I will now discuss, betrays several lovers
during her spectacular criminal careeer.

Published in penny numbers,[15] the fifty-two instalments of Edward
Ellis' *Ruth the Betrayer* chronicle the adventure of Ruth Trail, who
begins life in a London slum and rises via robbery, forgery, murder and
illicit gambling to become 'one of the queens of fast, fashionable London
Society'.[16] Ruth's criminal career begins at an early age:

> When she was little better than a baby, then, she ran away
> from her friends and turned thief.
> A year afterwards, when she was not more than ten years
> old, we find her the mistress of a boy thief, in some vile
> lodging-house in Kent Street.
> Not long after that, the youthful lover falls into the hands of
> the police. His 'widow' appears in handsome clothes and,
> living in squalid splendour, and a rumour gets around that
> she had given information to the police.[17]

Ruth thus transgresses the expected norms of childhood as well as
those of femininity. Even in an era when the age of consent was twelve,[18]
a sexually active girl of ten would have been shocking to readers. The
sexual shock-value is deliberate on Ellis' part: *Ruth the Betrayer* is mildly
pornographic in parts,[19] which no doubt boosted sales. However, the
children's slum background has strong resonance with other fictional
genres. As well as having echoes of Fagin's gang in *Oliver Twist*, it
foreshadows *fin-de-siècle* concerns about the way slum children were
supposedly forced into a life of crime by their environment. Although he
has little sympathy for his heroine, who is presented as the incarnation of
evil, Ellis does not mince words in his descriptions of her early years:

> this wretched woman endeavour[ed] to think herself a
> martyr, and her memory carried her back to the days of her
> infancy – those days spent in the noisome alleys and squalid
> courts in the vilest and filthiest of Whitechapel purlieus!
> Again, to her hideous childhood – a childhood of precocious
> infamy, debauchery and prostitution!
> Again, to a girlhood spent among the thieves and vagabonds,
> among hellish revelries in the damnable haunts of the lowest
> and grossest vice and profligacy!

> The glare of the gin-palace – the sodden, drunken orgies of
> the shameless night-house – the nameless horrors of her
> street life – came back to her recollection ...[20]

Ellis represents Ruth as irredeemably evil, but at the same time implies
that she was driven to crime in childhood: prostitution and betrayal
offered her only way out of the slums. Ruth prefigures the slum viragoes
of later texts such as Gissing's *The Nether World* and Morrison's *A Child
of the Jago*. [21] She also has similarities with her middle-class counterpart,
the sensation villainess: Lady Audley pleads extenuating circumstances
because of poverty and Lydia Gwilt's career is shaped by her criminal
involvement at the age of twelve.

Ruth uses her beauty and sexuality to further her criminal career Her
exploits continue for over 400 pages, during which she becomes involved
in all kinds of criminal activity, double-crosses her lovers, and is shown
to be a deep-dyed villainess who exploits her sexual attractiveness and
has been the mistress of several different men. Like Lady Audley, Ruth
comes to a bad end, going 'raving mad, beyond all hope of recovery',[22]
and being immured in a convent, her beauty ruined and her body crippled
as a result of falling from an upper-storey window while trying to escape
the vengeance of a murderous ex-lover whom she had betrayed to the
police.[23] The penalty for her misuse of her sexuality is incarceration in a
community of celibates. Her fate is as much the punishment for her
predatory sexuality as for her crimes, a form of moral retribution which
was to recur in the sensation novel.

In the widely popular sensation novels of the 1860s the melodramatic
plots of penny fiction were echoed in mainstream fiction read openly by
the middle classes. Critics had looked down on the broadsheets, Newgate
novels and 'Penny Bloods' of the early part of the century as vulgar
productions for the lower classes, but sensation novels elevated crime
fiction into middle-class reading-matter. Mary Elizabeth Braddon was
aware of the strong resemblance between the sensation novel and penny
fiction. Describing a writer of penny fiction in her 1864 novel *The
Doctor's Wife*, she pointed out:

> That bitter term, 'sensation' had not yet been invented for
> the terror of romancers in the fifty-second year of this
> present century; but the thing nevertheless existed in divers
> forms and people wrote sensation novels ... unconsciously.[24]

Like the 'Penny Bloods', sensation novels depended heavily on crime
and sexual misconduct as mainstays of the plot, and the sexually
attractive, transgressive woman was a central figure. Despite the fact that
many of its exponents were women, such reading-matter was felt to

200

violate accepted norms of femininity. In an article in *Blackwoods* in 1867, Mrs Oliphant complained that:

> one of the earliest results of an increased feminine influence in our literature [has been] a display of what in women is most unfeminine.[25]

By 'unfeminine' Oliphant meant the move from the romance plot to a plot dependent on crime, melodramatic incident and sexual transgression. In an 1863 review of 'Popular Novels of the Year', *Fraser's Magazine* commented that:

> a book without a murder, a divorce, a seduction or a bigamy, is not apparently considered worth either writing or reading; and a mystery and a secret are the chief qualifications of the modern novel.[26]

Despite such 'unfeminine' subject matter, the sensation novel was largely a female genre. For many years previously, women readers had enjoyed sensation and melodrama in the form of Gothic novels: the sensation novel brought these closer to home by placing the action in a domestic rather than an exotic setting: as Henry James said of Wilkie Collins, sensation novels 'introduced into fiction ... the mysteries which are at our own doors'.[27] Lyn Pykett describes this process as a bringing together of different popular forms:

> The sensationalists brought together, in varying way and proportions, the dominant female forms of the early nineteenth century: female Gothic, melodrama and domestic realism.[28]

Women such as Mary Elizabeth Braddon and Mrs Henry Wood were among the genre's most successful exponents, and attracted a large female readership. Elaine Showalter,[29] Anthea Trodd[30] and Lyn Pykett[31] have discussed the sensation novel's preoccupation with domestic crime. Unlike her predecessors in penny serials or her descendants in *fin-de-siècle* crime fiction, the sensation anti-heroine usually confines her crimes to the domestic sphere. She is not so much the angel in the house as the demon in the house.

Arguably the best-known fictional villainess of the 1860s was Mary Elizabeth Braddon's Lady Audley. The exploits of Braddon's murderous bigamist proved highly popular, and the book was an immediate success, running to nine editions in the first three months after its publication in serial form.[32] Lady Audley caused a sensation. Critics were horrified by the beautiful blonde bigamist, but their reaction only served to give the novel more publicity, and the public bought it in their thousands. Two stage versions of the novel were produced within two years of its publication.[33] In both of these, Lady Audley dies at the end. The transgressive woman is punished more severely on the public stage than in the privately-read novel. Conversely, both Sylvia Freeman's strongly feminist 1988 adaptation of the novel[34] and Donald Hounam's 2000 television version[35] ended with Lady Audley escaping from the asylum and taking on a new identity. Her transgressions are evidently more acceptable to a twentieth century audience than they were to a nineteenth-century one.

Shocking though Lady Audley was to middle-class Victorian readers, she is in fact a remarkably mild and unsuccessful criminal compared to her predecessors in the penny press. Her murder attempts fail: although she believes she has killed George Talboys, Robert Audley and Luke Marks, all three men survive. Sensation villainesses tend to be not so much successful super-criminals as domestic murderesses, forced into crime by their circumstances. Perhaps the nearest approach to a female super-criminal in sensation fiction is Lydia Gwilt in Wilkie Collins' *Armadale*, who is involved in forgery, blackmail and attempted murder in a criminal career which begins in childhood. As Lyn Pykett points out:

> The actions of Braddon's Lady Audley (hitherto the type of the beautiful and deceptively demure sensation villainess) pale into insignificance beside the passionate intensity and sophisticated, scheming criminality of Lydia Gwilt.[36]

Lydia shocked reviewers. The *Athenaeum* condemned her as 'one of the most hardened female villains whose devices and desires have ever blackened literature'[37] and the *Spectator* complained that the novel:

> gives us for its heroine a woman fouler than the refuse of the streets, who has lived to the ripe old age of thirty-five [sic], and through the horrors of forgery, murder, theft, bigamy, gaol and attempted suicide, without any trace being left on her beauty.[38]

Lydia perhaps prefigures Wilde's Dorian Gray, in that this career of crime and dissipation leaves no outward trace on her attractive physical appearance. This apparent contradiction was particularly significant in a society in which belief in the 'sciences' of phrenology and physiognomy was widespread, supposedly offering a way of reading the mind's construction in the face.[39] The combination of outward beauty and inward corruption which was so shocking to the *Spectator*'s critic relates specifically to Lydia's gender. Jenny Bourne Taylor sees Lydia as a *femme fatale* whose 'villainy is mediated through her femininity'.[40] Like Ruth Trail and Edith Vandeleur, Lydia uses her femininity and sexuality to manipulate men. Like Lady Audley, she appears in the role of passive, submissive governess. Behind her facade of feminine modesty and passivity, she is, in Taylor's words, 'a figure of all-embracing, disarming, and suffocating female power'.[41] Pykett sees Lydia Gwilt as 'the extreme form of the demonic sensation heroine'.[42] Lydia Gwilt's roots lie firmly in the cheap fiction read by what Collins famously termed 'the unknown public'.[43] However, as Andrew King[44] and Jennifer Carnell[45] have pointed out, even the most demonic of sensation heroines is not so extreme as her predecessors in penny fiction, nor is Lydia Gwilt such a one-dimensional character. Collins portrays her as an intelligent, resourceful woman, tormented by her past: the archetypal sensation 'woman with a secret'. Like Lady Audley, Lydia is a remarkably unsuccessful murderess. She is arrested and tried for killing her first husband, but the text makes it clear that it was likely to have been her lover who killed him, leaving her to take the blame. Although she makes three attempts to murder Allan Armadale,[46] all three fail. Her marriage to Midwinter may or may not be bigamous, as it is doubtful whether her second marriage was legal.[47] As a murderous bigamist, she is a pale reflection of her penny dreadful predecessors.

Early detective fiction also featured female master-criminals, who, unlike their contemporaries in sensation fiction, frequently transgressed the bounds of the domestic sphere. The first assignment of Andrew Forrester's 1864 detective Mrs Paschal is to investigate the rich and beautiful Countess of Vervaine, who has an extravagant lifestyle but no obvious source of income. The police suspect that the Countess obtains her money illegally, but cannot prove it. A woman has baffled the male police force, so they set another woman to catch her.

Mrs Paschal persuades the Countess to take her on as a lady's-maid, which enables her to keep her suspect under close watch. The Countess is that stalwart of the sensation novel, a woman with a secret. She is lively in company, but sinks into 'fits of melancholy'[48] in private, from which Mrs Paschal deduces that 'she had a secret – a secret which weighed her down and crushed her young, elastic spirit, sitting on her chest like a nightmare and spoiling her rest by hideous visions'[49] – a deduction which may owe less to observation than to reading of sensation novels! The description could apply equally well to Aurora Floyd, eponymous heroine of Mary Elizabeth Braddon's best-selling novel of the previous year.[50] The image of the nightmare is drawn from another highly imaginative source, John Henry Fuseli's painting 'The Nightmare' in which a demon is shown crouched on the chest of a sleeping women. Fuseli painted several versions of this scene in the years 1781-90, and the picture was well-known to educated Victorians. Thanks to Mrs Paschal's efforts, sufficient evidence is found to arrest the Countess for robbery, but she commits suicide as soon as she is captured. The transgressive woman's final transgression is to deprive the law of its prey. Like Ruth Trail and Lydia Gwilt, the Countess wins a grudging sympathy from the law because of her beauty: Mrs Paschal, '[does] not regret that so young and fair a creature had escaped the felons' dock, the burglars' doom'.[51]

Another villainess who escapes the dock is Mme Katherine Kolouchy in L.T. Meade and Robert Eustace's *The Brotherhood of the Seven Kings*, which was serialised in the *Strand Magazine* during 1898. The Seven Kings of the title is not a reference to the London district of that name, but to a secret society set up by medieval Neapolitan aristocrats. The *fin-de-siècle* leader of the society is the mysterious Mme Kolouchy. 'A scientist of no mean attainments',[52] this beautiful young woman is 'chief and queen'[53] of the secret society which is responsible for a range of crimes including blackmail, robbery and murder. The narrator, a former member of the Brotherhood, says that, 'I never hear of any crime being committed in London without instantly associating Madame Kolouchy with it'.[54] He turns detective, and tracks her across Europe through ten episodes, but is continually defeated in his attempts to bring her to justice. Eventually it is a female detective who brings about Mme Kolouchy's downfall.

Like her predecessors in penny and sensation fiction, Mme Kolouchy cheats the gallows. She appears to have killed herself rather than face arrest but, like Holmes' adversary Moriarty, she leaves no body. The manner of her death combines those of two of the *fin de siècle's* best known fictional characters: Moriarty and Rider Haggard's *She*.[55] The final confrontation takes place in her labouratory. Perhaps foreshadowing her fate in the afterlife, she literally descends into a pit of fire, immolating herself in what appears to be a do-it-yourself crematorium oven.

> [H]er hand moved to a small lever on the bench beside her ... there leapt up, straight before our eyes, what seemed like one huge sheet of white flame. So fearfully bright and dazzling was it that it struck us like a blow ... [Beneath the trapdoor on which she had been standing] was the mouth of a big hole, from which ... radiated a fierce heat. By degrees it cooled sufficiently to allow us to examine it. It was about 8ft deep and circular in shape. From its walls jutted innumerable jets. Their use was evident to me at once, for upon the floor beside us stood an enormous iron cylinder, such as are used for compressed gases. These had presumably been used before to create by means of the jets one vast oxyhydrogen flame to give the intensest heat known, a heat computed by scientists at the enormous temperature of 2,400deg. Centigrade.

It was evident what has happened. As Ford sprang forward Madame must have released the iron trap and descended through a column of this fearful flame, not only causing instantaneous death, but simultaneously causing an absolute annihilation.

At the bottom of the well lay a small heap of smouldering ashes. These were all the earthly remains of the brain that had conceived and the body that had executed some of the most malignant designs against mankind that the history of the world has ever shown.[56]

The reader is irresistibly reminded of Haggard's Ayesha and her apparent death in a pillar of fire.[57] Like Haggard, Meade leaves the way clear for a sequel: there is no way of proving that the 'smouldering ashes' are those of Mme Kolouchy, who has made supposedly impossible escapes in previous episodes. Like madness, death by fire is a common punishment for the transgressive woman of nineteenth century fiction, perhaps hinting at her supposed eventual fate in the flames of hell. The archetypal example is of course Bertha Rochester, who dies in the blazing Thornfield Hall.

One of Meade and Eustace's most successful creations was the evil Madame Sara, *The Sorceress of the Strand*, who made her first appearance in the *Strand Magazine* in 1902-3. Like Mme Kolouchy and Rider Haggard's *She*, Sara is beautiful and apparently ageless, possessing 'the knowledge of centuries'[58] and the 'wisdom of the ancients'.[59] She uses 'secrets' obtained from primitive tribes[60] in her work as a 'beautifier'.[61] She moves in the cream of London society even though she is far from aristocratic, being openly 'in trade' as a beautician, dentist and cosmetic surgeon. and is a highly successful businesswoman. Behind this facade however, Sara is a master-criminal, using her skills as a surgeon and hypnotist to gain a fortune by a mixture of theft, blackmail and murder. She repeatedly challenges her male antagonists, investigator Dixon Druce and police surgeon Dr Vandeleur to defeat her, but although they continually foil her schemes, it takes a woman to bring about her final downfall.

Sara runs rings around the two middle-class male sleuths who are on her trail. Although they succeed in bringing her to trial for murder in the first episode, nothing can be proved and she gets off scot free after impressing the judge with her beauty and apparent innocence. However, she eventually comes to a well-deserved sticky end when she tries to double-cross a female accomplice. The equally formidable Julia Bensasan is an animal-tamer, who plans to murder Sara with a set of metal false teeth made to imitate the bite of a savage wolf in her private menagerie.

In the event, the weapon is unnecessary: the wolf itself kills Sara. However, Sara is victorious even in death: her final act is to shoot and fatally wound Julia, who then confesses with her dying breath. Both women are finally defeated by another woman rather than a man. It may be significant that a wolf is the instrument of Sara's downfall. She has tried to defy nature by keeping age at bay, but in the end it is a force of nature which destroys her.

As I have demonstrated, the female version of Moriarty had three incarnations: the super-criminal of penny fiction, the anti-heroine of the sensation novel, and the criminal mastermind of *fin-de-siècle* crime fiction. The last of these was perhaps consciously modelled on Moriarty, but with important differences which create a strong gender politics. The criminal's seductive powers give the intellectual duel between criminal and detective strongly sexual overtones. In all of the *fin-de-siècle* texts I have discussed the criminal is a beautiful female and her antagonist is male, adding sexual tension to the plot. By creating female super-criminals, writers of popular fiction were seeking to both mediate and contain the demands of early feminisms. The assertive, transgressive woman is portrayed as criminal. Like the heroines of New Woman fiction, she is liable to be punished for her intelligence and refusal to conform, as much as for her crimes. For female readers, however, she was to prove a figure of lasting fascination.

Endnotes

[1] Anon, 'Sensation Novelists', *Medical Critic and Psychological Journal* No 3, 1863, 513-518, quoted in Andrew Maunder's appendices to *East Lynne* (Ontario: Broadview, 2000), 723.
[2] Cited in Alan K. Russell, introduction to *Rivals of Sherlock Holmes* (New Jersey: Castle, 1978), x.
[3] Eliza Lynn Linton, 'Little Women', *Saturday Review*, 25 April 1868, 545.
[4] Edward Ellis, *Ruth the Betrayer; or the Female Spy* (London: 'Published for the proprietors, at the office, 25, Wellington Street, Strand', 1863), 410.
[5] Wilkie Collins, *Armadale* (1866; Harmondsworth: Penguin 1995), 529-530.
[6] Peter Haining, *The Penny Dreadful Or Strange, Horrid & Sensational Tales* (Gollancz, 1975), 32.
[7] Letter to Bulwer Lytton, quoted in Jennifer Carnell, introduction to Mary Elizabeth Braddon, *The Black Band or, The Mysteries of Midnight* (1861-62; Hastings: Sensation Press, 1998), vii.
[8] Mary Elizabeth Braddon, *The Doctor's Wife* (1864; Oxford: Oxford University Press, 1999), 40.
[9] Carnell, Introduction to *The Black Band*, xiii.
[10] Ascott R. Hope [i.e. Ascott Robert Hope Moncreiff], *Sandy's Secret* (Edinburgh: W.P. Nimmo, Hay, & Mitchell, 1900], 18. The novel is set some years before 1900, though the exact date is not given.

[11] Jennifer Carnell, *The Literary Lives of Mary Elizabeth Braddon: A Study of Her Life and Work* (Hastings: Sensation Press, 2000), 207.

[12] Braddon, *The Black Band*, 583.

[13] For a detailed discussion of the sensation novel's supposed bad effect on female readers, see Kate Flint, *The Woman Reader, 1837-1914* (Oxford: Clarendon, 1993).

[14] Ellen Wood, *East Lynne* (1861; Ontario: Broadview, 2000), 334.

[15] Ellis, *Ruth the Betrayer*, spinal note on 409.

[16] Ellis, *Ruth the Betrayer*, 410.

[17] Ellis, *Ruth the Betrayer*, 409.

[18] The Offences Against the Person Acts of 1828 and 1861 stated that carnal knowledge of a female beneath the age of 12 was unlawful. The 1875 Amendment to the Offences Against the Person Act redefined the age of consent for girls as 13, and the 1885 Sexual Offences Act raised it to 16.

[19] For example, there is an account of the sado-masochistic lesbian flagellation of a pregnant nun on 58-61. The errant nun is then buried alive with her dead child and, not surprisingly, goes insane.

[20] Ellis, *Ruth the Betrayer*, 385.

[21] Arthur Morrison, *A Child of the Jago* (1896; London: Panther, 1971).

[22] Ellis, *Ruth the Betrayer*, 410.

[23] Ellis, *Ruth the Betrayer*, 407.

[24] Braddon, *The Doctor's Wife*, 10.

[25] *Blackwoods Magazine*, CII, (September 1867): 257-8, quoted Winifred Hughes, *The Maniac in the Cellar: Sensation Novels of the 1860s* (Princeton: Princeton University Press, 1980), 45.

[26] Quoted Hughes, *The Maniac in the Cellar*, 4-5.

[27] Henry James, *Nation*, 1, 9 November 1865, 595.

[28] Lyn Pykett, *The Improper Feminine: The Women's Sensation Novel and the New Woman Writing* (London and New York:, 1992), 6.

[29] Elaine Showalter, *A Literature of Their Own* (1977; London: Virago, 1982).

[30] Anthea Trodd, *Domestic Crime in the Victorian Novel* (London: Macmillan, 1989).

[31] Pykett, *The Improper Feminine*.

[32] Pykett, *The Improper Feminine*, 6-7.

[33] William E. Suter, *Lady Audley's Secret: A Drama in Two Acts* (London: Thomas Hales Lacy, 1863) and C.H. Hazlewood, *Lady Audley's Secret: An Original Version of Miss Braddon's Popular Novel in Two Acts* (London: Thomas Hales Lacy, 1864).

[34] Sylvia Freedman, *Lady Audley's Secret*, Gloria Productions, Lyric Theatre Hammersmith, 1988-1989 (text unpublished).

[35] Donald Hounam, *Lady Audley's Secret*, Warner Sisters, broadcast on Carlton TV, 17 May 2000 (text unpublished).

[36] Lyn Pykett, *The Sensation Novel from The Woman in White to the Moonstone* (Plymouth: Northcote House, 1994), 27.

[37] *Athenaeum* no 2014, 2 June 1866, 732.

[38] Cited in John Sutherland, Introduction to Wilkie Collins, *Armadale* (1864-1866; Harmondsworth: Penguin, 1995), xix.

[39] For a discussion of physiognomy in relation to sensation fiction and Pre-Raphaelite painting, see Taylor, Introduction to *Lady Audley's Secret*, xxii-xxiii.

[40] Jenny Bourne Taylor, *In the Secret Theatre of Home: Wilkie Collins, Sensation Narrative and Nineteenth Century Psychology* (London and New York: Routledge, 1988), 167.

[41] Taylor, *In the Secret Theatre of Home*, 167.

[42] Pykett, *The Sensation Novel*, 27.

[43] Wilkie Collins, 'The Unknown Public', *Household Words*, Vol XVIII, 21 August 1858, 217-222.

[44] Andrew King, 'Literature of the Kitchen: *The London Journal* 1845-1883' (Unpublished paper given at *The Amusements of the People: A Study Day on Victorian Mass Culture*, London University Institute of English Studies, 2 July 1999); and 'Sympathy and Subversion: *Lady Audley's Secret* in *The London Journal*' (Unpublished paper given at *Mary Elizabeth Braddon and the Culture of Sensation*, Birkbeck College, 13 May 2000).

[45] Carnell, Introduction *The Black Band*, xiii.

[46] Collins, *Armadale*, 559ff, 568ff and 650ff.

[47] Collins, *Armadale*, 534-536.

[48] Andrew Forrester, *Revelations of a Lady Detective* (London: Ward Lock, 1864), 12.

[49] Forrester, *Revelations of a Lady Detective*, 12.

[50] Mary Elizabeth Braddon, *Aurora Floyd* (1862-1863; Oxford: Oxford University Press, 1996).

[51] Forrester, *Revelations of a Lady Detective*, 38-9.

[52] *Strand*, Vol 15, 86.

[53] *Strand*, Vol 15, 86.

[54] *Strand*, Vol 15, 381.

[55] H. Rider Haggard, *She* (London: Longmans Green & Co, 1887).

[56] *Strand*, Vol 16, 428-429.

[57] Haggard, *She*, 292-294.

[58] *Strand*, Vol 25, 72.

[59] *Strand*, Vol 25, 284.

[60] *Strand*, Vol 24, 389.

[61] *Strand*, Vol 24, 390